RUSSIA OBSERVED

Advisory Editors

HARMON TUPPER   HARRY W. NERHOOD

TRAVELS THROUGH PART
OF THE RUSSIAN EMPIRE

Robert Johnston

ARNO PRESS & THE NEW YORK TIMES

New York • 1970

Reprint edition 1970 by Arno Press, Inc.

Library of Congress Catalog Card No. 72-115549
ISBN No. 0-405-03036-3

Russia Observed
ISBN for complete set 0-405-03000-2

Reprinted from a copy in
the Harvard College Library

Manufactured in the United States of America

TRAVELS

THROUGH PART OF

THE RUSSIAN EMPIRE

AND THE

COUNTRY OF POLAND;

ALONG THE

SOUTHERN SHORES OF THE BALTIC.

BY ROBERT JOHNSTON, *A. M.*

[From the first London edition of 1815.]

NEW-YORK:

PUBLISHED BY DAVID LONGWORTH,

At the Shakspeare-Gallery,

11 *Park.*

1816.

J. Desnoues, *printer*, No. 7 Murray-st.

CONTENTS.

Page

CHAPTER VII.

CHAPTER VIII.

CHAPTER IX.

CHAPTER X.

CHAPTER XI.

CHAPTER XII.

PREFACE.

—◦◆◦—

If we inquire into the history of European nations, even as far back as Charlemagne, never shall we find, perhaps, an æra of more universal interest than the present, both to those nations in general, and to Great Britain in particular.

The constitution of governments, like the constitution of man, must have its periods of vigour, and decline ; it must rise and fall, flourish and decay ; and, although it abound in *physical*, it may fail in *moral* strength, and thus perish.

From this failure in the moral constitution of their governments, more than from any other source, has flowed that vast and mighty stream of desolation, which, like a torrent, swept along the face of modern nations and nearly overwhelmed them in its gloomy tide ; from this has the recent map of Europe presented so melancholy and so degenerate a picture. The iniquities of civilized man and the corruption of Courts had opened a wide and yawning abyss ; nations were on the brink ; the light of life and liberty had fled ; the storm was gathering ; the angry eye of Heaven looked down, formed a being for the scourge of man, and sent him abroad to desolate the land.

What scene then did the continental map of Europe present ? Its nations chained, as if by one common spell of thraldom ; their governments, their laws, their religion trampled on ; the ties of society torn asunder ; the rights of thrones trodden down ; their Kings degraded, and upstart vassals polluting, with their vile touch, the sacred sceptres of royalty. No longer did the age of chivalry throw its light around ; that of blood, rapine, and desolation was at its zenith ! a long and dreary night of Vandalism overshadowed the earth : the only light it shed was caught from the burning pile where nations lay expiring, and gleamed on the gore-spotted arena, where the common gladiators of despotism were mangling their warworn frames.

These times are past—the sad picture is no more—a new light bursts in—the spell is broken, and that being, whom it pleased the Almighty ruler of nations to send as a scourge to mankind, is hurled into his original den of darkness. How changed is the scene, a new order of things succeeds—the rights of thrones and nations are respected, and peace is restored to a suffering world ! No blood-stained star shoots its troubled ray o'er the horizon, and sheds its horrid gleam on ruined cities and desolated lands—all is calm, tranquil and serene.

To inquire even slightly into the causes, remote or proximate of so grand and universal a change, is a task of no small labour : it is not our business here however,—it is not the business of the traveller —his only aim is to pourtray the principal features in the character and country of those who have been most instrumental in its agency, and, to add to that interest, which we must all feel in the fate of those who have so largely contributed to put an end to the sufferings of mankind.

When we look to our own country, what just cause of pride and dignity do we behold ! Never did her eagle-wing soar higher—never did she beam in brighter splendour ! Amid the ruin and wreck of demoralized nations she has stood out the firm and generous pilot— when others slept and were worn with their woe she ever watched at the oft giddy helm ; her greatness grew with the madness of the gale ; her swiftness hung on the wings of the storm ; her proud pendants floated aloft o'er the majesty of the Heavens ; her course was steady ; her track was secure, and she still pointed to that beacon, where peace and salvation shewed their hallowed, but expiring flame.

But it is not to Great Britain alone that we are to look in the glorious struggle. The nations of the north have poured down their legions : to these we are to turn our eyes. The flames of Moscow have burst a new light on man ; the falling towers of the Kremlin have chimed the tyrant's parting knell, and proclaimed aloud that Europe is free ! And never did his towering genius soar to such a flight as when first these ill-fated towers caught its glance ; never did his blood-stained pinions dart on a more hapless victim. If the memory of future ages had but this alone of his mighty conquests to dwell on—if the giant strides of his vast career had ceased to be remembered, and been swept down the common stream of time, this alone would remain on its banks an imperishable monument of lawless ambition.

The traveller, however, must not confine himself to political views—it is not for the diplomatist or statesman he writes; for al-

though he has traced war's ruthless paths, and trodden on the yet
smoaking ruins of a bleeding country, yet its theatre is too vast to
present more than a mere outline. He is well aware that his province is a very peculiar one, his views of man and country must be
rapid and hurried ; the impressions made on his senses, by these
views, must necessarily be rapid also ; although perhaps vivid in
colouring, they must be light and delicate ; they must present all
those lights and shades which were passing across the mind of the
author when writing, and which, by a correspondent transition, must
throw their tints over that of the reader, and thus keep his attention
constantly excited. He knows that it is out of the nature of his pages
to be heavy and prolix ; they must not be impressed with the stamp
of lucubration, they must not be tinged with the gloom of the closet.
He must bid adieu both to theory and to contemplation, and, as he
mingles with new scenes, his mind expands and illumines, his pages
catch the kindred spark ; they grow, as it were, with the subject, and
the sacred light of truth marks them with its unerring stamp. His
works are not to be judged by the standard of schoolmen. His facts
are collected under many disadvantages. He has " to look that he
may learn," not " to learn that he may look." He must draw his
information from uncertain sources; the answers he may receive to
his questions may be as different and incongruous as the people from
whom he asks them. He has no alternative : he must adopt the one,
explode the other, or draw conclusions from both. He must think for
himself and himself solely. Opinions and characters of man and
country must be taken on the spot, and according to the exact stamp
of the moment. They must not go *before* the moment, because it
shews a reference to other authorities, and thus weakens that spirit of
originality, which ought to be the very essence of his pages : they
must not come *behind* the moment, or it will be loading the memory
uselessly.

Each individual spot, which the traveller traces, has its peculiar
character; the very nature and disposition of the rocks and mountains, the shape of the lakes, the surface of the soil, the numerous
errors of the maps, as well as the manners of the people, ought to be
particular objects of his remarks.

Amidst all that vast mass of observation which these northern
regions stretch out to him, none can be more interesting than the

influence of climate on the *physical*, and its corresponding influence on the *moral* constitution of their natives.

In a political point of view, never perhaps was there a period in which the affairs of the North, and particularly Russia, could be of more interest than the present. Every Briton must feel a conscious glow of pride in looking at the glorious alliance of Russia with his country; long have they been joined in the bands of a holy and sacred war, and long may they be kindred in the spirit of peace!

There is no æra, in the history of nations, more interesting to inquire into, nor more difficult to delineate, than that which intervenes between their ruin and their restoration; between their subjugation and that new existence, which they derive from a recovery of their rights, &c. At this critical period, their character, with that of its people, undergoes various changes; it assimilates with the nature of the existing revolution. Their moral existence becomes tied down by their political creed, and vibrates with its fluctuations. All is in a state of uncertainty, and there is no fixed standard, by which to judge of its identity as a nation.

Most particularly has this been the case, at least in many respects, in those countries in which the author has travelled, and most precisely has this been the period at which his observations were made. The time when he travelled was indeed critical and embarassing both to the countries and to himself. Scarcely had they begun to heal from their wounds, scarcely had the storm of war ceased to thunder through them, and scarcely had that pivot rested, on which their fate had been so long vacillating.

To these points therefore he lays principal claims for the interest of the following pages. Let it not be supposed, however, that their character will be merely political : his chief object is to develope the principal and prominent features of that vast line of country along which he travelled; to point out their present state, and notice those objects most worthy the attention of their rational visitor. He treads lightly and rapidly. His views, characters and impressions were taken on the spot, at the moment, and under many disadvantages. His labours and privations were many, his paths were dark, dreary and intricate; but the bright star of enthusiasm, like the clue of Ariadne, has carried him along, and if even one gleam of its sacred light can dawn on him who turns over these pages, their labour will be forgotten, and the author rewarded.

TRAVELS,

&c. &c. &c.

CHAP. I.

Dantzick, June, 1814.

WHEN a traveller first sets out from his native land, and afterwards publishes his tour, it generally happens that the pages of his book keep pace with the stages of his journey, and that, whether in idleness or amusement, in dulness or instruction, both correspond and sympathize with each other. This may be very well, when he arrives at a certain distance from home, and visits countries which cease to be familiar; but to devote his pages to the oft trodden tracks of his own country, and those immediately around it, is too often an useless evaporation of their interest, and an idle fatigue to their reader.

After a short, and not unpleasant, residence in Denmark, having made the necessary arrangements for our journey to the Russian empire, we took leave, and not without regret, of our Danish friends. It is not the object of the following pages to attempt

3

illustrating a nation so well known as Denmark, nor a metropolis so splendid, and whose features have been so often portrayed, as Copenhagen,—where elegance of taste,—social virtues, and the most liberal institutions of charity, equally claim the attention, respect, and admiration of every stranger.

Yet we cannot but behold, in this little nation, a striking instance of the mutability of events. The Danes were the greatest people of the north, after the destruction of the Roman empire, and continued, for a length of time, to plunder, destroy, and even to give laws to countries now the first in the world. When it had risen to the plenitude of its power, and its flag rode triumphant from the Baltic to the Mediterranean seas, a combination of commercial towns under the name of the Hanseatic league, opposed its daring outrages, and overcame what all the powers of Europe could not effect: from that time Denmark gradually diminished in power, wealth, and territory; and, from having once stretched from the banks of the Rhine to the North Cape, it is now confined to the peninsula of Jutland and the duchies of Schleswig and Holstein, with the islands of Zealand, Funen, Laaland, Falstaff, etc. scarcely a shadow of its former greatness, but still valuable, in point of local situation, to commerce.

As the power of nations now depends both on the number and bravery of its people, it might be an advantageous exchange to Denmark and Great Britain, were the island of Zealand delivered to the latter power for the electorate of Hanover. Zealand, under the protection of Great Britain, would soon become the mart of the northern commerce, as it was in the beginning of the sixteenth century, when the commercial power of the Hanse towns was diminished. The Sound dues, collected at Elsineur, might be raised to a sum sufficient to defray the expenditure of the colony. The value of Zealand, at present, is at its lowest ebb. The whole island, from agricultural neglect, does not produce any thing in sufficient quantity for exportation. One half of the island is covered with excellent wood, and little more than one fourth of its surface is cultivated. At present the average purchase of land is, from seven pounds to fifteen pounds an English acre. Its situation, strengthened by the power of Great Britain, would become the key to the Baltic commerce; and, if in friendly alliance with Russia, would be connected with that of the Caspian and Black Seas, independently of the Mediterranean communication. Thus the British might claim the exclusive privilege of navigating the Baltic. Denmark, on the contrary, would acquire extent of dominion and population, and might fix the royal residence in Hanover. Her commerce would be increased, from the facility of trading with Copenhagen, besides the internal trade, by means of the Elbe and the Weser; and her interest would be best secured in maintaining a strict alliance with Great Britain. Were the northern nations to shut their ports against Great Britain, they must soon find that they alone would be the sufferers. Their chief exports, though highly useful to Britain, is what they would have the least use for, and which can be equally procured from the British colonies in America; therefore the profits are on their side, and it becomes their interest to maintain a commercial intercourse with Britain.

We cannot shut our eyes to the increasing advantages, and the prodigious wealth which the north of Europe is annually opening to our view. While war has ravaged and left the fairest portion of Europe almost a desert, and a race of men returning to barbarism; the once bleak and unknown wilds of Scandinavia are now becoming the land of freedom, of riches, and of the arts and sciences.

The winter had been unusually severe, but, towards the end of May, it had disappeared:—spring now burst out in all its brightest bloom;—the woods assumed a new form;—the meadows sported their varied charms;—and, on all sides, were seen the delicate and endearing plant "forget me not," covering the rude soil with its virgin leaf, and spreading a beauteous carpet over the face of nature.

It is impossible for the traveller in these regions, not to notice those singular fluctuations of season which seem to separate the spring and winter from each other. The leafless tree may be seen to-day in all its withered form,—to-morrow, clothed in all its richest foliage. The birth of vegetative life seems as sudden as its decay : that beauteous and lingering approach, by which the joys of spring are so truly felt in England, is here quite unknown. The lakes and rivers, and even the sea, are covered with ice half the year, and "nature reigns in all the varieties of sublime disorder."

From the vast mass of frozen land which the winds, coming from the east and the north, have to travel over, and from the sudden and irregulai heats which the sun, now and then, throws out, there is a constant interruption to that regularity of course which, in tropical regions, is marked by so distinctive features.

From Copenhagen, we proceeded, through Holstein, to Hamburg; thence, along Pomerania, and the shores of the Baltic, to Dantzick. In traversing this large tract of country, although its general outline is somewhat familiar to our countrymen, more particularly from the commercial relationship subsisting between the ports of the Batic and those of Great Britain, yet it would be depriving these pages of a large portion of interest, if we passed over, unnoticed, those broad and striking features which must arrest the attention of every intelligent and thinking traveller,—and those more particularly which are connected with the late unhappy and desolating invasion to which it has been so long a prey.

Among these there are none which more particularly claim notice, and which more immediately strike the eye of the stranger, than the fortified towns and cities. It is here that the iron hand of invasion has laid its coldest and most cruel grasp; these are the spots which give colour and character to its sad and melancholy picture. Among these, the first which is worthy of notice, and the first we arrived at, was Hamburg.

Nothing can be more destructive to a commercial town like Hamburg, than to maintain a military rank. Late events have proved how ineffective such means of defence are, when unsupported by a proportionate force. In the modern art of war, fortified towns, only expose a concentrated point of lives, to suffer the utmost effect of destruction.

This city fell a sacrifice to the treachery of the Danes, and the inactivity of the Swedes; but not before it had made a most gallant resistance. The French army, under Davoust, kept possession of the town for eleven months, and, after a loss of twenty-two thousand men, made an honourable capitulation.

The French will ever be execrated for the cruelties they have committed. To prevent the approach of the Russian soldiers, not only the villas of the rich and the villages of the industrious, but even the humble cot of the peasant, and the aged avenues of trees, formerly the admiration of travellers, have all been erased from the earth, and exhibit a shocking scene of ruin and desolation.

As a city, Hamburg has neither claims to beauty nor regularity. The streets are narrow, and, in general, intersected by canals of stagnant water. The houses are lofty, clumsy, and irregularly built. The lower floor is converted into warehouses, and, before a person can reach the apartment destined to receive visitors, he must wade through innumerable bales of merchandise. The principal and most commanding buildings are its churches: from the remarkable height of the spires, and the extreme flatness of the surrounding country, they are seen at great distances.

The city, with a certain extent of territory, is formed into a little republic, governed by the citizens, under its own laws, and, with Lubeck and Bremen, retains the rank and privileges of the Hanseatic league.* The senate and college of burghers

* In the thirteenth century, when this part of Europe became a prey to the daring outrages of northern banditti; Hamburg, in conjunction with many other towns, formed a treaty of mutual

regulate the laws of the city; levy taxes and preside at the courts of civil and criminal jurisdiction. The taxes are levied in proportion to the exigency of the times. The militia and the pensions of the senators, etc. are paid from the public revenue;— all houses are taxed, and every place of public amusement pays one-eighth of its receipts, particularly the theatre.

One of the principal branches of exportation, from Hamburgh, was the manufactured linens of Silesia, Brunswick, Westphalia, etc. also the refining of sugar; but which last, during the usurpation of Napoleon Bonaparte decreased, and was partly removed to Gottenburg. The bank of Hamburg is conducted on a singular and excellent plan, which affords the greatest facility to the commerce of the place. Each individual deposits a quantity of silver specie, which is transferred from one to another, without being removed from the bank. The present state of commerce exhibits a lively scene of ships and bales of goods, but a dejected gloominess

commerce and defence, which was afterwards known by the name of the Hanseatic league; and the towns which composed it were called the Hanse-towns. This association extended from the North Seas to the Mediterranean, including not less than eighty-five cities. From their number and monopoly of trade, they excited the jealousy of the other powers, which soon dissolved the union. The only cities which now retain the rank and privileges of the league, are Hamburg, Bremen, and Lubeck.

in the aspect of every agent and merchant. Speculators have too rashly intruded their merchandise into the continent, through the means of Hamburg, before the country has had time to recover from its former oppression to sudden freedom; in consequence,—all colonial goods are sold at a loss of nearly forty per cent. The rigid laws of Napoleon against the use of coffee, turned the attention of the people towards procuring a substitute. Parched rye has been used by the common people, and, from custom and its cheapness, it is not likely to be immediately disused.

From the nature of its republican government, and the general influx of foreign merchants, but, perhaps, more particularly at this time, from the recent effects of its invasion, it presents a varied group of strangers, and occasions a difficulty in fixing the decided *character* of the place. Here no sovereign is acknowledged: neither precedency nor prerogative above that of a citizen. Title and rank are avoided, in consequence of which, an intrusive familiarity is allowed to prevail.

The amusements and recreations of the town consist in theatric exhibitions, dancing, and tobacco smoking. The theatre is tolerably large, and the proscenium is lighted up, and not allowed, like the Danish and Swedish theatres, to remain in utter darkness. The performers are *mediocre*, and appear

4

to study the mechanical part of the drama, more than its pathos or sentiment. The German language, though harsh to an English ear, is yet considered more agreeable and better adapted to the stage than the Danish. The evening we visited the theatre we met general Benningsen, a Russian, who has performed a most conspicuous part during the present campaign. He commands a division of the Russian army quartered in the city and neighbourhood. The appearance of the Russian soldiers must excite a lively interest. It is surprising to observe the rapid improvements that remote country seems to have made towards the formation and maturity of its military character. The infantry are most gracefully dressed, and admirably drilled. Their discipline is taught in a manner most severe. No punishment nor cruelty seem to be spared in the education of a Russian soldier. The officers, at first sight, dazzle the beholder with the exuberance of finery, and the dangling orders of merit, etc.; however, on longer acquaintance they appear the mere outward puppets.

Attached to the division here are several regiments of Cossacks and Baskirs; a race of men worthy of presenting terror in their very looks;—they are the most irregular of soldiers, and, in appearance, the most shocking ruffians which the imagination can picture. They are mounted on small active horses, which are trained to go through extraordinary degrees of fatigue;—the Cossack and his horse may almost be said to be one animal, divided, and endowed with different powers. The Baskirs use the bow and arrow;—the Cossacks the pike, sword, and pistol.

From Hamburg to Harburg, across the Elbe, extends the famous wooden bridge, erected by Davoust, for the retreat of his army, in the event of its necessity. This extraordinary work of a few weeks, extends nearly three miles in length. The whole is built, over a morass, on large piles of wood, with a neat platform and side railing laid over them. The bridge is about ten feet high and twenty-four wide, and finished upon an exact level. If we consider its simplicity, elegance, strength, and extent, it will appear as one of the great curiosities of the present day, and a monument of French ingenuity and labour. The whole of the wood was forcibly taken from the merchants; however its advantages are such that they are now resolved to keep it in repair.

The number of inhabitants in Hamburg, before the invasion, were estimated at nearly a third more than its present population. The suburbs, which were destroyed, between the city and Altona, contained not less than ten thousand individuals; all of whom were barbarously banished from the reeking ruins of their houses, and sought a temporary

shelter, during the inclement months of winter, from
those friends, whose distance alone from the scene
of havoc, preserved them from a similar fate.   The
French, as enemies, took from them their little property with a degree of national politeness; the Russians, as friends, severe in every thing, in a manner
which marks the character of an unrefined people.
The Cossacks gallop through the gardens, and
every where mutilate the shrubs, while the halls
and passages of every house in the environs of the
town, are strewed with the servants of the officers,
reposing like so many filthy pigs.   In short, the exchange from enemies to friends is felt equally op-
pressive.

The distance from Hamburg to Lubeck is about
forty-five miles; the intermediate country is flat and
uninteresting.   The road is probably one of the
worst in Europe; and, though our landaulet was
one of the easiest hung carriages, yet, from the number of loose stones, and inequalities, together with
the insufferably bad driving of the postillions, it was
almost impossible to bear the fatigue.

Lubeck is built at the confluence of three small
rivers, about twelve miles from the sea.   This city
is of considerable antiquity, and exhibits the houses,
built in that style of architecture peculiar to the
fifteenth century, with the gable end towards the
street, and of the most irregular order.   The en-

tries to the houses are so large as to admit their carriages. From a distance the town has a singular appearance, owing to the number of its lofty spires, grouped together in so small a space. The ramparts, like those of Hamburg, are built after the old Dutch fashion, extremely broad, with rows of trees planted on them, forming a cool and agreeable shade. Formerly it took the lead of the Hanseatic league, and, at one time, engrossed the entire trade of the Baltic. Its commerce is now but trifling; and, from the easy communication, by the canal, from Kiel to Tonningen, it is still more diminished. How the Hamburg and Lubeck merchants could neglect the advantages of opening an inland navigation between their towns is a most extraordinary circumstance, and betrays an obvious want, both of enterprise and of industry. The labour of such a work must indeed be trifling, when compared with the immense advantages resulting. By means of it, a tedious, difficult, and often dangerous navigation would be avoided, and vessels, sailing from the British and Dutch ports, instead of taking the long and circuitous voyage by the German Ocean, through the Sleeve, Categat, and Sound, into the Baltic, and thus encountering all the dangers of these narrow and obstructed passages, would enter the Baltic, from the Elbe, by a passage of about fifty miles instead of nearly five hundred. It is to be hoped

that, now, this immense benefit to commerce will
not be lost sight of, and that, what is already
begun at Lubeck, may be carried through. The
country is peculiarly fitted, from its flatness and
plenty of water, to facilitate the business.

A small canal is formed from Lubeck to the Elbe,
by a southerly direction, passing by Möellen, and
supplied with water from the lake of Ratzburg;
but, from the narrowness of the cut, its circuitous
passage, and the boats being dragged by men, the
expenses and delays are considerably increased.

From Lubeck we entered the principality of
Mecklenburg, in Lower Saxony. The government
of this country is divided between the house of
Mecklenburg Schwerin, which is the eldest branch,
and the house of Mecklenburg Strelitz. The duke
of Mecklenburg Schwerin resides, during the summer months, at Dobberan, a small village, esteemed
from the excellence of its baths, and the fashionable
resort of company.—The second daughter of the
duke *was* married to prince Christian of Norway,
but now is separated from him, on account of the
infidelity of her character.

The duke's subjects complain of the severity of
the taxes, but which it is said will be abolished, and
a new system of taxation will be laid on incomes,
arising from hereditary property. When Napoleon
planned his conquest of Russia, this little territory

was compelled to contribute nineteen hundred men
to his mad ambition. Before the grand army
reached Dorogoburh, only thirty of the Mecklen-
burghers survived. Wismar and Rostock are the
only towns which derive any immediate advantages
from commercial navigation. The former, with its
lordship, at one time, was subject to the crown of
Sweden, but is now restored to the duchy. Rostock
is the capital; it is surrounded by an earthen mound
and ditch, and contains some elegant churches and
a college. In the college, is a small library of German books, and a trifling museum of birds, among
which were excellent specimens of the *otis tarda*, and
the *tetrao uragallus*.—Before the war there were
from two to three hundred students; at present they
do not exceed the fourth of that number. The
French kept possession of the town for six years;
their decrees against the introduction of English
merchandise were fully executed. The largest
churches were converted into custom-houses, and,
at the gates of the town, English manufactured
goods were publicly burnt. The churches, which
the French converted into custom-houses, are at
present used by the Swedish soldiers, as barracks,
and those sacred melodies, which once breathed
through its vaulted aisles, are now changed for the
horrible blasphemies of soldiers.

The whole of the duchy of Mecklenburg appears to be well cultivated; and, though composed of a soil not particularly rich, yet produces luxuriant crops of grain.

We entered Swedish Pomerania at Damgarten; before we could pass the boundary line, we were obliged to pay a small tax on leaving the one country, and a similar compliment on entering the other This is one of the many modes by which the revenue of these states is kept up. The country, towards Stralsund is remarkably flat, and, in general, covered with fine, loose, drifted sand, yet, occasionally, relieved by small plantations of oak and fir. The roads can only be considered as tracks; and, from the quantity of loose sand, the average rate of posting does not exceed three miles an hour, besides the loss of time a traveller has to expect in procuring horses at the different stages. The posting is under the regulation of the government, and the postillions wear the respective livery of their countries. That of Sweden is blue, with yellow facings. They always ride the *near* wheel horse; the leaders are yoked, at an extraordinary distance, before the others, and are guided by only one rein from the near leader. The tresses are made of ropes. Instead of using breechings to back the carriage, a leather strap is fixed around the neck of the horse, and fastened to the pole. From this barbarous custom the necks of the horses acquire a hollow form; or, what is termed among jockies, *ewe-neck*. Each postillion has the appendages of a horn and tobacco-pipe suspended from his neck. The first he uses to announce the arrival and departure of a traveller. The other is constantly fixed to his mouth; except when he shares his enjoyment between it and his *schnaps.**

Stralsund is separated from the island of Rugen by a narrow channel; and is the capital of Swedish Pomerania, in the circle of Upper Saxony. It is strongly fortified both by nature and art, and is said to be among the strongest fortifications along the coast of the Baltic. The town is surrounded, on the one side, by an arm of the sea, and, on the opposite, by two small lakes, which have been joined. The centre of the town is considerably elevated. The large square spires of the churches add to its picturesque appearance. Its finest church is, at present, converted into a military storehouse; its religious ornaments are allowed to be shamefully mutilated.

This province has been long subject to Sweden. In 1812, when that power concluded a peace with Great Britain, Bernadotte incurred the displeasure

* A dram.

5

of Napoleon, who, in consequence, seized this country.

The amusements of the town are very circumscribed. There are public gardens without the walls, where the company regale themselves with coffee and tobacco-smoking.

The trade of Stralsund is less than that of Rostock. It exports a considerable quantity of grain, and the numerous flocks of geese, reared on the commons, constitute a branch of its trade. They are hammed, and are esteemed an exquisite treat, through many parts of Germany.

Before we entered Prussian Pomerania, we could not avoid remarking the rigour with which the Swedish laws are enforced. The hideous deformity of the Bonapartean code has crept in, and reigns throughout. Though now in a period of profound peace, and, at a moment when all military barriers should be levelled with the fallen usurper, in this country alone it is retained. Passports, though now granted to travellers as a matter of form, are here considered of the utmost utility. Nothing can appear more contemptible, than the appearance of a wretched town, encompassed by a ditch, with scarcely a gun to defend it, refusing admittance to the traveller, without the formal ceremony of obtaining the permission of a *maitre de police*, an animal whose soul is centred in a tobacco-pipe, and whose honour and integrity is the *pretium argenti*.

The small town of Anclam, on the river Pene, divides Prussian from Swedish Pomerania. The country towards Stettin, continues flat, with alternate morasses and plains of loose sand, and extensive plantations of excellent oak and fir trees.

Stettin, the capital of Prussian Pomerania, is built on the west bank of the Oder, and is surrounded by strong fortifications. The houses are old and irregularly built. On the north side of the town is an agreeable parade, in which is seen an excellent statue of Frederick the Great of Prussia. He is represented in his military dress, with huge boots and a cocked hat, etc. The execution is admirable, but the caricature of the dress renders the whole truly ludicrous. The surrounding country is extremely flat and marshy, through which the Oder is seen in its dull and winding course. The environs, like those of Hamburg, exhibit one general scene of ruin, and the poor families are now living under temporary sheds. Some fine avenues of trees, leading from the north gate, which were cut down by the French, are replanted.

> " Ye fallen avenues, once more I mourn
> " Your fate unmerited; once more rejoice
> " That yet a remnant of your race survives."

The French had possession of this town for six years; and, though they exercised the most severe tyranny, yet they have a party in their favour equal to the opposite.

From Altham, the road passed over a plain of fine, loose sand, scarcely giving life to a blade of grass; yet, in many places, covered by a profusion of fir trees, though of a sickly and slender appearance. Excepting on the marsh, between Stettin and Altham, the whole country, from Anclam, is a continuation of forest trees. This is a proof, that trees, particularly fir, (the species here, is the common Scotch fir) oak and lime, will grow in sand, though as loose and fine as that found on the sea shore.

The tracks are very irregular, and only of a sufficient breadth to admit the wheels of a carriage. The ride, through these forests, partakes of all those fancies, which the flights of an unbridled imagination conjure up; and a mind, given to romance, may here enjoy delightful reveries.

The little town of Gullnow shows the ruins of a brick wall partly standing;—the gate had mouldered away with the wall, but was substituted by an old veteran, whose hoary head and mangled looks bespoke the hardships of many campaigns. Passing the barriers of the town, we drove through a street of execrable pavement, and wretched houses; and crossing at a right angle, passed through another equally bad.

From Gullnow we proceeded, in a northerly direction, towards Colberg; passing the small towns of Naugard, Griffenberg, and Triptow; each of them similar to the other in decay and wretchedness. Triptow excited some degree of interest, as being lately the residence of the gallant general Blucher. The distance from Stettin to Colberg is about one hundred miles. This extent of country does not excite any interest, beyond its general state of cultivation. Considerable quantities of rye, barley, and potatoes are reared; also an excellent breed of horned cattle, but, singular to say, of all one colour, a yellowish red. Hogs and sheep are less numerous.

The manners of the common people are more sprightly than those in Swedish Pomerania, though they still partake of that cold indifference, so conspicuous among the different classes of these northern countries.

Colberg is situated on a river, named Persante, about a mile from the sea. It is surrounded by strong and regular fortifications, which are kept in excellent order. The streets are wide, and the houses, though old, are strongly built, and not inclegant. It carries on a considerable trade in the manufactory of salt.

We changed horses at Corlin, the second stage from Colberg, and could not avoid remarking the superior neatness of the houses. In the reign of Frederick William I. the town was destroyed by fire; but it was rebuilt under his directions: in gratitude for which the inhabitants erected, to his memory, a statue, which stands in the centre of the town.

The general flat appearance of these countries is remarkable. From the duchy of Holstein to this spot the surface of the country is extremely level, and consists alternately of sandy plains and marshes. In a geological point of view, they bear strong marks of having been, at some former period, a part of the sea, and the evident traces of marine exuviæ and the long bent or sea grass growing on the surface, strengthen the supposition. The only interruption to this general level is a narrow ridge of clay-marl, about one hundred and fifty feet high, near Corlin, and which may, without extravagance, be called the " *Alps of Pomerania.*" From its summit, a prospect boundless as vision is beheld. The broad expanse of the Baltic is seen stretching along its flat and sedgy shores, while the little town of Corlin appears below, surrounded by its extensive plains, which, towards the south, becomes sheltered by a diversity of woodland scenery.

It is surprising to find the unequal distribution of the population throughout this country. Instead of the farmers residing in the country, they generally collect together in villages, or in the towns. By this means the *country* seems to be unpeopled. Nothing can be more offensive than the closeness and stench of the houses; let the weather be never so hot, not a window is opened nor a room ventilated. Every apartment has its huge downy beds, and filth is in every corner. No deference nor attention is paid to a stranger in this country; whether he rides in a carriage or a wagon, he meets with the same cold reception. A stranger may reside for weeks at one of these houses, and, on his departure, not a single adieu is offered. At every stage he is liable to be imposed on, and the most common imposition is a charge for one horse above the usual allowance.

As we approached Dantzick we could not but behold with pleasure the beauty of the surrounding scenery. On the north side, a broad and sheltered bay stretched towards the mouth of the Vistula, while a beautiful avenue of trees, about four miles in length, conducted us to the suburbs. This was the scene of several skirmishes between the French and Russian armies; scarcely a tree seems to have escaped the shots of the troops. Their wounds have been carefully cleaned, and covered over with pitch and bandages of coarse linen.

The first object which arrests the stranger's attention, on entering the town, is the prodigious thickness and height of the ramparts. The situation of the town is flat, and, from the height of the ramparts, only the numerous spires of the churches can be seen. The streets, though badly paved, are regular; and cross each other at right angles. Many of them are agreeably shaded by rows of trees. The houses are large, and built with the gable ends towards the street; before the doors a clumsy kind of railing is contrived, to keep off carriages, representing huge monsters, such as crocodiles, serpents, etc. supported on globes of stone. The cathedral is a building of great size, but heavy and irregularly constructed. It is built in the form of the cross, and has not less than fourteen roofs and nine lofty spires. In the church are several good paintings, though it is said the French carried off the most valuable.

Several bomb-shells fell on the cathedral during the siege, but regularly passed through the roof and sunk in the floor, without further injury. The church has suffered many instances of a similar kind of violence. Every spot, where shots have passed through the roof, is carefully painted, and the date marked over it.

The exchange stands in the centre of the town. In it is seen an excellent statue erected to the memory of Augustus III. of Poland. Around the walls are several hunting paintings; and, to give effect to the game, huge antlers are stuck on the head of each representative! Formerly there was an university in this city, but which is now gone to decay. The sciences are certainly not encouraged here. There are only two small bookseller's shops, containing a paltry collection of pamphlets, and not a map of the country. The public amusements are, a German theatre, assembly rooms, and public gardens. The environs and walks around the city are extremely pleasing. On the west, the ground rises to a gentle ridge, covered with trees and skirted with neat villas. The east is bounded by the two branches of the Vistula. This space is extremely flat, and about twelve miles square. To prevent the advance of the Russian army, during the late siege, the French opened the eastern embankments of the river, and inundated the whole of it. From the spire of the cathedral we could easily discern the vast extent of this lake. The water had somewhat subsided, and we could discover the steeples of churches, chimnies of houses, and tops of trees, peeping above its surface. It is said the French opened the sluices, without apprizing the inhabitants of their intention, who would have been swept away, had not part of the Russian army saved them by boats.

The history of Dantzick has been long memorable as a commercial and fortified city. It originally belonged to Poland; but in the subsequent division of that unfortunate kingdom, it was annexed to Prussia, and forms a town in West Prussia. At the formation of the Hanseatic league, it was the first in riches, commerce, and strength. In 1793, when the last division of Poland was planned and executed by Catherine, the king of Prussia obtained this city and Thorn. It has since remained to that power, as the great depot of naval, military, and commercial stores.

At one time the population of Dantzick, with its Hanseatic territory, amounted to upwards of an hundred thousand persons. At present it scarcely contains half that number. The French kept possession of the town during five years. The history of the last years of the situation of Dantzick, will be long remembered in the annals of its sufferings. From the memorable discomfiture of Napoleon in Russia, Dantzick was declared in a state of defence; and general Rapp, at the head of thirty thousand French soldiers, shut himself within the walls.

The town was surrounded by a division of the Russian army, who closely invested the fortifications, and prevented all egress. In consequence of this hardship the inhabitants suffered every privation. The cruelties of the French, *within* the walls, and the destructive necessity of the Russians in the suburbs *without*, completed the scene of wretchedness and horror. Provisions became so scarce, that horses, dogs, and cats were the only subsistence of the common people. It was the object of the French to diminish the population as much as possible; and, though the poor and helpless part of the inhabitants were not turned out, as at Hamburg, yet if sickness attacked them, assistance was refused, and death relieved the miserable object from its sufferings.

The inhabitants were taxed most oppressively. Those who were not base enough to sell the honour of their families, were most oppressed. Can any action express the infamy of French principles more than this? The account of their vices here is shocking. While it stamps a disgrace on their moral character, it plainly appears to have left a strong infection on that of the people.

CHAP. II.

Memel, July, 1814.

In the neighbourhood of Dantzick, we visited the monastery of Oliva. Its situation combined all which the most agreeable scenery could produce; and its structure, the rudeness of the age in which it was established. The one, contrasted with the other, appeared as the venerable relic of piety, which had braved the shocks of past ages, and yet afforded protection to its pious devotees.

The sight of these religious edifices always carries us back to distant ages. In these asylums, the seducing pleasures of the world were renounced; the germ of knowledge was fostered, until time ripened it to perfection, and spread its genial influence around. Hither flocked the aged and unhappy. Here they sought that comfort and consolation which their sorrows demanded, while the sick and poor crowded round, to crave the boon of charity from the pious fathers.

The lapse of ages has sunk in oblivion the history of each individual action, and only the bolder features, like the strong lights and shades of the landscape, can now be discovered.

The monastery of Oliva was founded as early as the twelfth century. It was richly endowed with many privileges and immunities, by the sovereigns of Poland. In the intestine revolutions of the country, it was seven times demolished; yet, like a spot too hallowed to be lost in ruins, was as constantly restored. In the sixteenth century, the inhabitants of Dantzick, in a fit of frenzy, carried the torch of destruction and razed it to the ground. The king of Poland, for the irreligious act, compelled them to rebuild it on the plan of its former magnificence.

The present disturbances in the country have again affected this monastery. Before the invasion of the French it contained seventy fathers. Of that number only fourteen are survivors, and but five of these now reside in the establishment. It was shamefully despoiled of its paintings, and the riches of its altar, by the French. During the siege of Dantzick, the Russians converted it into a barrack for their soldiers, and left it in a sad and mutilated state. The cloisters communicate with the cells, in which the monks reside. We visited one of the brothers, who showed that the gloomy wall of a monastery, or the austerity of its laws, had not made many ravages on his person. Instead of the lank care-worn devotee, we beheld the plump, cheerful father of gayety and satisfaction.

It was now the beginning of July, and the weather had become so oppressively hot, during our stay at Dantzick, that we proposed to travel during the night, in order to avoid the excessive heat of the day. The evening we took our departure proved dark and rainy, in consequence of which the postillion lost his way, and upset the landaulet in a deep swamp. The accident was trifling, and a small village being near to the spot, our German servant went in quest of assistance.

The few poor families who inhabited the villages were Poles, and unacquainted with the German language.—*Frederick* not being able to make himself understood, or to rouse them from their couches, returned in rather an indignant manner, and exclaimed " that they could not speak a word of German, and did not deserve to live !" As a last resource, the postillion rang the church bell, which soon collected a number of uncouth, ragged Poles, who, in a short time, extricated the carriage, and conveyed us to the road. Nothing could be more miserable than the appearance of these poor men. They were wrapped up in sheep-skin jackets. Several of them were afflicted with that offensive disease, the *plica polonica*, or matted hair. The hair hangs over their necks in thick and clotted lumps. The disorder is supposed to proceed from a viscous humour, exuding from the head into the tubes of the hair, which dilates to such an extent as to admit small globules of blood.

From Dantzick, we proceeded, through a flat country, along the west bank of the Vistula, and reached the small town of Dersehau, chiefly inhabited by Poles. The wretched appearance of these people excited no other feeling than disgust and pity. They carry on a considerable inland trade, by means of the Vistula; large rafts of wood and barges of grain are constantly seen floating down the river.

The grain boats are navigated down the river, from the interior of Poland, etc. and are often from one to three months on the voyage. These boats are very clumsily put together; and, when the cargo is sold, they are broken up and sold for firewood. A strange custom seems to prevail among the boatmen, in using no precaution whatever in covering the grain from the inclemency of the weather. The grain is raised up with sloping sides; and from the moisture of the air soon assumes a green roof of vegetation, which answers the purpose of a tarpaulin. As these boats float along the stream, numerous flocks of birds regularly accompany them, and may be seen perched on several parts of the cargo, without the least molestation.

At this stage we crossed the Vistula by a ferry. The river here is about one thousand four hundred feet in breadth, and sixteen deep. Its stream is dull and muddy,—the banks low, marshy, and covered with sedges and brush willow. From the ferry the road crosses the marsh to Marienburg, a small town of ancient respectability situated on the Nogatt, but more properly the east branch of the mouth of the Vistula.

Over the river an excellent floating bridge of boats conducts the traveller to the town. Marienburg possesses no other interest than the remains of an old castle and church, once the residence of the knights of the Teutonic order; besides some remains of Roman antiquities.

From Marienburg to Elbing, the country is a continued flat, insipid morass. The road passes along the south side of the Nogatt, which is confined within its proper bed by immense embankments. From the soft, clayey state of the roads, and the want of stones or wood to form a foundation, they become deeply rutted, and very unequal in the surface, resembling a regular series of ridges. The uneasy motion given to the carriage, in passing over these ridges, occasions a sensation similar to

7

that of a boat at sea, and is apt to create a disagreeable sickness.

The appearance of Elbing, from a distance, is by
no means inviting. The high embankments of the
river, and the extensive morasses, exclude all views
of the town. On entering the town the traveller is
pleased to find the regularity of the streets and
neatness of the houses. The town is unfortified,
but appears to have been once encompassed by a
slight brick wall.

Elbing exhibits a convincing proof of the destruction which fortifications produce in a commercial
town. Here were no means of defence or shelter
for the French troops, and the inhabitants only suffered the temporary severities of the armies passing.
Had Hamburg and Stettin been similarly exposed,
they probably would not have undergone the hun-
dredth part of their sufferings.

From Elbing to Dantzick there is a regular communication, by means of a canal, which joins the
Nogatt to the town of Elbing. By the river Vistula an extensive commerce is carried on with the
interior of Poland. Numerous barges of grain and
earthen-ware are brought here from as far as Cracow. From the number and extent of the granaries at Elbing it must be evident that the corn trade
is very considerable, though not nearly equal to that

of Dantzick. These granaries are built on a small
island on the west side of the town. No fires are
permitted to burn in them. Retail trade is conducted on a small scale, at extravagant prices.
Every article of the mechanical arts is chiefly
brought from Berlin.

The warehouses here, as in Dantzick, are guarded during the night by a number of ferocious dogs,
and to prevent their prowling beyond a certain distance, keepers are stationed at certain places with
whips.

Wood is here, as in the former towns, the common fuel. From the number of men and horses engaged in carrying it to the town, it appears to be a
part of their summer employment, or *home trade*.
The horses are small and slender, yet active. The
wagons, to which four of these horses are generally
yoked, consist of four small wooden wheels, with an
extraordinarily narrow body, nearly twenty feet
long, and not more than twenty inches wide. The
sides are formed of two thin boards, which are
taken off at pleasure. The driver, similar to the
postillions, rides on the near wheel horse, and guides
the others with a long whip, without any reins.

The local costumes here, among the lower orders, differ only in the head dress. They, not un-
gracefully, fold a black kerchief round the head,
tied, in front, into a knot. Their appearance and

manners are rather pleasing; they show more delicacy and modesty, than the intrusive immorality of
those at Dantzick, and less indelicacy than those at
Stettin or Hamburg.

The surrounding country is extremely beautiful
on the western side of the town. Nothing can be
more agreeable than the gentle inequalities of its
surface, the richness of its verdure, and straggling
plantations. An excellent new road is forming
from the town towards Frauensberg; about four
miles of it is finished.

The nature of the soil immediately changes, at
Dantzick, from what it had hitherto been. From
that city to Frauensberg, it abruptly becomes, from
loose sand, to a blackish loam, mixed with clay,—
hard and cloddy. The crops are rye, barley, some
wheat, and a small quantity of potatoes, which is
the only green crop we have remarked. They are
planted in narrow ridges, similar to the mode practised in Ireland. The tops do not grow to any
height, or luxuriance, and the roots are generally
small, but keep uncommonly well throughout the
summer. The other crops vary in luxuriance according to the soil. We have hitherto remarked
none equal to what is seen in England.

The mode of farming is extremely simple, and
the implements of agriculture are rudely contrived.
A plough, with two heavy wheels, and the forked

coulter, fixed to the axletree, in a perpendicular manner, is used to cross-plough the fallow land. It has no stilts, and is drawn by four horses. The ploughman rides on the near wheel horse.

In July, grass fields are manured, ploughed down, and allowed to remain until the rye is sown in October; by this means the valuable advantages of grazing are lost. In consequence of this practice, but few black cattle are observed throughout this part of the country.

At the wretched village of Truntz, the first stage from Elbing, we left the territory of West Prussia, and entered that of East Prussia, in Prussia Proper. The second stage brought us to the beautiful town of Frauensberg, on the shores of Frische Haffe. The town is partly built under a sandy ridge, which stretches in a parallel line with the bay. On the summit of this rising ground is seen the Romish cathedral, a large, and not inelegant Gothic structure. This cathedral belongs to the diocese of the bishop, who presides over the monastery of Oliva. Besides two residing bishops, it contains fifteen canons. During our visit at Frauensberg we had the pleasure of forming an acquaintance with the bishop Marcellus de Szuyski. This reverend prelate gave us much valuable information as to the present state of the country; he also showed us the costly robes of the priests, and riches of the church.

Frauensberg is celebrated, as having been the birth-place and residence of Nicolaus Copernicus, the astronomer. He lived in the sixteenth century, and died, as one of the canons of the cathedral, in the seventy-third year of his age. Nicolaus Copernicus flourished after the discoveries of the Pythagorean and Ptolemaic systems were produced.

The word *system*, as is well known, in astronomy, means an hypothesis of a certain arrangement of the different parts of the universe, in order to account for the appearances of the heavenly bodies, their motions, changes, etc.

Claudius Ptolemy, the Egyptian astronomer, supposed the earth immovably fixed in the centre of the universe, and that the sun and planets revolved round it. In this early age, it was believed that all the stars were fixed in one concave sphere, at an equal distance from the earth; and that the *primum mobile*, the imaginary sphere which gave motion to all the rest, was the celestial paradise.

Tycho Brahe, a noble Dane, flourished about the same time with Copernicus. He partly corrected the Ptolemaic hypothesis; he supposed the earth had no motion; that the sun and moon revolved around it in twenty-four hours, and that the other planets revolved round the sun as a centre.

The system of Copernicus, or the revival of that of Pythagoras, is founded on demonstrative proofs, and accounts for all the phenomena of the heavenly bodies, in a natural manner. According to this system, the sun is placed in the centre, and the planets and comets are supposed to revolve round it, at different periods of time, and in orbits, at different distances from it.

In the church a plain slab, with the figure of a globe on it, marks the spot where the ashes of this celebrated astronomer repose. His observatory forms one of the angles of the wall, which surrounds the church. At present it is occupied by a fat jolly canon, who, instead of imitating the heavenly pursuits of his predecessor, employs his time in a trifling display of shell work.

In our hotel we could not but feel interested in the fate of a young female, the only daughter of our landlord, a man of a surly and morose disposition: she had lately lost her mother, her sister and brother,—the icy hand of death seemed to have marked her as its next victim,—she was in a rapid decline, and had even fixed the time of her dissolution.

It was not without feelings of regret that we quitted the scene of Copernicus' discoveries, the

kindness of father Szuyski, and the unhappy state
of poor Antoinette!

Leaving Frauensberg we travelled along the
southern shore of the Frische Haffe, towards
Konigsberg. The intermediate country is flat, of
a dark rich soil, and remarkably well cultivated.
At the different stages, we found triumphal arcl.es
erected in expectation of the emperor Alexander's
arrival, on his return to St. Petersburg. At every
stage, where it was supposed the emperor might
pass, were collected from sixty to one hundred
horses, ready harnessed and grazing on the sides
of the road. At some of the stages the horses had
been in waiting for several days.

Before we entered Konigsberg, our luggage
was carefully inspected by the custom-house officers. This ceremony every traveller must submit
to, otherwise he is sent under a military escort to
the post-office.

The situation or appearance of Konigsberg is by
no means inviting. The scite of the town is somewhat lower than the surrounding country, which is
flat and cheerless; it is encompassed by an earthen
rampart, possessing neither strength nor beauty.
The Pregel divides the town into several parts, and
falls into the eastern extremity of the Frische
Haffe, whereon is situated Pillau: the harbour of
Konigsberg is about thirty miles from the town. It

is evident that the sea has retired from its original station. The former port of the town was only two miles from it. From this spot to the Haffe, a distance of fifteen miles, is now dry land. This change has probably been occasioned by the large quantities of sand and mud brought down by the Pregel at different floods; and, there being no tides in the Frische Haffe to wash it away; it would remain and accumulate.

The streets of the city are irregularly planned and badly paved. The principal buildings are the churches and palace of former kings, in front of which is seen a statue of Frederick William the elector, who crowned himself in 1701 as the first king of Prussia.

The religion of the inhabitants is nearly divided between the Lutherans and Roman Catholics, and the morals of the people are similar to those of other fortified towns which have been a prey to invasion. The theatre had been repeatedly burnt down, and money was immediately subscribed to rebuild it; but if a church were destroyed, it remained in ruins.

On the banks of the river, towards the centre of the city, public gardens are laid out and opened every evening for the amusement of the inhabitants. They are occasionally illuminated; and, with the addition of a concert and fireworks, gambling, and tobacco-smoking, the company seem to be highly delighted with its *recreations*.

A portion of the French prisoners, from Russia, are now passing through this place on their return to France. Nothing can exceed the wretchedness of their appearance both in dress and looks; —many of them have only the covering of a tattered blanket, and scarcely any possess the comforts of either hat, shoe, or stocking. The description of their return, during the winter, from Russia, is a frightful picture of the horrors they suffered from the severity of the climate. Many of these men are without fingers and toes; and many exhibit large blotches on their faces. The king of Naples reached Konigsberg, with a part of his division; but the inhabitants, expressing their dislike to the French interest, he immediately sought his safety in flight, and went to Elbing.

Konigsberg is the capital of Prussia-proper, and was the residence of the sovereigns, until the seat of government was removed to Berlin.

About the thirteenth century a war broke out between the German knights of the Teutonic order and the Prussians. They subdued and peopled the country with Germans. A part of the country was ceded to Casimir IV. of Poland, for his assistance, and the other part they retained, as vassals to Poland. The sovereignty of the Teutonic knights continued to the sixteenth century, when Albert, margrave of Brandenburg, was created duke of East Prussia. In the seventeenth century the elector, Frederick William of Brandenburg, released the country from its vassalage to Poland, and crowned himself at Konigsberg. In the succession of the kings, the elector, Frederick William the Great, was father of Frederick I.; who was the father of Frederick William I.; who was the father of Frederick II. (or the Great); who was uncle to Frederick William II. the father of the present king, Frederick William III.

In consequence of the arrival of the emperor's *avant courier*, we were detained two days at Konigsberg, before horses could be procured. The posting horses in Prussia are under the management of the post-office, and belong to the king. Each postillion receives a hat, jacket, belt, whip, and horn. The livery is dark blue, turned up with orange colour. On the road, private carriages, etc. must give way to the postillion, when he sounds his horn. On entering the towns, they do not fail to announce, by the loudest sounds, the arrival of travellers.

Caimer, the first stage from Konigsberg, is a small picturesque village, embosomed among trees. The post-house is kept by a countess, who gleans a scanty pittance from the hire of her horses.

The next stage is Lablau, situated on the shores of the Curische Haffe, and the canal called Fredericks Graben, which connects the Niemen with the Pregel; thus affording an easy and direct communication from Konigsberg to the Black Sea, by the Niemen and the Dnieper, which rivers have been joined together at Pinsk. This interesting inland navigation is only performed during the summer months, when the produce of the Baltic is exchanged for that of the Black Sea.

Proceeding through a flat, but beautiful country, well cultivated, and diversified with trees and shrubberies, we reached Tilsit. The houses, along this part of the country, are rudely built of wood, neither so large nor so comfortable as those in West Prussia. The inhabitants are chiefly Jews, who reside in the country, and cultivate the land. Their figures are tall and thin, with a huge unshapely beard; over their persons is wrapped a long loose black cloak, and, on their heads, a black velvet cap, over which is worn a large one of fur.

Tilsit stands on the west bank of the Memel; it consists of two streets, running parallel with the river, badly paved, with a collection of mean brick, and wooden houses.

On the south side of the town is a small lake, surrounded by a few straggling buildings, called the Liberty. The river is crossed by a floating bridge of boats, which is removed in winter to allow the passage of the ice. The Memel is a noble river, it discharges itself into the Curische Haffe, by two branches which are navigable for small vessels. This river, about forty miles above Tilsit, takes the name of the Niemen, by which it is better known.

We now beheld the spot, where, in 1807, the treaty of peace was concluded between the emperor of Russia, the king of Prussia, and Napoleon Bonaparte, on a floating raft expressly contrived for the occasion. The grandeur and *eclat* evinced on this occasion were indeed worthy a meeting of monarchs. What a day of exultation to the autocrat of France! what a day of insult to Russia! Never did the destiny of Napoleon know a prouder day. Never was the war-winged genius of modern Gaul more pre-eminent than at that moment; and never did the power of France seem to rest on a surer basis. But how are the mighty fallen! This once favoured child of war, who so shortly before humbled the greatness of this northern empire, once more attempted its complete overthrow. He who thought the world too narrow for his boundless ambition, has fallen at one blow to insignificance and Elba! and now drags on a career, seemingly as pitiable as it was once unbounded.

From Tilsit to Memel is fourteen Prussian miles. The road, after crossing the river, keeps a north-westerly direction, passing through a flat country, extensively beautified by tracts of cultivation, meadow lands, and numerous plantations of willows. On the meadows are raised prodigious quantities of hay, which, with the grain, forms a part of the exported produce of the country.

Around Tilsit is seen the most productive land in this country. The soil throughout is dry soft sand, which occasionally varies into a mixture of clay-loam. The crops of barley and oats grow most luxuriantly, though the barley is as late in ripening as the oats. The produce is far beyond the consumption of the country; an immense quantity of grain is therefore annually exported. The cottages, though neither large nor subtantially built, are yet comfortable; and, in general, surrounded with willow trees, which, in these flat plains, give an extremely pleasing air of shelter.

The second stage from Tilsit is remarkably fascinating, and must gratify every admirer of rural nature. The road is flat, smooth, and shaded on each side by aged willows, trained to grow in an outward direction; on each side, the extensive plains appear as a soft lawn, covered with the richest verdure, on which securely graze its numerous flocks; while the humble cottages, under the shades of trees, afford a general scene of calmness and retirement. Here the parade of wealth does not intrude itself, neither does the humble hut retire to give room to the stately palace.

However favourable the soil, in this country, is to agriculture, yet little attention is bestowed on it. If properly tilled, it is capable of producing the heaviest crops. The farmers generally take one or two crops from the land, and afterwards allow it to remain two or three years to rest. Manure they rarely use. It is not an unusual practice, among the small farmers, to allow the dung, in the cattle yard, to accumulate to such a quantity, as to occasion a difficulty in living beside it, during the hot months of summer. Instead of removing the dung, and applying it as manure to the fields, many allow it to remain, and remove their dwelling-houses from *it!*

This country was formerly considered under the same laws as Russia, with reference to the peasantry. They were slaves to the noble, and farmed his lands; but, within these few years, the government of Prussia has abolished these laws, and given an enlargement of freedom to the people. Whether it is productive of immediate good, is difficult to decide. As slaves, under the nobles, the land was portioned out to them, and overseers were appointed to inspect their daily labour, and attention to their stock. When they carried the produce of their farms to the market, they were obliged to sell it to the best advantage, and to preserve its value. By these means they were kept from idleness and dissipation.

Those who have procured their freedoms, either rent their farms annually, or, by industry, become enabled to purchase the perpetuity of them. At present the *free* farmers are careless in the improvements of the land,—sell its produce at a trifling price, and, in the knowledge of being under no restraint, squander it away in drunkenness.

Those who are slaves receive a certain portion of land, and cows. For this they are necessitated to give three days' labour in the week, to their master, and the rest is at their own disposal. When any of their cows die, the master supplies the loss. In consequence of this grant they are less attentive to their live stock.

The cattle are herded together in flocks: each farmer sends his stock to the general pasture, where a common herdsman is employed to watch the whole. In these flocks, horned cattle, horses, sheep, and swine, are promiscuously mixed, and graze together. These grazing commons are very extensive; and they are, in many places, covered with forests. It is not an unusual thing, in West Prussia, while passing through these forests, to find little spots cleared of the wood, and settled into farms. The appearance of these woods and farms is extremely agreeable. When the traveller has passed through many dreary miles of a forest, he suddenly enters, when most unexpected, a circular spot, shaded from every storm, by the natural form of the forest; while the open space is filled with crops of rye and barley, shooting their slender forms into the unruffled air. In the centre of the farm stands the humble dwelling of the poor secluded peasant, who dreads no enemy, unless it be the brutal inhabitant of the forest, or the oppression of his lord.

However agreeable the journey from Tilsit to Memel might appear, yet the instant the latter town is approached, all softness of ideas is overturned, every object of picturesque beauty vanishes; and nothing is beheld but a wretched town, surrounded, on the one side, by a wilderness of loose sand, and, on the other, by the sea.

Memel is the last of the Prussian towns on the coast of the Baltic. It is situated on the east shore

9

of the Curische Haffe, within three leagues of the
Russian frontier. The town is old, clumsily built,
and contains about six thousand inhabitants. The
streets are irregularly formed, and, like the rest of
the Prussian towns, are badly paved. The manner of
paving the streets in these towns, consists in laying
three rows of large unshapely stones, parallel with
the houses. These rows are about four feet asunder from each other,—the intermediate space is
filled up with smaller stones carelessly thrown in.
The middle row of large stones is places in the centre of the street, which generally affords the best
footpath; but, from the frequent interruption of
carts and horsemen, a passenger must be constantly
on the watch. The stones acquire so fine a polish
that, were the horses shod, they could not, without
considerable difficulty, pass over them. Shoes are
seldom put on the horses feet here; besides, they
are so small and light, that they get over these
pavements with uncommon facility. I have frequently seen parties of the peasants, when intoxicated, mounted on their little horses, without stir-
rups, trot and gallop along the street with extreme
alacrity.

Memel formerly belonged to the Hanseatic
league, and seems to have been partly fortified.
The ramparts, though repaired about a year ago,
are, at present, in an useless state of defence. The

town does not appear to have been regularly fortified, nor could it be done but at an enormous expense. Between the town and the sea, on the north
side, the distance is equal to three English miles.
This space is a level plain of dry, loose, sand, without any vegetable decoration. All the houses, extending from the town, in a parallel direction with
the harbour, are built on loose sand, and the streets
consist of nothing else.

Memel is the great depot of timber brought down
the Niemen. The harbour is formed by the entrance of the Curische Haffe, which is only a quarter of a mile broad, and not more than thirteen feet
deep. In consequence of this, large vessels take in
part of their cargo about a mile out at sea. Around
the suburbs are erected a number of windmills,
which are used as saw-mills to cut up the timber,
before it is exported.

The quantity of timber exported from Memel
was calculated at three hundred and fifty thousand
pounds sterling per annum;* but this has considerably decreased, partly from the effects of the late
war, and also it is said, from the diminution of the
forests in Poland.

Immense rafts of wood are annually brought
down the Niemen from Poland and Lithuania. On

* Oddy's European Commerce; a very important work.

these rafts small temporary covers are raised, under which the *voyageurs* repose. They also bring along with them carts, horses, poultry, etc. When the cargo of wood is disposed of, they return by land with their horses. A raft often consists of more planks than are sufficient to load the largest vessel which sails from Memel. These rafts appear on the water like a floating island, on which are men, women, children, and cattle, with all the implements of their household and travelling machines.

The greater part of this country is peopled by the descendants of the ancient Lithuanians, though considerably intermixed with the colonies of various nations, which Peter the Great of Russia introduced. The Jews, in particular, almost seem to have fixed the land of the New Judea here !

The Lithuanians are a coarse, clumsy, and stupid class of people ; their ideas, manners, dress, and actions are those of the dullest, heaviest, and most inanimate description. The women seem to perform all the laborious part of the work. They navigate and row their little boats down the rivers with the produce of the country, particularly green vegetables and poultry. While these poor women are toiling under these hardships of the day, the men idly loiter about the public houses swallowing vast quantities of raw brandy. The quantity of this pernicious liquor drank by these people is almost incredible. Every house on the road sells spirits, and regularly at each the postillions and peasants stop and take their schnaps. Even the women carry with them a private bottle, and, as they meet in the streets, or on the road, they first salute by kissing each other's cheek, and then apply the bottle to each other's mouths, and finish by another salute of kisses.

The women ride on horseback, after the manner of men, with their petticoats tied round the knee. Nothing can be more ludicrous than to see a woman thus mounted meeting another on foot. They stop, salute, and present the bottle to each other, with all the grimaces of a complete caricature.

The boys dress in a manner similar to old men. A group of these may be seen with their backs to an observer, and scarcely known from old, decrepit men. Their hair is allowed to hang over their shoulders; they wear a broad flapping hat, also a jacket with a broad skirt; coarse stockings and sandals, made of the bark of trees, complete their dress. These boys may be seen bartering at a common stall for the smallest trifle, with all the careful coldness and distrust of penurious old age. They want that life and thoughtless gayety which prevail in youths of other countries. The boys in Sweden are almost similar to them in disposition and manner.

It is highly worthy of admiration to observe the marked difference between the appearances of the people of these countries. In West Prussia, the women are particularly fair, and even pretty. From Elbing to Memel, every stage exhibits coarser features, both in men and women: there seems to be a progressive increase of ugliness; and, from Konigsberg to Memel this ratio still further holds good.

CHAP. III.

St. Petersburg, July, 1814.

On reaching Memel, we learned that our passports, from St. Petersburg, had not arrived, and
that we might probably remain several weeks in
the expectation of them. No stranger is admitted
into the Russian territory, without a passport being
regularly procured from the metropolitan police.
It is necessary that a traveller should write to St.
Petersburg for a passport, several weeks before
he reaches the Russian frontier, otherwise he is
placed in a very awkward situation. During the
war, it required several months before they could be
obtained; and they were, it is said, sent to the emperor, when he was in France, for his signature.

Our passports from Hamburg were made out to
Memel and St. Petersburg. The Russian consul
at Memel particularly assured us, that they were a
sufficient protection to our entering St. Peters-

burg, if we went by sea, and that they did not require his signature. To avoid this detention, as
well as the disagreeable sensation of continuing in
a place void of every attraction, and without society;
we resolved on taking the advantage of a small
Prussian galliot on the eve of sailing to Cronstadt.
Before we sailed, another cause of regret occurred;
we were expressly assured that we could not take
our English carriage with us, by sea, without its
being seized by the officers of the custom-house:
in consequence of this information, we were obliged
to leave it behind.

The Christina being a small galliot, scarcely of
an hundred tons burden, could not accommodate so
many passengers in the cabin; besides, it only contained one sleeping place for the captain. A second cabin for the sailors was situated on the deck,
in which the apparatus of cookery was placed. The
vessel carried no cargo; and, as a substitute for a
cabin, the hold was allotted to us, as our apartment. We had the advantage of four small ham-
mocks, slung from the beams, but which were un-
provided with either beds or blankets. The cross
beams of the deck formed the ceiling, not more than
six inches above us, while the sand-ballast, and coil-
ed cable formed the floor. The motion of the vessel rocked us from side to side, and the bubbling

noise of the passing wave, lulled us to sleep. Even on the plainest couch, a mind at ease will sink to rest, and forget the inconveniences of the moment. When the morning dawned, we were awoke with recruited spirits, by the cackling noise of some fowls, which roosted in the same apartment.

There were neither tables nor chairs on board,—in short these are often unnecessary luxuries at sea, as, not unfrequently, the floor of the cabin, or deck, proves the most comfortable; as a substitute for a table, a large box was used. Ease and freedom were here triumphant; there was no ceremony as to precedency; no formality as to places; no delicacy nor fastidiousness. Necessity compelled us to relish what, under other situations, might have been felt as a punishment,—so true it is, that self-punishment and privations are comparatively easy to those really severe, when inflicted by others.

The tedious operation of breakfast being over, that of dinner soon followed. The kitchen of the Christina was enriched with only one pot; it was the general cauldron of the captain's feasts, and the sailors' mess. Its hungry cavity daily received the salted ribs of Lithuanian pork, or the less savoury junks of Courland beef. The presiding Comus of this Pandemonium was one of those

10

abortive imps, which required only to be seen, in order to derange the internal economy of the stomach. Apollo had not smiled at his birth, nor had the Graces hailed his entrance with any approbation;—deformity claimed him as her own, and the extremes of filth, and littleness of mind, formed his character.

The voyage along the gulf of Finland, though pleasant in summer, must, in stormy weather, prove both intricate and dangerous. The gulf is extremely narrow, and, along its course, are scattered several small islands and rocks, rendering the navigation often hazardous. On many of these islands are erected light-houses, which tend greatly towards assisting the course of the mariner.

The water of the gulf is extremely light and clear, of sparkling appearance, and perfectly sweet and fresh to the taste. The Baltic is less salt than the ocean, and which, from the Sound, increases in freshness towards the extremities of the gulfs of Finland and Bothnia.

The Baltic sea being of so small an extent, compared to the ocean, and having no tides, and constantly supplied with so vast a number of large rivers, may be the principal cause of its freshness. In short, the Baltic may almost be called a large lake. During the intensity of the frost, in January 1814, the greatest part of it was frozen over, and some merchants actually crossed in sledges, from the Russian to the Swedish coast. The guides could not be prevailed upon to remain; in the mean-time the thaw had taken place, and they found a watery grave under the ice.

The water of the Baltic is extremely cold to the touch; when the temperature of the air (in July) was equal to 73° of Farrenheit, the thermometer, when plunged a few feet under the water, fell below 50°. This great degree of cold in the water, when the temperature of the air is so elevated, might be attributed to those immense masses of ice, which, on its breaking up, become specifically heavier than the water, and sink to the bottom; and thus, by constantly expelling a stream of cold, prevent the immediate influence of the sun's rays.

Our voyage continued prosperous; and, although our progress was slow and somewhat fatiguing, yet, from the fineness of the weather, we had some compensation. The winds were light and fresh,— the sea calm and serene. Its blue face stretched around to immeasurable distance and left us scarce an object to relieve the wandering eye, unless perhaps when a distant sail would show its sunny tints, —or when a grey rock would point its shady brow on the passing wave.

In rolling along these wide and watery wastes, where ocean and sky blend in the far stretched horizon, and where eternity seems to hold its visionary realms, we naturally look around us; we ask where those mighty waters came from? from what vast abyss have they rolled? what is their use? In these inquiries we are naturally led back to the ages of chaos,—to those times when nature first threw creation out of her hands, and gave new forms to the wreck of matter. We hear, that, by these waters, the earth was once deluged and again may be dissolved.

On this subject I cannot avoid inserting the following elegant hypothesis of a valuable friend. " Here o'er the level and wide stretched ocean do the springs of the earth find their everlasting source. Here do we see the grand centre of their circulation, the bed from which they arise, the bed to which they return. Here is to be seen that vast reservoir in which, for ages past, and ages to come, have been crumbling the fragments of perishable matter, yielding back their primary elements to give new forms to other beings. Here we see illustrated the doctrine of the Metempsychosis; we see the death of organic, giving birth to inorganic matter, and *vice versa:* the fabric of the one reared on the ruins of the other; and thus the wheel of eternity constantly going round. Above all, here may we not contemplate that vast and unfathomable abyss, in which this perishable globe will one day leave its mouldering relics."*

The fatigues of our voyage were now to terminate; and at last we were to tread on the *terra firma* of Russia. On the evening of the eighth day of our voyage, we approached the shores of Cronstadt, the grand harbour and naval depot of the imperial capital. From the low situation of the town, and its want of steeples, we were unable to obtain a distinct view until within a league of it. At seven o'clock in the evening, we anchored within half a league of the pier, but, from some delay in the examination of our passports, we were unable to reach the docks until midnight.

Before we were allowed a pilot, the police officers, from the fleet, came on board to inspect our passports. This was the first instance of a Russian character we had seen. and which could not, indeed, impress a stranger with a favourable opinion, either as to sobriety, intellect, or moral principle.

* See Dr. T. C. Speer.—Tract. inaug. de Aquæ Natura. Ediñ. 1812.

The Christina being safely moored at the outside of the great dock, the captain permitted his
little scullion to escort us on shore. With the utmost difficulty of navigation, we wandered through
endless canals formed by vessels moored in the
docks. The moon shone in full splendour, and the
numerous masts and shrouds of the ships, and the
shades they flung around, presented the picture of
a vast floating forest. We reached the end, and
signs being of much more use to us than words, by
these we were conducted to our hotel,—a house
exteriorly boasting of much magnitude, but *interiorly*
one vast mass of filth, irregularity, and vermin,—
where the whole five senses, particularly that assigned to the most prominent feature of the face,
were constantly engaged in the most distressing
species of warfare. The house is kept by an An-
glo-Russ. However meritorious his individual attentions may be, and however valuable those properties, which he has inherited from his mother
country, yet, when adulterated with such raw materials as the creatures around him, they lose their
virtues; and the traveller must neither expect comfort, cleanliness, nor satisfaction.

Here we lay, or rather languished, for one
night; and the rudeness of our couch was indeed
but a sorry recompense for the fatigues of our

voyage. Next morning we took a walk through the town, imperial arsenal, round the dock yards, etc. and were enabled to form a hasty sketch of it.

The present appearance of Cronstadt must astonish every beholder. He will see the most extensive ranges of elegant buildings, intended as storehouses and barracks, it being a strong naval station, and the grand marine depot. These barracks are capable of containing a force equal at least to six times the population of the town, which latter is about six thousand. In front of the storehouses great canals are cut, and dry docks formed for clearing and repairing the imperial fleet. Connected with these and projecting into the sea, long stone piers are raised, forming a kind of square. These form the wet docks, where all merchant ships, etc. are moored, and but ill-protected from the swell of the gulf. The fortress is strongly defended, but absurdly flanked with redoubts out at sea, which could easily be taken by gun-boats, and turned upon themselves.

Outside of the docks is moored the Russian fleet, which returned a few days ago from England. These ships are in a line extending from the dock in a southerly direction, and occupying a space of five or six leagues. There are twenty sail of the line in excellent condition ; they evidently show the effect of an English polish.

It is a singular circumstance that the three commanding admirals of the Russian fleet are foreigners,—two of them are Englishmen, the other an American ; many of the captains are also Scotch and Irish. It must be an awkward situation for these gentlemen, in the event of a war with England. In the late war they resigned their commissions, and were ordered to reside at Moscow. At its termination, they were restored to their former rank.

The Russian navy must ever be liable to great disadvantages, in the event of a war with any foreign powers. Their northern situation excludes them, during six months of the year, from getting out, or returning to the Baltic ports, in consequence of ice. Even if they were stationed in the Black Sea, they would be at too great a distance from the capital, in a remote situation, and liable to all the obstacles of the Turks, and the passage of the Dardanelles.

Russia can never support a great naval power; her coast is too limited, and she possesses no colonies, nor the means of forming expert sailors. It is only from her internal commerce that she can acquire strength and riches.

From the irregularities and delays of the custom-house, our vessel, though only in ballast, could not be cleared out for two days. Our portmanteaus and packages were all noted, and our passports carefully examined. The useless and frivolous ceremonies attendant on the last operation, afforded great vexations and delays. We were told that our Hamburg passports were of no use, as they were not signed by the Russian consul at Memel, though we were there particularly assured that his signature was of no importance! From hour to hour we were detained, and, in some fruitless attempts to wait on the admiral of the police, we received the first instance of Russian *politeness*, by being denied any explanation. In the mean time our passports arrived from the capital; and, as a packet-boat was under way for St. Petersburg, we got on board. These boats are large and open, and provided with light awnings, to protect the passengers from the sun's rays. They are rowed by twelve stout fellows; but, if the wind is favourable, they are managed by two clumsy lug-sails. They carry about thirty passengers, and the voyage is usually performed in from three to eight hours. We could not avoid being struck with the comeliness of our boatmen, and still more by the peculiarities of their costume, manners, etc. They are all natives of the south-western provinces of the empire, and regu-

larly at that period, when the ice breaks up, flock
to Cronstadt, like birds of passage, and remain there
until winter, when they return back to their own
country. They are a small class of men with broad
open countenances, bespeaking great good humour
and affability; but, like all untutored people, are
easily provoked and revengeful. Their dress consists of a coarse shirt, without a collar, and open
down the right side of the breast where it is secured by a button,—over a pair of loose trowsers,
is worn the shirt, which is fastened, round the waist,
by a rope; on the head they wear a low crowned
hat, with a broad brim, turned up at each side;
the hair of the head is cut strait across the forehead, in a line with the eye-brows, from which it
hangs perpendicularly down, so as to cover the
ears, whence it is cut square across the neck, from
ear to ear.

While engaged at their labour they generally
sing and seem to forget it. Their voices and their
oars go together; the one in keeping tune, the other
in keeping time. The clapping of their hands forms
an interlude, and thus, of a hardship, they make a
pleasure. Their execution in music is very respect-
able, and their melodies are, I think, very sweet:
they strongly remind me of those I have heard in
the Highlands of Scotland, and brought me back to
those happy scenes, where the hardy Scot,

Free as the winds that play on his mountains,
And wild as the streamlet that flows from his fountains,

ranges along his desert path,—unknown to luxuries, unknown to cares.

" *Caledonia!* thou land of the mountain and rock,
    Of the ocean, the mist, and the wind;
Thou land of the torrent, the pine, and the oak,
    Of the roe-buck, the hart, and the hind.
Though bare are thy cliffs, and though barren thy glens,
    Though bleak thy dun islands appear,
Yet kind are the hearts, and undaunted the clans,
    That roam on those mountains so drear."

Ettrick Shepherd.

Having left Cronstadt, at a late hour in the evening, we were unable to judge of the surrounding
landscape; but, early on the following morning, the
proud towers of the Russian capital burst on our
astonished sight; their domes, glittering in the
rising sun, and throwing their rich tints on the pla-
cid bosom of the Neva: nor pen, nor pencil, nor
tongue, can give adequate effect to the glorious
coup d'œil. It was more like the bright vision of
an eastern night,—more like the light which gilds
the poet's dream, than the cold morning realities
of common life.

Every where around us lay palaces, temples, and monuments, and we beheld a city, as if reared by magic and designed by the gods. No ugly nor deformed heap obtruded itself on the eye,—no mean nor disfigured speck violated its fine stretched film, —all was grandeur, majesty and arrangement.

Here we could not but contemplate the distant glories of this young and vigorous capital,—the struggles she has suffered for the deliverance of Europe, and the era she has made in the history of the world. We could not behold, without reverence and wonder, the grand reservoir, whence have flowed those vast and mighty streams, which have swept away the tyrant's desolating legions. We could not but gaze on those glorious banners, under which the brave and good Alexander reared his mighty hosts and sent them abroad to give peace to mankind.

It is totally out of the reach of language to give adequate effect to the splendid outline of picture which here first strikes the stranger. We generally associate the painting with the time taken in its execution, and we conceive they correspond with each other. Not so here,—our principles of association will be totally deranged, and our astonishment will be greater than ever. If we consider the rapidity with which this city has been raised; the

harlequin transportation by which the reeds of a
morass were changed for the spires of a capital ;—
if, with this, we consider its population, its buildings
and its extent, we are really confounded and lost in
admiration. But, when we learn that this spectacle
of human labour and ingenuity was accomplished
by the genius and industry of one individual, it re-
quires indeed very peculiar powers to appreciate
the vastness and qualities of that nature which the
Almighty has given us.

The first and grandest object which will strike
the traveller's notice, on entering the Russian capital, is the majestic and deep flowing Neva. By its
divisions and ramifications, several islands are formed, on which stand portions of the city ; these are
connected with each other by means of floating
bridges of boats. The river is one-third of a mile
in breadth, deep, rapid and clear as crystal. Its
mouth is obstructed by fishing nets and stakes placed
in the water to decoy the fish into them. The
banks, below the town, are flat and marshy, but, in
many places, relieved by trees and wooden huts.
The circumjacent country is so flat that only partial
views of it can be taken at once.

Scarcely had we landed in the capital before we
were summoned to the police, to enrol our names,
professions, etc. and to receive a ticket of residence

also' to return the passports which had been forwarded to us at Cronstadt. So extremely requisite is it, to be provided with these certificates, that any foreigner, attempting to enter the capital without it, is liable to considerable inconveniences.

An English merchant happened to arrive at the same hotel, at the same time we did ; and, not being aware of the impropriety of trespassing against the laws of the police, accepted the offer of a courier's conveyance from Memel, then returning to St. Petersburg from the court of London. On their arrival he soon found his error, and being unable to present the necessary certificates of his admission into the country, was, without any ceremony, conveyed to a loathsome cell, and confined, until his friends heard of his situation, and relieved him.

In a general survey of this city, every thing surpasses and dazzles the attention. The streets are long and spacious, neatly paved and kept remarkably clean. In some of them gravelled walks are laid out along the centre, shaded by rows of poplars, which form a safe and agreeable promenade, from the carriages passing along on each side. Others are intersected by broad canals, and massy bridges of granite, giving life and activity to numerous bargemen, and bearing, on their loaded bosoms, the treasures and labour of the country. The houses are large exteriorly, and splendid in appearance; they are in general plaistered with stucco, in imitation of stone, or painted either yellow or white, with roofs covered with sheets of iron or tin, and, not unfrequently, painted green; while the fronts exhibit numerous ranges of windows, balconies, endless collonnades, virandas, and porticos. The numerous and fantastic-shaped domes and spires of the churches, covered either with gold or silver gilding, every where reflect their metallic lustre, and dazzle the eye, while the ear is as constantly assailed by the jingling of their bells.

The admiralty stands in the centre of the town, on the south side of the Neva. It exhibits a light square building of immense extent; on every side forming a front of nearly six hundred feet in length, but of no height, and that considerably concealed by a heavy earthen mound, thrown up around it. In the centre of the south front, the principal entrance passes under a magnificent arched gateway, supporting a splendid square basement of Doric pillars, surmounted by a rich gilt cupola, and slender spire, the top of which is crowned by a vessel under full sail, emblematic of the building. Along the outside of the earthen mound and ditch, delightful gravelled walks are laid out, shaded by double rows of clipped poplars, while the borders are beautifully

relieved by low green painted railings, and sweet
scented flowers. The extreme care with which
these walks are kept, reflect the greatest credit on
the police, and forms one of the most delightful
lounges imaginable. Every morning the inferior
officers of the police are regularly seen cleaning and
sweeping these walks, and trimming the flowers.
It is a matter of surprise to witness those delicate
plants, in the crowded streets of a metropolis, growing, without once meeting with the slightest injury,
beyond what the changes of the weather produce ;
not a tree is scratched, nor a plant trampled upon.

From the admiralty, the principal streets diverge,
as from a general centre; so that from each, its gilded
spire forms the terminating view. Among the streets
leading from the admiralty, that, called the Per-
spective, is the longest and most elegant in the city.
A gravelled walk, shaded by trees, extends along
its centre, occasionally interrupted by the massive
granite bridges over the canals. About three miles
from the admiralty this beautiful street terminates
at the monastery of St. Alexander Nevsky. In it are
seen some superb palaces and churches, also the
market or place allotted for shops in general.

The principal church to be seen here, is the Casan, the St. Paul's of Russia. It was founded as a
rival to that at Rome, and named after the govern-

ment of Casan, the first province in the Russian empire which embraced Christianity. The building, though not completely finished, exhibits an outline sufficient to denote its extent and proportions. The body of the church is built in the form of a cross; while the front represents a part of a great circle, formed by a quadruple row of grooved pillars, supporting a massive square capital. In this circle there are one hundred pillars, each forty feet in height, built of brick, and plaistered to imitate stone. The effect of this part of the building is certainly grand; but the body of the church is too small in proportion, and is concealed by their superior height; the dome is neither of sufficient height nor size. It is covered with block tin, and crowned with a cross of exquisite workmanship, supported on a large gold, gilded ball. The inside of the church surpasses its exterior, both in beauty and proportion. The roof is arched, richly ornamented with flowers in relief, and supported by fifty-eight magnificent pillars of polished granite. Each of these pillars consists of one solid stone forty feet in height, and four feet in diameter, surmounted by a rich capital of brass, and supported by a massive pedestal of the same metal. Nothing can exceed the beauty and elegance of these pillars; they have a polish and reflection equal to the finest crys-

tal. The expense and labour of transporting them
from Finland, must have been immense; and,
while they reflect the greatest credit on the perseverance and labour of the people, it also is an instance of the rapid improvement which the government seems to aim at. But what are these pillars,
compared to the rock on which the statue of Peter
the Great is placed!

The altar and religious decorations equally correspond in magnificence: the altar differs from that
of the Catholic church, in being concealed behind
folding doors of silver, in the *sanctum sanctorum*,
where no woman has permission to enter, and,
between the altar and the folding doors, only
the priests are permitted to pass. On each side of
the doors are paintings of the Holy Family, and
particular saints; before each of them are placed
large silver candlesticks, with a circular plate on
the top, on which are placed numerous wax tapers.
Only the faces, hands and feet of the paintings of
the saints are to be seen, the other parts are covered by a rich gold drapery, thickly studded with
pearls and costly gems. Above the altar is a large
painting, representing the last supper of our Saviour; here Judas is drawn with one finger at his
mouth, denoting treachery, while, in the other
hand, he holds a bag of money! Around the walls

of the church are displayed the various flags taken from the enemy, the keys of captured cities, etc.

On account of the great riches contained in this church, persons of tried fidelity are constantly kept in it as a watch against any sacrilegious attempts: even the priests are not permitted greater freedoms than others, and probably from a good motive. Among the warlike trophies hung up in the church was a splendid *baton* of one of Napoleon's marshals, taken during the late campaign. Its value was too tempting to be resisted, and it was stolen by one of the officiating priests,—a model of the original supplies its place.

In this church the body of Kutousoff, the late commander-in-chief of the Russian army, is interred. This veteran was the saviour of his country from the invasion of Napoleon. He was unanimously called to the chief command of the army by the nobles, though it is said, against the private wishes of the emperor; but who showed sufficient wisdom and judgment in approving of their choice. His tomb consists of a plain iron railing, in the west angle of the nave of the church; over it is formed a warlike trophy of French flags and the eagle of Napoleon; a device very appropriate to his character.

Such is a short description of the Casan church, which is, to St. Petersburg, what St. Paul's is to London; but as inferior in magnitude, chasteness of design and execution, as the cell of the *Meve-lavites* to the temple of Diana at Ephesus.

Splendid as this church is in appearance, and imposing in the.effect which it must always have on the beholder; yet when we contrast with its grandeur, the filthy figures of those who bow at its altars, we feel more emancipated from that pure and holy spirit of devotion, which otherwise, its shrines are well calculated to create, and which seems to hover around its consecrated aisles.

Beyond the Casan church, is the place allotted for the merchant's shops and the fruit market. They are allowed in no other part of the city, and are so mechanically arranged, that a customer has the advantage of selecting any particular article of manufacture, etc. from several shops, dealing in the same trade, and placed under one view. A range of building, occupying nearly half a mile square, is entirely filled with these shops. They form two stories, with covered piazzas in front, where the company parade and view the various manufactures of foreign nations. All articles of one description are placed in shops adjoining to each other. In

the first range are seen the booksellers, which occupy twelve shops; next to these are the station-
ers. In these shops are innumerable volumes of
books, almost all in the Russian language, and entirely of religious tracts, and German romances.
Next to the booksellers' shops are the ranges of
haberdashers, dealers in silks, dealers in hardware.
boot and shoe-makers, dealers in leather, hat-ma-
kers, fur shops, etc., and lastly the apothecaries
shops, which are the most numerous and most disgusting. These venders of medicinal herbs and
drugs, exhibit the lowest and most melancholy picture, which the whole and manifold tribe of Galen
presents; they seem really the last and most pitiable link in the chain; their very physiognomy and
the superjacent filth under which it struggles to
peep out, cannot but remind one of the synopsis of
a *materia medica.* It presents the most varied
group of character, and must often *operate* on a
stranger, as much as his drugs; indeed, it is impossible for the stomach of any other animal than a
Russian, not to be somewhat put out of its usual
arrangement; even the lower regions must sympathize, and the whole inward man become dreadfully disconcerted.

Every shop has a boy stationed at the door,
whose constant attention is directed to allure passengers to enter and view the goods. No jealousy

seems to subsist between them, and the extreme
attention and civility with which they exhibit the
goods, are no less pleasing, than praiseworthy.

Adjoining to the retail shops, is that of the fruit
market. Here the finest display of different kinds
of fruits and flowers is exhibited. Melons, peaches,
nectarines, ananas, grapes, apples, cherries, straw-
berries, raspberries and gooseberries, with a variety of heath and woodland berries, are in the utmost abundance, besides various kinds of foreign
fruits. These fruits are all forced, excepting the
class of berries; and, in so northern a climate, we
cannot but applaud the success of the Russian
horticulturist.

The numerous private orchards, kitchen gardens,
and hot houses, which are daily established by the
nobility and gardeners, have contributed much to
the great abundance of vegetables.

The only fruit which seems to succeed indifferently, is the common gooseberry. The red variety
is the sole kind which is seen, and it is of a small
and sickly form. The beauty, fragrance, and regularity of this market, must excite the admiration
of every stranger.

Beyond the fruit market is that for poultry, sing-
ing-birds, rabbits, etc.; also, mushrooms and cucumbers. All the varieties of the fungus tribe are in-

discriminately sold, and the quantity of cucumbers
raised is almost incredible. The common people
are constantly seen eating them raw, or preserve
them in dry salt. The proportion of cucumbers raised in this country, is almost equal to that of potatoes.

The theatre is situated near to the market. Its
exterior is perhaps the most inelegant of any public
building in the city. The interior of the house is
large, neatly decorated, and well lighted up. The
stage, scenery and dresses are equally well arranged,
and the performers by no means deficient in the his-
trionic art. The Russian language, when heard
from the stage, sounds remarkably soft and pleasing; at a little distance it has a strong similarity to
the English language, particularly in the theatres.
At present a popular melo-drama is performed,
which is intended to represent the return of the
victorious Russian army from the late campaign.
The appearance of the various tribes which com-
pose the army, their different dresses and mode of
attack, etc., is an excellent epitome of this extraordinary large nation.

The part of the house, allotted to the company,
consists of the boxes and pit. The first is the private property of individuals, and the last the *reservoir* of the very refuse of elegance. The pit is an
open space, without seats, and where every degree

of rank and rude contact is suffered.   If a stranger
happens once to get wedged in, he will soon lament
his unfortunate destiny: All his senses will be engaged in the most distressing state of hostility; the
zephyrs of garlick and onions will be constantly hovering around his nose; myriads of vermin will be
wafted on their balmy wings to his racking touch,
and no longer will the *sesquipedalia verba* of the drama charm his ear.

At the west side of the admiralty is situated the
Hermitage, or winter palace of the emperor.   This
huge edifice of stuccoed brick forms a square, on
each side representing a front, lost in a confusion of
pillars and statues of every order.   Nothing is so
difficult as an attempt to describe these public buildings; no regularity of architectural rules is observed,—the exuberance of all is combined, to form one
confused mass.   Here the emperor occasionally resides; and here the late Catharine gave free scope
to the unbridled licentiousness of her reign.   Part
of the palace forms the royal gallery of paintings;
in the collection are several excellent original paintings by Teniers, Leduc, Wouwerman, da Vinci,
Rembrandt, Porter, etc. etc., with the celebrated
collections of Crozat and Houghton.

The paintings are arranged in separate rooms,
with the name and age in which the artist lived,

affixed to each frame. This collection is very extensive, and well calculated to dazzle the eye of a
passing stranger; but the artist will be compelled
to behold innumerable daubs and many forgeries,
unblushingly exhibited as originals.

Part of the gallery is appropriated to mineralogy.
The collection is tolerably large, but indifferently
arranged. It consists of polished specimens of
agate, jasper, crystallized sulphur, and some specimens of native metals, particularly large masses of
malachite, or the carbonate of copper.

Within the palace are artificial gardens, denominated the winter and summer gardens. The
first is roofed with glass, laid out in gravel walks,
and planted with orange trees, and several parter-
res of flowers, and filled with birds of various countries. The summer garden is exposed to the air,
and placed on the top of the palace. At one corner of
the palace is the riding school, a covered room four
hundred and fifty feet long, by one hundred and
twenty in breadth, but very low in the roof, and
by no means equal to the one at Copenhagen,
which is probably the largest and best proportion-
ed *manege* in the north of Europe.

In front of the palace is the largest square in the
city; one of its sides is formed by a magnificent
building, erected by the late Catharine for her fa

vourites, but which is now changed to a private club-house by the English and German merchants, and on each side terminated by the public hotels.

To the west of the Hermitage, and fronting the river, is the palace of the grand duke, partly built of hewn granite and Siberian red marble, and is probably one of the chastest buildings in St. Petersburg. In the vicinity of this palace are laid out extensive gardens, in every corner of which are exhibited statues, which are condemned to be buried six months in the year, under snow. Between the garden and the river, is one of the finest and most superb iron-railings, perhaps to be found in any part of Europe. It is supported between thirty or forty massive columns of granite, upwards of twenty feet in height, surmounted by large urns. Between the granite columns the iron spears are placed, of the same height, and gilded with gold at the top.

An anecdote is related of an Englishman, who, having heard of the grandeur of this railing, undertook a journey to St. Petersburg for the express purpose of seeing it. The instant he arrived he proceeded to the summer gardens, and having satisfied his curiosity, immediately bent his course back to England, without even examining the beauty of the city!

At the south end of these gardens stands the palace of the late emperor, wherein he was strangled.

This colossal and clumsy edifice, was one of the many eccentric labours of that unfortunate monarch. To avoid inhabiting the same palace which his royal mother had occupied, and, as a secure asylum against the too just suspicions which he entertained of the attachment of his nobles, he raised this building in the short space of three years. For the completion of this palace, he appropriated the marble, which the empress Catharine had ordered to be used in the building of the great church of St. Isaac, and, by way of insult to her memory, he ordered this beautiful church to be finished with bricks, in a most disfigured manner, which gave rise to the following epigram.

De deux regnes voici l'image allegorique ;
La base est d'un beau marbre, et le sommet de brique !*

From this palace he hurled out mandates, which menaced the very existence of his empire. Here his eccentricities rose to their highest pitch, and here he met with that fate, which must always endanger the madness of despotism.

It is said the death of Paul might have been prevented, had he not forgotten to pull a bell wire

* This church is an emblem of two differing reigns ;
The marble marks sense,—the brick, want of brains!

which communicated under ground, with the room where his body guards were assembled. Whenever he used to give this signal, every one flew to the palace with the utmost speed, whether dressed or not, and whoever first arrived was richly rewarded, while the last was as certain of destruction!

Returning to the west quarter of the admiralty, a similar square to that in front of the Hermitage is laid out, and which contains the humbled and disfigured church of St. Isaac, as a striking example of the cultivated taste of Catharine, and the rudeness of her successor. The interior of the church is partly finished with marble, but altogether gloomy and somewhat neglected.

In the same square is the prodigious rock, on which is placed the elegant equestrian statue of Peter the Great. This great rock of granite was drawn from the neighbourhood of the capital, on cannon balls, placed in a grooved railway, which corresponds with an opposite grooved space, fixed to the basis of the rock. It was moved forwards by means of ropes, pullies and windlasses, drawn both by men and horses. A drummer was stationed on the rock to give a signal to the workmen. Its size, when brought to St. Petersburg, was between forty and fifty feet in length, upwards of twenty in breadth, and as much in height.

When the artist, Falconet, had finished his statue of Peter the Great, though as admirable a specimen of the art, as ever graced the followers of a Phidias or Praxiteles, yet, from the giant rudeness of its pedestal, it could not but be rendered too minute in the general outline; he, therefore, in order to assimilate their dimensions, mutilated the rock, and thus gave an imaginary measure of bulk to the figure. The attitude of the statue represents the monarch, as having gained the summit of a precipice, and restraining the violence of his horse, which is seen rearing on its hind legs, with a full and flowing tail, touching the writhing body of a serpent, on which the horse tramples. The head of the figure is crowned with laurel, and a loose flowing robe is thrown over its body. The left hand holds the reins, while the other is stretched out in the act of giving benediction to his subjects. On the rock the following short, but expressive inscription, is fixed in golden letters, both in the Latin and Russian language,

" CATHARINE II. to PETER I."

Connected with this square is the elegant street, known by the name of the English-line, from its being, at one period, the principal residence of the

English merchants; its extent is upwards of a mile,
and separated from the river by a broad street and
a massive pier of hewn granite, through which are
cut flights of steps in order to descend to the numerous boats and barges.

This short description gives an account of the
principal features of the city, on the south side of the
river, which contains the most elegant buildings,
and is the residence of the court, the nobles and
gentry, with a population of one hundred and
eighty thousand persons. In the quarters of the
admiralty all the finest buildings are situated. As
we approach towards the barriers of the town,
much open space is seen, partly covered with
wooden hovels and marshes, while the streets are
laid with planks of wood.

On the north side of the river is situated the opposite division of the city, which is built partly on
two islands formed by the different branches of
the Neva. The most conspicuous of these buildings are the citadel, the academy of arts, the military institution, the exchange, custom-house, etc.

The exchange and custom-house are situated on
the west end of the lower island, called the quarter
of Vassili Ostroff, at the separation of the branches
of the river, and immediately fronts the citadel,
which is situated on the opposite corner of the up-

per island, named the St. Petersburg quarter. A new exchange was erected a few years ago, but, from some singular motive, has never been opened; the merchants, in consequence, continue to meet in the open air, in front of the old house. The new exchange consists of an oblong square, surrounded with a broad piazza, supported on numerous pillars. In front of the building are placed two extraordinary monumental pillars, with large figures emblematic of ships, but more like some nondescript monster. Nothing can be more ludicrous. Behind the exchange is the custom-house, warehouses, quay and docks; this range of buildings is probably more contemptible than those in any other of the trading towns along the barren shores of Sweden.

Every vessel, bound to the capital, must be cleared at Cronstadt, before it is permitted to enter the Neva. From the inactive and irregular manner, in which every department of public business seems to be conducted in this country, it is impossible not to feel chagrined at the vexatious delays and losses sustained by it. A redundancy of persons is employed in every official situation, and a disregard to method or system is pursued by every one. While one obeys, another seems afraid to command. This must in part arise from the despotic nature of the government; it is only by comparison that we judge of the excellencies or defects of governments, and the nearer they approach to simplicity, and the more unrestricted they are, the more they ought to be admired.

The galliot, which brought us to Cronstadt, though only in ballast, was detained there two days before it could be cleared out for the capital. With the vessel, was detained our luggage, without our being permitted to take any part of it. On her arrival at St. Petersburg, not less than ten days were consumed in the necessary arrangements of granting a license for their being landed, and even this indulgence was accomplished by the irresistible power of money!

No laws are stricter than those of the customs of this country, against the importation of prohibited goods, yet no where is a law more evaded. To encourage the manufactory of Russian woollen cloths, those of other countries are rigidly prohibited; yet not a noble or foreign merchant is seen without his dress being the work of an English loom!

If a ship is consigned, and not acknowledged by its agent, within a given time, she is liable to be confiscated. The agent must specify the goods, and pay the duties accordingly, without seeing them. If the cargo is more than what is specified,

the surplus is detained,—if less, the money is kept,
and the goods are returned.

In consequence of this measure, there is abundance of law disputes, but no justice. Any person
who chuses, becomes a lawyer, and the client who
pays the highest is certain of gaining the cause. A
case may be decided immediately, or may be protracted *ad infinitum*. Every merchant becomes, in
rotation, a magistrate, in which capacity they act
as judges in the courts of civil law. From a singular law of Peter the Great, every judge is answera-
ble for his decision. Their term of acting is three
years, they therefore postpone every case from
time to time, until the period of their jurisdiction is
finished, when they resign the office to the succeed-
ing magistrate, who carries on the same method.
In this respect a client might never get redressed.
However there is a substitute, in an inferior sort of
illegal court, which is allowed to practice, by paying
an annual sum to the government. This court consists of a president and a numerous set of pleaders,
self-educated, and self-enrolled. A case must be
paid for by previous agreement, and the most generous client is generally the most successful. The fees
are equally divided among the members of the court.
Over the head of each member is written the word

14

Siberia! and thus, like the sword hanging over Da-
mocles,—they are kept in constant terror.

Near the exchange is an old clumsy building containing the royal museum, and which is open to the
public by paying a small fee to the attendant. The
only person who conducted us through the museum, was an illiterate Russian boor, who, the one
day shows the cabinet of curiosities, while the other
he is perhaps employed in sweeping the streets.
The museum is divided into several apartments; the
first is a circular room, gloomy and neglected; this
contains the library. The collection was tolerably
large, and chiefly written in the French and German languages, with a few in English, but scarcely
any in the language of the country. The Russian language is a dialect of the ancient Sclavonian, and is
perhaps spoken over a greater extent of country than
any modern tongue. Its alphabet consists of for-
ty-one characters, not unlike, in their form, to those
of the Greek. It is spoken by the natives with extreme quickness, and has a soft and hissing sound.
The language in common use among the nobles is
French, and it is a notorious fact that many cannot
write their own. Russian literature must ever be
cramped until their language is altered. Independently of many other reasons, their authors have

too much *verbiage* in the very structure of their sen-
tences and words; and even in the characters of
their alphabet there is a kind of barbarism which is
truly revolting. Hence the few books it has will
not be read by foreigners, and, if men of real genius
are to be found, and wish to communicate their
ideas, they must adopt a garment less rude and
more fashionable to dress them up, and send them
into the world. French or German is the medium
generally adopted; thus the natives are prevented
from receiving that instruction which they might afterwards communicate and improve upon. But this
is only one source among many others of the poverty of Russian literature; to enumerate them,
would be to go through a melancholy catalogue of
moral infirmities.

The second apartment contains some exquisite
models of wooden bridges, invented and executed
by a common Russian slave, to be thrown across the
river. This beautiful model was finished about
forty years ago; but from the great expense attending the erection of it, the attempt had been abandoned. The model is nearly one hundred feet in
length, and consists of a single arch. The breadth
of the river over which the arch was intended to
be thrown is one thousand feet. The model is
roofed at the top, and covered at the sides. The

road passes under the top arch, or appears to be
suspended from it.   Another model is formed on
pontoons, and which has been approved of, in preference to the other.

The adjoining apartments are allotted to the classes of insects and quadrupeds.   The former are mechanically grouped together, to form figures in imitation of flowers, etc. without attention to any zoo-
logical arrangement; equally unclassic is that of
the quadruped class.   Elephants and badgers, tigers
and the Greenland bear, wolves and eagles, etc. etc.
are all indiscriminately blended together; while the
stuffed skin of a giant and anatomical preparations
are exhibited in the most indelicate manner, and
yet there were many Russian ladies visiting all
parts of this gross exhibition!

Among the rarest productions of the class Mammalia, was an excellent specimen of the hairy and
spinous duck-billed animal denominated *Ornithorin-
chus*, presenting new and strange conformations,
contrary to all former rules.   This animal has been
lately discovered in New Holland; it exhibits the
perfect resemblance of the beak of a duck engraf-
ted on the head of a quadruped, with the webbed
feet of the duck.   It is an animal about fourteen inches long, and about four pounds weight.   We also
saw several of the *Mustela Erminea*, principally

caught in the wilds of Russia, from whose skin the valuable ermine fur is procured. As might be expected, the white bear (*Ursus Maritimus*) occupied conspicuous stations in the exhibition. The *Tetrao Tetrix*, or black grouse, and the *Falco-Melanœtus*, or black eagle, were also very common.

The last apartment contains a wax-figure of Peter the Great, dressed in one of his court-dresses, a light blue silk trimmed with silver lace. On each side of the figure is his common dress, which appears to have been often patched. In another room are his turning machines, models of ships, etc. also his favourite horse and dogs. In short every relic of this extraordinary monarch seems to be preserved with a degree of religious veneration.

In one of the apartments of this museum is the entire skeleton of some extraordinary large animal, said to have been dug out of the banks of a river in Siberia. This skeleton is larger than that of the elephant, and the principal character between them is the shape and position of the tusks. Those of the elephant form a straight perpendicular outward curve, with its trunk or proboscis inserted between them. In this skeleton, the tusks present an elevated circular shape, and so closely united at the roots, that no trunk could pass between them.

This skeleton is asserted to belong to that of an animal called a *mammoth*. If such an animal ever existed as a distinct genus, and only found in the northern latitudes, we may safely conclude the climates of these countries to be the same at this moment that they were at the end of the general deluge, consequently they could not find sustenance sufficient for their size. Some great revolution might have brought their bones, etc. to these regions : but may not the mammoth be an amphibious animal ? In the sacred writings mention is made of an animal, which partly partakes of the character of the elephant, and that of an amphibious animal. Job, chap xl., verse 15. " Behold now *behemoth* which I made with thee; he *eateth grass* as an ox." Verse 23. " Behold he drinketh up a river, *and hasteth not :*"—

Many teeth and bones of animals have been found in a fossil state, both in Siberia, and on the banks of the Ohio, in North America, also in Peru and the Brazils. Those discovered in America belong to the *great mastadon* described by professor Cuvier. Those found in Siberia have been called by the Russians mammoth's teeth, or mammout bones, and mammon's horns, which they supposed to have belonged to an animal, which they describe as being of a monstrous size, and living in caverns

under the ground. To whatever class of animals
these bones belonged, they are certainly at present
unknown. The French academicians, on compa-
ring some of these with the bones of the real elephants, concluded that they belonged to the same
species of animal. Mr. Pennant also assents to the
opinion of those who think they once belonged to
the elephant. " It is," says this elegant writer,
" more than probable that this animal yet exists in
some of those remote parts of the vast new continent unpenetrated yet by Europeans. Providence
maintains and continues every created species, and
we have as much assurance, that no race of animals
will any more cease, while the earth remaineth,
than *seed time and harvest, cold and heat, summer and
winter, day and night.* However the mere anatomical structure of the animal is sufficient to mark its
difference from the elephant. Dr. Hunter discovered on a more accurate examination, that they are
very different from those of the elephant, and belong to another animal. The tusks of the true elephant have a slight lateral bend, but these have a
large twist or spiral curve. Those teeth which
have also been found in North America, evidently
belong to a carnivorous animal, whereas those of
the elephant are flat and belong to graminivorous
animals. In the present specimen there were no

perfect teeth. The thigh bone is also of a very disproportionate size to that of the elephant, besides some other anatomical variations.*

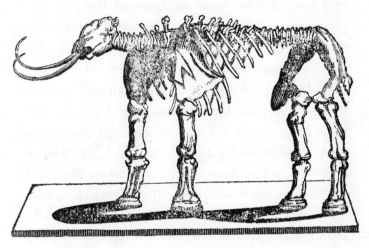

The following scale is an accurate measurement of the skeleton.

	Feet in length.
From the mouth to the root of the tail . . .	21
Length of the tusks	10
From the top of the shoulder to the hoof . .	12
Width of the thorax	5
————— pelvis	4
Diameter of the hoof, 14 inches.	
Thigh	4
Legs	3

* Phil. Trans. vol. lviii. art. 5.

Spine including the joints of the tail, composed of forty-three vertebræ,—ribs not perfect.

M. Cuvier, in his admirable osteological descriptions of several of the larger species of quadrupeds, mentions that two species of elephants are at present known as inhabitants of the earth. The one, which is confined to Africa, is named the African elephant; the other, which is a native of Asia, is named the Asiatic elephant. Only one fossil species has hitherto been discovered. It is the *mammoth* of the Russians. The following discovery is given by professor Cuvier, from a report in the supplement to the *Journal du Nord*, No. XXX, by M. Adams.

"In the year 1799, a Tungusian fisherman observed a strange shapeless mass, projecting from an ice bank, near the mouth of a river, in the north of Siberia, the nature of which he did not understand, and which was so high in the bank as to be beyond his reach. He next year observed the same object, which was then rather more disengaged from among the ice, but was still unable to conceive what it was. Towards the end of the following summer, 1801, he could distinctly see that it was the frozen carcase of an enormous animal, the entire flank of which and one of its tusks had become disengaged from the ice. In consequence of the ice beginning to melt earlier and to a greater degree

15

than usual in 1803, the fifth year of this discovery, the enormous carcase became entirely disengaged, and fell down from the ice-crag on a sand bank, forming part of the coast of the Arctic ocean. In the month of March of that year, the Tungusian carried away the two tusks, which he sold for the value of fifty rubles.—Two years afterwards, or in 1806, M. Adams went to examine this animal, which still remained on the sand bank where it had fallen from the ice, but its body was then greatly mutilated. The *Jukuts* of the neighbourhood had taken away considerable quantities of its flesh to feed their dogs; and the wild animals, particularly the white bears, had also feasted on the carcase; yet the skeleton remained quite entire, except that one of the fore-legs was gone. The entire spine, the pelvis, one shoulder-blade, and three legs, were still held together by their ligaments, and by some remains of the skin; and the other shoulder-blade was found at a short distance. The head remained, covered by the dried skin, and the pupil of the eyes was still distinguishable. The brain also remained within the skull, but a good deal shrunk and dried up; and one of the ears was in excellent preservation, still retaining a tuft of strong bristly hair. The upper lip was a good deal eaten away, and the under lip was entirely gone, so that the teeth were distinctly seen. The animal was a male, and had a

long mane on its neck. The skin was extremely
thick and heavy, and as much of it remained as required the exertions of ten men to carry away, which
they did with considerable difficulty. More than
thirty pounds weight of the hair and bristles of this
animal were gathered from the wet sand bank, having been trampled into the mud by the white bears,
while devouring the carcase. Some of the hair
was presented to our museum of natural history,
by M. Targe, censor in the lyceum of Charlemagne.
It consists of three distinct kinds. One of these is
stiff black bristles, a foot or more in length, another
is thinner bristles, or coarse flexible hair, of a reddish brown wool, which grow among the roots of
the long hair. These afford an undeniable proof
that this animal had belonged to a race of elephants
inhabiting a cold region, with which we are now unacquainted, and by no means fitted to dwell in the
torrid zone. It is also evident that this enormous
animal must have been frozen up by the ice at the
moment of its death." " It is worthy of remark,"
adds the accurate translator of M. Cuvier, " that
although fossil bones of the elephant were described
as such in the middle of the sixteenth century by Al-
drovandus, it was not until two centuries afterwards
that his opinion was credited. In the intermediate
time they were described as lusus naturæ,—bones of

giants—*skeletons of fallen angels,*—remains of marine animals or of colossal baboons."*

It is not improbable but this animal had been conveyed down the stream, on some piece of floating ice, and deposited at the place where it was discovered. We have seen a similar fact noticed by some late travellers who had ascended the Missouri river, in North America,—that frequent instances had occurred where the buffaloes were carried down the stream on shoals of floating ice, and the bodies of several of them found embedded in the ice banks. This supposition might tend to explain why the mammoth's skeleton was found on the banks of a river in so northern a latitude. But from what part of the continent such an animal had taken its departure, must remain in impenetrable darkness, until further discoveries tend to elucidate the certainty of its existence. Those bones of elephants and other animals still in existence, which have been found in Siberia, might with more probability be accounted for, by the circumstances of their wandering from their own country in the summer months, and being overtaken by the storms of a more northern climate, and carried down the streams of those rivers which flow from the con-

---

* Cuvier, Theory of the Earth.

fines of China to the Artic sea. The river Yenessa
receives a tributary stream from the lake Baikal, in
Chinese Tartary, and disembogues itself into the
Frozen Ocean at about eighty degrees of east longitude. The lake Baikal is supplied by other rivers
which flow from the south, and through a country
inhabited by elephants. It is not improbable then,
that the bones of these animals have been thus conveyed from their native country to these remote
places. Perhaps if a careful search was made at the
mouths of the Oby, the Yenessa, and the Lena,
more remains of such animals might be discovered
than on the plains between those rivers,—particularly bones of elephants, and such large animals
as are peculiar to these south-eastern countries.

  We cannot close this interesting inquiry, without
turning our attention to the fact that such animals
once existed. The bones of the mammoth are not
the only instances of the remains of a singular race
of animals being discovered. Those of the *great
mastadon*, found in an imperfect state in the new
continent, prove them to belong to a distinct genus ;
also the singular skeleton found at Buenos Ayres,
called the *megatherium*, which evidently belongs to
the carnivorous species, with cloven feet (didac-
tylus) and long claws. This extraordinary skeleton is preserved in the royal museum at Madrid,

and of which M. Cuvier has given a very accurate drawing.

The academy of arts is situated on the north side of the river, in the Vassili-Ostroff. This is an immense quadrangular brick building, forming in the centre, a large open circle, in which the students amuse themselves after the hours of study. The students of this excellent institution are clothed, educated and maintained, at the expense of the government. The younger students seemed to have acquired considerable proficiency, but those of the higher classes seemed to be stationary at the same standard of improvement. There are scarcely any original paintings in the academy. Its principal subjects are the copies of native artists, which entirely relate to the exploits of their own heroes, etc.

In the architectural hall are several elegant models of the public buildings in the city, also one of the great rock, on which the statue of Peter the Great is placed, and the manner in which it was moved. Likewise several excellent models of various Greek and Roman edifices. The collection of statues is rather defective both in arrangement and chasteness. It is singular that every object, both of art and nature, are named in the Russian language, which seems to convey an ignorance of the

Latin language.—Here, as in the museum, a drunken servant was the *showman!*

Although the exhibitions of this academy may impress us with an high idea of the rapid strides which this country has made towards refinement; yet they cannot but equally impress us with an idea, that the standard at which they aim, is borrowed from those of other nations. In short, they are merely copyists, and though abounding in *talent* and industry, they are deficient in *genius*. Their exhibitions indeed, when compared with those of other nations, are, for the most part, paltry and puerile, decked out more as baubles to catch the eye, than as solid specimens of art. There is a want of classic arrangement about them, which evidently indicates a want of science.

The citadel stands on the north side of the river, immediately opposite to the exchange. This was the first part of the town which Peter the Great built, being then only designed as a plàce of arms in the Swedish war; but after the battle of Pultowa, in 1709, when Charles XII. of Sweden was entirely defeated, he determined to render it the foundation of his infant capital. The citadel is walled in, adjoining the river, by a massive front of granite, and strengthened with five regular bastions. On the opposite sides it is defended by an earthen mound, and broad ditch, filled from the river, over which is thrown an extensive wooden bridge. The citadel does not appear to be a place of much strength, and is useless as a means of defending the city. Within the walls are several small houses for the accommodation of soldiers, and officers under the employment of the crown, also dungeons for the confinement of state-prisoners. In the centre stands the church of St. Peter, in which the ashes of Peter the Great repose.

This is the only church in the city which has a regular spire; it is about two hundred and fifty feet in height, and richly gilt. Its interior decorations were removed, in consequence of some alterations, now taking place in the building. The tomb of Peter the Great is placed near the altar.* It is formed of a plain greenish marble sarcophagus, without any ornaments whatever, but a gold plate on one end, with his name and title engraved on it. On the opposite side of the altar are similar tombs, with the bodies of his wife Catharine, the beautiful Livonian, Anne, Peter III., etc.

The gold and silver sent from the mines of Siberia are here coined; and the machine for stamping the coins, is said to have been the invention of Catha-

---

* This great prince was born at Moscow, 12th of June, 1672, and died at St. Petersburg in 1725.

rine II. but which has yielded to the superior power of the paper stamp.

Here is also shown the boat which Peter the Great used to amuse himself with when a boy, at Moscow, and which led to the formation of a navy.

Without the walls of the citadel, is the hut in which Peter the Great resided when laying the foundation of his capital. It is about thirty feet in length, and constructed in the rudest manner. To preserve this memorable house, a brick building is raised over it upon arches, through which the original house can be seen, yet protected from the severity of the climate. From this hut the most extensive, as well as the most beautiful views of the river and town are visible, particularly on the north side, the fortress, the academy of arts and sciences, with an extensive range of buildings and ships, while the two floating bridges stretch to the opposite side, where the eye beholds with equal pleasure the palace, admiralty, church of St. Isaac, and the statue of Peter the Great, also numerous gilded domes glittering in the horizon.

What is here mentioned includes a general description of the most prominent features of this beautiful city. Many elegant churches, and other public buildings on a scale of great magnificence, every

16

where invite the attention and admiration of the stranger, and on which the eye agreeably reposes; added to these, several excellent institutions of charity, which reflect the greatest praise on the government, and on many amiable individuals.

CHAP. IV.

St. Petersburg, August, 1814.

In the general description of a city, objects which are the most conspicuous become the leading features in a traveller's remarks, and though perhaps not more interesting than many minor ones, yet as their uses are more or less assimilated with the public interest, it is a matter of information to bring them before the reader, and to contrast them with those improvements and revolutions to which such places are subject; in this respect, those observations become a dry detail, and can only amuse, in proportion to the interest excited.

Among the many grand objects, which here arrest the attention, is that of the Neva. If we consider its breadth, the rapidity of its course, and its extreme transparency, it will almost stand unrivalled. This noble river is discharged from the southwest corner of the great lake Ladoga; and, after forming a circular course of nearly fifty miles, it

joins the eastern extremity of the gulf of Finland,
below the city of St. Petersburg. The lake Ladoga,
which gives origin to this beautiful river, is the
largest in the north of Europe; its shape is nearly
that of an oval, and its entire circumference, including the irregularities of its shores, comprises nearly
three hundred miles. From several appearances,
it is not unlikely but that it once formed part of the
gulf of Finland. In a direct line between the gulf
and the lake, the distance is only twenty miles, and
the intermediate space low and marshy. From the
exit of the Neva to its junction with the gulf, its
course is over a rugged bed of red granite, which
is the cause of its transparency; no tributary
streams add to its bulk. The river is nearly of one
breadth, except that part of it which flows through
the city, and which divides into two branches, called
the great and the little Neva. Its depth varies from
twenty-four to twelve feet. Its stream runs about
three feet and a half per second, or nearly two miles
and a half an hour; but is considerably regulated
by the state of the winds. If a strong easterly wind
takes place, the current is considerably affected,
the river immediately begins to rise, and, not unfrequently, inundates many parts of the city. To
avoid this occurrence, the banks of the river are
lined with walls of granite, which are elevated

several feet above the level of the street. Again,
a strong westerly wind tends to lower the stream
considerably below its usual standard, and often
prevents loaded vessels from passing over the bar.
A singular aperient quality attends the use of this
water, which proves very unpleasant and often
dangerous to strangers.

The two bridges thrown across the river are
formed by a series of flat boats or pontoons, anchored at both ends parallel to each other, at regular distances, and covered by a broad platform,
with side railings and footpath. Many of the boats
are fitted up as places of residence for various workmen. Barges and small boats can easily pass between the pontoons, but trading vessels are only
permitted to pass during certain hours of the night,
when a drawbridge is opened for that purpose.
During the breaking up of the ice, in the spring,
the bridges are removed, to avoid their being damaged by it. Over the smaller branches of the
river, around the suburbs, neat wooden bridges, on
arches, in imitation of stone, are used. The ice
preserved from the river is as clear and transparent
as the finest crystal, and is considered among the
greatest luxuries, during the hot months of summer. Innumerable pleasure boats, gondolas, and
common wherries, are constantly gliding along the

stream, in every direction, some with music, and others with coloured awnings,—while huge rafts with pyramids of fire-wood and hay slowly move onwards to their respective stations. In winter, when the river is frozen over, the bodies of individuals who are robbed and murdered, are frequently thrust under the ice, to prevent detection.

The environs of St Petersburg are extremely beautiful. The villas and gardens are laid out in the neatest manner, and in the most showy and fantastical forms. The general landscape is undoubtedly pleasing, as far as mere fore-ground is brought into view, which, in this instance, is all that can be seen. There are neither hills nor distant views, to relieve the studied regularity of lengthened avenues and formal walks.

> " Grove nods at grove, each alley has a brother,
> And half the platform just reflects the other."

It is a remarkable circumstance that in this part of the country, birch, poplar, and some fir, are the only trees which have yet been reared. So severe is the climate that only the hardiest plants of the forest have succeeded in braving its rigour. In a country so uniformly flat, and by no means romantic, these grounds are said to be very beautiful. On the whole it shows perhaps the effect of too much study and design. The views are merely those of neat villas, trees, water, and its lively scenery of boats. Nature is not seen sporting in her fanciful freedom, but every where tied down, with painted railings and other ornaments, as showy as the dangling orders of rank suspended round the necks from the common soldier, up to the prince.

The variety of railings, both in their form and mode of painting, is as fanciful and grotesque as the productions of rude uncultivated genius must always be. All the public railings, lamps, lamp-posts, mileposts, etc. are painted in black and white squares, similar to a harlequin's dress. This peculiar arrangement was the fancy of the emperor Paul. The order of the present day is yellow, and the harlequinade dress of Paul, is now yielding to a dead sombre yellow.

These mechanical and uniform dresses every where meet and fatigue the eye. A few weeks ago a fruiterer employed a celebrated artist to paint the figure of Pomona on his door. The enraptured votary of the goddess daily watched the magic touches of the pencil, and the last finishing stroke was given, when an imperial order blazoned through the city, that all doors and windows, etc. were to be painted yellow. There was no resistance, the beautiful figure of Pomona was effaced, and the poor painter was left to mourn in silence over her memory.

The suburbs present a singular contrast of wooden houses built in a very straggling manner, and which must require future ages to complete. From every appearance, the buildings of the town seem at present to be carried on with less activity, and on a scale less magnificent than formerly. The town is divided into eleven quarters, as follows,

1. Admiralty quarter.
2. Do.   do.
3. Do.   do.
4. Do.   do.
5. Foundry quarter.
6. Moscow quarter.
7. Rojestvensky quarter.
8. Carriages quarter.
9. Vassili Ostroff quarter.
10. Petersburg quarter.
11. Wiburg quarter.

Each of these quarters is under the management of a certain portion of the police, who regulate their respective districts; in the cleaning and repairing of the streets, the regulation of the public vehicles, etc.

The streets of the metropolis are beautifully paved with small round stones, in angular squares, but which is the repeated labour of every summer. From the severity of the frost in winter, the pavement of the streets is often displaced; none of the streets has the advantage of a footpath. The postillions drive as close to the walls as they chuse. Another disadvantage is the want of water-pipes to convey the rain from the houses; but which is thrown from the roofs of the houses by waterspouts into the middle of the street. The streets are elegantly lighted up at night, with large square lamps, each having four wicks and reflectors. During the night the streets are paraded by guards, mounted on horseback, and in the day by police officers, armed with a long pole with an axe fastened to its point. These men constantly reside in small wooden houses, placed in different parts of the streets.

The orderly behaviour of the people, and quietness of the town at all hours, is astonishing. So carefully is this department managed that no one would run the risk of getting into a quarrel. Frequent instances of intoxication are seen among the lower orders, but even in that state they are neither noisy nor quarrelsome. This must partly arise from constitution, or partly the effects of despotism.

The houses, though extremely large and showy, are not very lofty, nor are the spires and domes of the churches conspicuous in height. In the town are

17

forty-four churches appropriated to the religion of the empire, and those of other sects, which are tolerated without any restrictions.

These churches are all more or less singularly constructed, and adorned with gildings and different colours. Many of them are surmounted with several domes and huge crosses.

The hotels are situated in the square opposite to the admiralty and palace: the rooms are but partly furnished, and that in a very inferior manner; neither carpets, curtains, nor bed-hangings are used, because these would form too many depots for vermin to lodge their stores. From this circumstance, carpets are scarcely used in any house, but, by way of compensation, the floor of every room is beautifully inlaid with various coloured woods. Besides the regular hotels there are many restaurateurs, pastry-cooks, and innumerable petty drinking-houses. Many houses, though splendidly finished in the exterior, are yet infested in the under story with these low haunts of debauchery.

In the southern suburbs is the elegant monastery of St. Alexander Nevsky, where the archbishop of St. Petersburg resides. The monastery consists of an extensive range of buildings, including, besides the great church, many minor religious edifices. The whole is surrounded by a ditch; in the church is the tomb of its saint, made entirely of silver. This saint was a distinguished military hero; who overcame the Swedes in a pitched battle near the spot where the monastery now stands, and, in commemoration of it, erected a small religious edifice. When Peter the Great founded St. Petersburg, in order to overcome the religious superstition of the people, and to induce them to settle in the infant capital, he removed the ashes of this saint from Moscow, and solemnly interred them here. The procession consisted of one thousand priests, who walked the whole way barefoot. In this church the body of Suwarrow is interred; a small plate of brass marks the spot; however to the memory of his sanguinary career, a statue is erected in the city. Here Potemkin immured himself, in order to excite the attention of Catharine; and how well this religious mask succeeded, his future character too well explains. This monastery is the residence of the most distinguished prelates, and who are styled popes. Their dress consists of a loose black cloak, and a round black cap: neither the beard, nor the hair of the head are cut; and no one can be admitted as a member until the age of thirty.

St. Petersburg is supposed to contain about two hundred thousand inhabitants, exclusive of the military. This would appear a small proportion in compa-

rison to the size of the city; but when the width of
the streets is considered, the size of the houses, and
extent of ground which the churches occupy, etc. it
will be found a large proportion.

The entire arrangement of the city, keeping the
streets in repair, laying out new plans, etc. are under the laws of the crown. For this purpose nearly forty thousand men are employed, who act as
scavengers, watchmen, police-officers, and imperial
guards.

The extent of the city is nearly six miles in length
and almost the same in breadth, including the irregularities of the suburbs; but if the solid connected
buildings are measured, its extent might be almost
reduced to one half. The city has been lately enclosed by a canal, and the principal entrances over
this barrier, are through the magnificent gateways,
and where a guard is stationed to examine every
passenger.

The nobility, merchants, and foreigners, are divided into three classes called *gilds*. The first class
are allowed the use of four or more horses to their
carriages; the second class can only use two horses,
and the third must use an hired carriage. For
these distinctions a proportionate tax is levied,
which is voluntary,—however those who pay a tax
for the third class, if discovered by the police offi-

cers, using their own carriage and horses, are subjected to a slight fine.

Every person who has an income sufficient to enable him to keep a horse or carriage, considers it as a necessary appendage to his comforts. To be seen walking on foot is looked upon as an instance of extreme vulgarity. In short, many would rather sacrifice their domestic comforts, than not retain this extraordinary fashion. Scarcely any attempt riding on horseback, which is too laborious an exercise for their general indolence. As an excuse for their not using this healthful exercise, they have a fixed observation,—that in winter it is too cold to ride on horseback, and in summer, too hot!

The town has little or no confusion from trade; the shipping being almost confined to Cronstadt, or in the neighbourhood of the exchange; and the markets being stationed in one distinct spot, few carts are seen in the streets: however, they are constantly crowded by a strange variety of vehicles, under the name of coaches, droskies, kibitka, and sledges, with the horses attached to each in a different manner and number.

The droskie is the most common as well as the most useful carriage in the town. It is a singularly formed machine, not more than two feet high, with four small wheels, covered with broad leather wings,

and which between the wheels forms a kind of open
stirrup for the rider's feet. The rider either sits
across, as on a saddle, or if in company with another person, they sit back to back, and are drawn
sideways. The driver has a small seat fixed between the fore wheels, nearly on a level with the
horse's knees. If there are two horses yoked to the
droskie, one is placed in the shafts, with his head
tightly braced up to an arched hoop,—while the
other is merely used as an out-rider for show. The
horse in the shafts trots, while the other canters;
the first is managed by the servant, the other is
guided by the master. There is a considerable degree of elegance in the appearance of the actions
of the horses, but when constantly practised it becomes formal and tiresome. These droskies are the
most numerous vehicles in the streets; they are
driven astonishingly quick, and at a certain distance
have an appearance somewhat like a *grasshopper*.
On a dusty road, they are certainly the most disagreeable machines in which a person could travel.

The coaches are either made to open like a lan-
dau, or, more generally, resemble in shape and
clumsiness the London hackney coaches. The number of horses attached to these carriages depends
on the rank of the proprietor, and are yoked according to different tastes. In some instances four

horses are yoked abreast to the carriage, with two leaders placed at an extraordinary distance in front of the others,—in many instances not less than twenty feet. Sometimes six horses are yoked abreast, with one leader in front. The traces of the leaders are fixed to the point of the pole, and the boy, who always rides the *off* leader, at every moment is seen looking back to the coachman, to be directed. This signal from the coachman is given by various nods of the head, and thus a telegraphic communication is kept up. The coachman on the box throws the reins over his head, and holds a corner in each hand, widely extended; at his wrist is hung a short whip, which is scarcely ever used. The horses are accustomed to increase their speed from the sound of his voice, and not by the lash of his whip. In this respect the Russians are a most humane people, and extremely kind to their horses. The harness and reins are sometimes made of coarse leather, but more generally of ropes.

The tails and manes of the horses are worn extremely long and bushy, particularly the manes, which are generally false, and carried to such a ridiculous length, as to sweep the streets, and become a burden to the suffering animal. These false manes are considered as extreme marks of beauty With black manes the deception can scarcely be perceived, but in lighter colours, the addition of every hair is immediately detected.

The horses are certainly animals of great beauty, and are kept in a state of fatness which is rarely seen in other countries. They are generally of a short round form, and extremely animated. To warn the people from being rode over in the streets, the postillions constantly call out *padee*. In those places where the hackney carriages are stationed, ranges of mangers are erected from which the horses are fed, that the streets should not be covered with hay or straw; there is also attached to each station a pump of water,—besides a circular building, used in the severity of winter, to contain a fire.

Nothing arrests the attention of a stranger more on his entering the Russian capital, than the appearance of the common people, their habitudes and manners of occupation. Their features, dress, language and implements of mechanical uses, are peculiar to themselves; or, perhaps a mixture between those of Asia and Europe, without any improvement on either. It is not within the reach of the passing traveller to attempt to describe every variation of peculiar appearances, it is only the bolder features of the general scene, like the stronger lights and shades of the landscape, which can be observed, while subordinate minutiæ are blended and lost in the general mass.

Every thing appears in the extremes of finery and rags. In the costume of the common people there is little or no variety, they are all clad alike. A long swaddling cloak, either made of sheep-skin or coarse cloth, is wrapped round their bodies. In hot weather it is sometimes changed for a coarse shirt and loose trowsers, over which the shirt usually hangs, and is fastened round the waist by a sash. The legs are bound round with pieces of sail-cloth, (instead of stockings), and shoes made of the bark of trees. The hair of the head is cut across, from one temple to the other, in a line with the eye-brows; from the temples it hangs perpendicularly down, so as to cover the ears, from which it is cropped directly across the neck. The hair is often combed and daily covered with grease. The lower part of the face is concealed by an hideous and filthy beard. The hat is also characteristic. Their countenances are open, and full of good humour; but not one, when carefully examined, can be called handsome. They are coarse, yet have something in the general expression which is pleasing. In their manners they are extremely animated, and considerably polished. They talk with rapidity, action and grace. In the town they are evidently addicted to drunkenness, gambling and indolence. The shop-keepers are generally seen playing at draughts, and the servants at chuck-farthing.

The only difference of costume remarkable among the common people, is that worn by the nurses of children. Their dress is singularly fantastic, but extremely clean. They wear a distinguishing badge on their heads, in the shape of a large yellow painted cap, and very wide shirt sleeves, fastened at the elbow. These women are in general procured from the country, and the extreme attention and kindness which they devote to their infant charge, is a laudable instance of affection. They are properly exempted from all religious fasts.

The habits of life in the common people are as simple as their modes of dress. They are contented to sleep on the floor of the room, the bare stones of the street, or between the wheels of a carriage. Their food partly consists of a slice of coarse bread, with a little salt and thick oil poured over it, with a kind of sour beer, called *squash*, made from oatmeal and rye-bread soured, and coloured with a red berry; besides vast quantities of raw cucumbers, onions, garlic, green beans and carrots.

From the quantity of garlic which they eat, its offensive smell every where pervades.

Of all the traits in a Russian's character, that of his religion is the most prominent. To this all his actions are devoted, and he becomes the mechanical slave of his devotions. In front of every church, and in many places in the streets, a painting of the Virgin is exhibited, which no one passes without uncovering his head, profoundly bowing, and crossing himself. In almost every room a picture of the Virgin is hung up. The moment a Russ enters the door, he performs his duty to the picture, before he addresses himself to any one. If he is accused of any misdemeanor, he asserts his innocence by repeated crossings and invocations to his favourite saint. If he receives any donation, he is expressively thankful, bows, crosses himself, and even kisses the ground. They are extremely good humoured, but rather indolent, except when excited by gain. Altogether the common Russ is a prepossessing character, cheerful and obedient.

No class of people seems to pay more attention to personal cleanliness than the Russians, taken *collectively;* yet, perhaps, there are none who live more filthily clad, taken *individually.* In various parts of the city public baths are established, and constantly frequented by all ranks, but particularly by the lowest. Their religion, in some measure, enforces the use of the bath; but, as they take little or no bodily exercise, they find the use of the bath act as a powerful remedy in carrying off the super-abundant humours, occasioned by the quantity and nature of their food, independently of the enjoyment they find in it.

In the public baths, the most curious specimens of the indifference of manners or delicacy are seen. No sight can be more disgusting than that exhibited in those places. Scores of individuals mingle together in an heated apartment, and after being sweated, switched and half boiled, rush into the open air like so many frantic *satyrs*, and plunge into the coldest water.

In these heated apartments a range of steps extend from the floor to the roof, which at the top is covered with bricks, and heated from a flue underneath. The heat is in proportion to the ascent of the steps; pipes are fixed in different parts of the room, conveying hot water, which is occasionally thrown over the heated bricks, and rises up in the form of hot steam.

In this heated room as many individuals enter as chuse. Each person is accommodated with a small wooden pailful of hot water, and a bunch of the soft twigs of the birch tree, with which he switches his body, at the same time pouring warm water over his head, which is increased in temperature, in proportion to the excess of perspiration. When the body has arrived at the highest state of heat, they suddenly rush into the open air, and scour themselves with soap and cold water. The operation of bathing occupies nearly an hour. The heat, at which these baths are taken, would be insupportable to a person not in the habit of using it. Here it is used summer and winter; and many of them rush out of the hot bath in winter; and roll in the snow. They look upon the bath as a sovereign remedy for all their diseases and complaints, but particularly in cases of indigestion. Adjoining to the bath appropriated to the men, is a similar one for the women, who, in hordes, perform the same ceremony.

From the attention which the Russians pay to the use of the bath, a stranger might be induced to believe that they are the most cleanly people in the world; whereas the very reverse is the case. However often they may wash and scour their persons, yet they never perform the same attention to their dress, which, being made of sheep-skins, contracts every sort of filth and vermin; and no sooner does a Russian quit the bath, than he is seen commencing hostilities against his manifold associates.

Every stranger must be pleased with the environs of the metropolis. The principal merchants generally reside in the summer months in neat villas, at some distance from the city, which are ornamented with beautiful gardens, and innumerable pots of flowers. The most common of these flowers are the holly-hock, and carnation; roses do not seem to flourish in this country. In the botanic garden, many exotics are to be seen growing most luxuriantly. Attached to each of the country villas is a flag-staff, upon which a small flag is displayed at those hours when the landlord is *at home,*

The most beautiful part of the environs is situated in the quarter of St. Petersburg, where the palace of Kamennoy-Ostrow, the country residence of the emperor, is. The house is low and irregularly built, but the scenery around it is extremely beautiful. It stands on the east end of a small island, surrounded on each side by different branches of the river. Here is displayed all that studied neatness of Dutch scenery, where neat villas, weeping birches, gravelled walks, and painted railings, water and pleasure boats, are seen. These islands are so low, that a strong gale of wind, from the west, is almost sufficient to raise the water to such a height, as partly to inundate them.

The amusement, in the summer months, in this

part of the country, is chiefly derived from a singular conical frame of wood, raised to a height of thirty or forty feet, with a grooved railway, leading from its summit, to a considerable distance along the plain. This is called the *flying mountain.* The company ascend by a flight of steps, and each individual, being seated on a low carriage, supported on four small wheels, is precipitated down the railway, with a velocity sufficient to produce giddiness. The force of the descent carries it along a level distance, equal to an hundred yards. At the termination of the level line, another elevated frame is erected similar to the other, which, on ascending, produces a retrograde effect. To vary the motion, the railway along the plain is sometimes made of a series of ridges, so that the velocity acquired in descending from the one, carries it up the other, and thus a sort of *perpetuum mobile* is kept up. When the Neva is frozen over, these *flying mountains* are erected on the ice, and receive an increase of velocity, in proportion to the decrease of friction.

During our residence at St. Petersburg, it wore the aspect of gayety and joy. The return of the emperor Alexander and his guards, after an absence of eighteen months, and the successful termination of the most dreadful contest which ever threatened the repose of the empire. This happy event pro-

duced a lively sensation of interest among all ranks.
The city and environs were splendidly illuminated
during three successive nights; good order prevailed every where, but it was not that spontaneous
and generous burst of warmth which we see in England. No huzzas rang the air, neither fun nor
frolic enlivened the crowd,—all was a general blaze
from the houses and pavement, while crowds in mechanical order, paraded along the streets, who
coldly and calculatingly gazed at the flaming pile.

The rejoicings were extended to the country palace of Peteroff, the once favourite residence of Peter
the Great, and his empress Catharine. This irregular pile of building is situated on the southern shores
of the gulf, about twenty miles from the city. Extensive gardens, pleasure grounds, and water works,
surround the palace on all sides. Here we witnessed a magnificent display of rejoicings, in honour of
the dowager empress' birth-day. In the morning
the emperor reviewed the guards; and, in the evening, there was a public masquerade, etc. The
whole extent of the gardens was brilliantly illuminated with fanciful displays of lights, and the water-works were exhibited to the greatest advantage.
The imperial fleet were moored opposite to the
palace, and exhibited each a flaming meteor. There
were no variations of colour in the lamps; all was

one dazzling white. The number of glasses employed to contain the tallow and wicks was astonishing. In a magnificent circle of arches, in front of the water-works, were placed twenty-two thousand glasses, and yet this was but a trifling spot compared to the whôle. The motley mixture of the mob was truly astonishing. It was a gala day, and moreover a favourite saint's day. In consequence every one, high and low, rich and poor, good or bad, were indiscriminately admitted and promiscuously blended together.

The day was extremely hot, and the road a bed of fine dust; the string of carriages of every form, and of every description; the various dresses of the company, the concentration of every nation as it were, seemed to be passing along to one common centre. Booths and marquees were every where erected for the accommodation of the company, but so numerous were the visitors that scarcely could the tents of the imperial army have sheltered them all. Every one carried provisions for the day; and parties of every rank were seen dressing and brushing off the dust in the exposed fields. Never was a scene so truly ludicrous; every one seemed to challenge the other in mirth, forwardness, and impudence. Royalty and slavery were blended together:—the common bearded Russ, in all his

filthy coverings, paraded through the royal apartments, and breathed the odour of royalty! It may
be proper to accustom the eye of the common people to occasional views of elegance and the effect
of refined civilization; but it does not appear to illu-
mine his mind more than the rays of a passing meteor, which dazzles the eye for a moment, and is
for ever lost.

After a short but pleasant residence in St. Petersburg, we turned our attention towards prosecuting
our journey through the interior of the country.
Though it was not without considerable difficulties
that we procured passports on our entering the
country, yet we had to encounter more in getting
permission to leave the capital. Every stranger,
before he is permitted to leave the city, is obliged
to insert his name and character, during three successive weeks, in the public newspapers, stating his
intention of leaving the country, and that he has not
contracted any debts. After this notification the
traveller applies at the police-office for the passports, which are made out exactly to the route he
is to travel, and for which he is under the necessity
of undergoing many vexatious delays. Along with
the passports, an order for horses is also granted;
and in it the number of horses to be used is also
mentioned. The charge for this order is in proportion to the number of horses the traveller wishes to

employ. This order comes under one of the distinctions of the *Gilds*, and the traveller can only use the number of horses, in proportion to his rank. But even the rigid strictness of the Russian police is not proof against the influence of money; and, like the courts of law, agents are to be procured who contrive to settle the business.

Three English gentlemen arrived in the capital at the time we did, and, being anxious to prosecute their journey, applied to one of those agents, who readily procured passes and an order (of the first distinction) for horses; with a charge of fifteen guineas; seven of which was to procure a passport for their servant, because he was a Dane! This very servant was refused admittance into the capital; but a small donation at Cronstadt readily effected the purpose. Nothing can be more odious than the despotic power of the police and its officers. Every valet de place is more or less a spy on the actions of his employer, and even in private families the most marked cautiousness and reserve is used before their servants.

During our residence in St. Petersburg we luckily met with a young Prussian, whom we took into our service. He had been a student at the university at Berlin, when the French invasion compelled him to fly from the conscript laws of Napoleon. He wandered to Moscow, and found a beneficent master in a British merchant, until the destruction of that ill-fated city compelled them both to seek an asylum elsewhere, from ruin and poverty. From his long residence in the country, he had acquired a knowledge of its language, with a purity scarcely inferior to the natives; added to this he was sober, obedient, and one in whom a considerable degree of confidence could be placed. A circumstance highly useful, in a country where so powerful and inquisitorial an engine is placed under the management of a despotic government. This person we engaged to travel with us as an interpreter, and he was granted a passport as far as the Russian frontiers.

From the circumstance of our being obliged to leave our travelling carriage at Memel, we procured a new Russian open travelling coach, heavy and clumsily built, yet very commodious, and with the advantage of a *dormeuse*. Though newly built, it detained us a whole week in repairing the accidents which every trial of its strength occasioned. It was not unlike the character of every thing here, highly varnished and showy externally, but flimsy and imperfectly constructed.

The weather, during the latter end of July and August, continued extremely hot and sultry, with occasional heavy showers of rain, accompanied with

thunder. At times, the temperature of the air underwent sudden and remarkable changes. On the
19th of August, at mid-day, Fahrenheit's thermometer stood at seventy-nine degrees; the air was
calm, and the sky cloudless. Suddenly, dark clouds
overshadowed the town, and the wind blew strongly from the ~~st: at five o'clock in the afternoon, the
mercury in the thermometer fell to fifty-five degrees. At midnight (of 20th), to thirty-five degrees;
and early in the morning a slight tinge of frost was
seen on the ground. The days are generally oppressively hot and sultry, and produces a sensible
degree of languor and debility, while the nights are
damp and chilling. The shortest day, in St. Petersburg, is five hours and a half long, and the longest
eighteen hours and a half.

Although the climate of Russia is so extremely severe to the constitution of man in general, and ap-
parently so congenial to that of the Russ in particular, yet it does not appear to produce in him that
hardihood, which its influence might be supposed to
occasion. The only manner in which we can judge
of the effects of climate externally on the bodies of
men, is by their wearing apparel. Judging by this,
we shall see that the Russ is most acutely and sen-
sibly alive to the variations of the weather, and is
constantly changing his dress. When it is hot, every

one is thinly clad, with very few exceptions; when the sky becomes clouded, or there are signs of wind, every one assumes his winter mantle. Thus the range of his sensibility is not confined to the mere effects of heat and cold; it is not only thermometric, but, in short, he is a barometer, a hygrometer, and an anemometer, all combined in one living machine.

Reasoning, however, in this way, as indeed in many other processes of reasoning, the effect may be often taken for the cause, and both become so entangled with each other, as to be scarcely separable. The increased sensibility of the Russ to the effects of his skies, may be the result of that changeful covering to which he accustoms his body, and which, by their means, acquires a delicacy of tact, which enables him to detect every change of weather. This is, perhaps, the solution of the problem; to suppose for a moment, that the delicacy of touch arises from an increased perfection of their nervous system, would be giving a credit which a Russian constitution is, indeed, far from deserving, and which every particle of their character tends to negative. The fact, however, is a singular one, and every stranger will notice it; the effects of cold and heat are much more felt by the natives than by others; their extremes produce an equal degree of debility on them. A foreigner, from a temperate climate coming here, will feel the cold more severely the second than the first year. This may arise from two causes, first, from that debility which its excitement has caused the first year; and, secondly, from his adoption of some articles of their clothing, and also the temperature of their heated rooms.

There is no feature in the Russian character perhaps more admirable, or more striking to a stranger, than their military system. A finer form, than that of the Russian soldier, cannot be seen; his figure is commanding, his gait erect, his evolutions like a machine, quick and accurate; his uniform simple and graceful, elegant and clean. Taken in a body no line can present a finer appearance than these men; their motions and their manœuvres are as simultaneous, as if one arm and one leg moved all; nothing is seen out of place; all is harmony, and the most disciplined arrangement. In short, the Russian soldier may stand as a pattern in dress, obedience and dexterity in the use of his arms, to all those of Europe.

Their present uniform consists of a long dark green coat, with red cuffs and collar, and long white loose trowsers, made with gaiters at the feet. The cap is worn extremely low, with a very flat broad crown; its sides are ornamented with white cord

and tassels.   The belts are black, and support both
a bayonet and sword, as well as the cartouche box.
The hair and beard are both cut off, except that on
the upper lip.   The moment a Russian becomes a
soldier, his beard is cut off; and to prevent recruits
from deserting, one side of their head is closely shaven.   Around the waist of every soldier is a belt
tightly worn, while the breasts of the coat are thickly padded.   This increases the manliness of the
figure, at the expense of the ease and health of the
individual.   Many of the officers are so tightly
twisted round the waist, as to appear something
similar to a wasp.   The purity of this fine military
system is dreadfully contaminated by the introduction of a set of common horse-soldiers, who are employed in the low branches of the service, carrying
despatches, aiding in the police, observing the motions of strangers, etc. etc. in short no work is either
too dirty or mean for them; and, like *jackals*, their
duties are confined to dregs and offal.   Their appearance is ragged, ruffianly, and disgusting,—their
horses like skeletons; and, thus armed with their
long pike, they present somewhat the appearance
of *Toledo's* champion, with faces equally rueful, but
without any of that generous pathos in it, which so
graced our ill-starred knight.

In a work of this nature, little can be said in regard to the state of commerce and exchange of this country, both of which are constantly fluctuating and depend on existing circumstances. Never, perhaps, was there a period in which the exchange of St. Petersburg was at so low a rate, and its market more overstocked with merchandise of every description, exported from the British ports. Such has been the spirit of imprudent speculators, since the sudden return of peace, that many individuals must suffer great losses.

The northern commerce of this country is chiefly confined to that of the metropolis, and its harbour at Cronstadt, and the ports of Narva, Revel, Riga, etc. The goods are conveyed from Cronstadt up to St. Petersburg by means of galliots and large open boats. Large vessels are prevented from sailing up to the city, in consequence of a bar of sand, which stretches across the mouth of the river, and the depth of the water over it often depends on the state of the winds. A westerly wind opposing the current of the river, increases the depth of the water, and an easterly wind the reverse. Ships of war, built at the dock-yards of St. Petersburg, are floated over the bar, by means of large flat-bottomed barges, called *camels*.

20

The produce of the country is generally what is
exported from St. Petersburg. It consists, particularly, of hemp, flax, tallow, oil, wood, iron, etc. etc.
These productions are conveyed down the rivers in
summer, and in winter on sledge-roads. Regular warehouses are erected for each class of goods,
to which the barges are floated, and the cargoes un-
loaded. Certain persons, called *brackers*, are appointed to inspect the goods; and when they are
sold, his name is affixed to them, to prevent an inferior quality being delivered. These inspectors are
paid by the purchaser, in proportion to the quantity
of goods bought.

The rate of exchange fluctuates according to the
state of the markets: a rouble at present is equal to
one shilling sterling. The Russian coins are divided
into gold, silver and copper.

Gold coins are {
Imperials of . . . . 10 roubles,
Half imperials of . . 5 roubles,

Silver coins are {
Roubles of . . . . 100 copecks,
Half roubles of . . 50 copecks,
Quarter roubles of 25 copecks,
15 Copeck pieces,
10 Copeck pieces,
5 Copeck pieces.

Copper coins are
$$\begin{cases} \text{5 Copeck pieces,} \\ \text{2 Copeck pieces,} \\ \text{1 Copeck piece,} \\ \text{Denuschka or half copeck piece,} \\ \text{Polushka or quarter copeck piece.} \end{cases}$$

Foreign coins are taken by the merchants, but the most useful are Dutch ducats. The notes issued by the imperial bank are on white, red, and blue paper.

The blue paper is valued at . . . . . 5 roubles.

The red . . . . 10 roubles.

The white . . . . 25, 50 to 100 roubles.

Besides the imperial bank, there are other banks called the aid and loan banks, which are intended to assist the nobility and towns, in paying debts, and the improvement of their estates, and for which they mortgage their slaves, until the loan is redeemed.

Before the foundation of St. Petersburg was laid, the whole external commerce of the empire was carried on at Archangel. It now not only embraces that of the White and Baltic, but even the Caspian and Black Seas. From the number and extent of its lakes and rivers, its internal productions are conveyed with the greatest facility to the most distant parts; and since many of these rivers have been joined by means of canals, the communication daily becomes more extensive, and the wealth of the country increased. A country which embraces such an extent of surface as that of Russia, must necessarily present a variety of climates, and soil capable of producing almost all the fruits of the world. From its northern tracts are drawn the most useful minerals; and though its climate is as yet somewhat unfavourable to the constitution of man, yet, as the forests are cleared away, and the marshes drained, it may become the abode of a numerous people.   Independent of the great quantity of iron which is annually exported from these northern regions, its forests also present various animals, producing the most delicate and valuable furs, while the seas are stored with fish of the most useful kind.   The quantity of iron produced from these mines about twenty years ago was equal to eighty thousand tons per annum, but which has since gradually diminished from the impolicy of too rapidly destroying the forests, and consequently of fuel in the smelting of the ore; and also the decrease of its importation into Great Britain.   Where the iron ore does not particularly abound, the manufactured wood of the extensive forests becomes an object of exportation, and which is sent down the rivers in the summer months in large floats; these floats or barges are rudely constructed with the largest fir planks, having the roots attached to the trunk, which forms the crooks of the vessel

The sides of the vessel are perpendicular, and about four feet deep, the bottom is perfectly flat, and their length about one hundred and fifty feet. Many of them are capable of carrying between three hundred to four hundred tons; the rudder is formed of a long tree; instead of using a pump to draw the water collected by leakage, a large wooden scoop, suspended from a cross-beam, is used to throw it out.

From the southern provinces of the empire are exported numerous flocks of cattle, fruits and wines. The most productive of these is the large quantity of tallow which is extracted from the black cattle. To such a length is this branch of commerce carried on, that every part of the animal is sacrificed for its fat; even the peasantry debar themselves from the enjoyment of tallow candles, and use as a substitute pine wood split into thin pieces. In 1803 the exportation of tallow from Russia was nearly equal to two millions pounds sterling; " a quantity and sum almost incredible, when we consider the produce of an ox for other useful purposes."*

It is not sufficient to enter on the nature of the internal commerce of this country, at present; it will appear with more interest and propriety, after a more intimate acquaintance with the interior of

* Oddy's European Commerce.

the country has been gained. This is a subject of such vast importance, that too careful an inquiry cannot be thought unnecessary; particularly on those points which may extend the commercial relation between Great Britain and Russia.

Such is a short and rapid sketch of the Russian capital, a city which, in extent, ranks with most others in Europe; in grandeur of outline perhaps superior to all, and in beauty of structure excelled by none. By none will the traveller be more dazzled at first sight, by none will he have his interest, his curiosity, and his admiration more excited. Its gilded domes and sculptured turrets, its huge colossal piles, the majesty and arrangement by which they are grouped, will present him with a picture, which, otherwise, he may have in vain sought for, except in the productions of his own fancy. This however is the distant view; he has not examined the picture closely, the charm is not to last long; the spell must soon be broken; the cup from which he has taken such bewitching draughts must be dashed from his lip, and his admiration will too often be turned into disgust. He will see every thing, as it were, in outline; nothing filled up; nothing perfect; nothing to please; every thing to astonish. He will see those lines harsh and strong; he will see their interspaces, void of that body, void of that softened colouring, on which the eye can rest; glitter and glare will render its film giddy; he will be dazzled, he will be overpowered, but he will not be pleased. He will here see a miniature of that picture which this vast empire presents; he will here see a mixture of splendid barbarism and mighty rudeness; while on the one hand he sees endless ranges of superb palaces, on the other he sees crowding around him, those more like brutes than human beings. Again, while he sees mean equipages moving along, he will see them crowded with the glittering courtier. He will see splendour in all its filth, and filth in all its splendour; he will see them in all the form and varieties of mixture; he will see them forming the alternate layers of the national character, stratum super stratum, the one ending where the other begins, and both so entangled with each other, that it is scarcely possible to see one at a time.

CHAP. V.

Zimogoire, August, 1814.

TAKING leave of this illustrious capital we were now to enter on those wild and desert plains, which separate it from its ancient rival and sister, Moscow; and as its towers faded from our sight, we could not but contemplate in our mind's eye, the glorious banners of war waving round them. We could not but feel interested in the fate of those young bulwarks, which, although yet in their cradle, have, like the infant Hercules, strangled the serpent and given peace to a suffering world.

In taking a retrospect of this capital, it is impossible not to feel astonished at its youth, and its perfection. In the short space of little more than a century, have been reared those splendid fabrics, which must dazzle and delight every eye.

In the same short space have the manners and customs of a vast nation been reduced to a new standard. Civilization has not required time for its

21

growth,—its seeds have shot up apace. Here,
every thing dazzles and bewilders the eye; on acquaintance they appear the same, and show the effect of study. If we approach closer the secret
spring is perceived, and little more remains than the
mere outline of a vast and superficial system, uncre-
ated, unconsolidated, and labouring under all the
defects of a government, which, from its vigour, has
become so unrestrained, and from its despotism, so
capricious.

From the structure of its government has arisen,
in a great measure, the moral structure of its inhabitants.   The ties of society are, here, not so connected, as in those towns whose character is purely
commercial.   The chain seems to be broken in different, and distinct pieces.   The military character
proudly predominates, and, although it does not carry along with it any of the finer traits of chivalry or
enthusiasm, still *rank* is the grand characteristic and
ultimatum.   To this all aspire, in their respective
degrees, and, for this, all other considerations are
neglected.   The commercial part of society is small,
and perfectly distinct.   The sources of wealth
chiefly arise from the sale of native produce, and its
exportation.   This sale is, comparatively speaking,
confined to the hands of a few.   Their agricultural
resources, unless in the immediate vicinity of the

capital, towns and villages, are very slender, and, were it not for the privations, which their religion inculcates, would scarcely suffice for their existence.

As in all countries regulated by military character, where rank bears so extensive a sway, and where the government is purely despotic, the system of farming is discouraged, and held in a degraded view. Every one, particularly the nobles, must, more or less, mingle in the politics of the court. He must, more or less, entwine himself in the fate, on which it hangs, and, when once they cease to bask in the sunshine of its favour, they are probably exiled to their native lands.

Taking leave of St. Petersburg, the road conducted us through the southern suburbs of the city, and passed along a country, flat, covered with straggling plantations of birch, and partly cultivated. The first stage is greatly relieved by the showy palace of Tsarsko-Selo, occupying a large space of ground, and surrounded by extensive, and well laid out gardens, and pleasure grounds. The palace of Tsarsko-Selo, like most of the other public buildings in this country, exhibits a strange combination of architectural orders. Towards the north it fronts the road, which, suddenly turning at a right angle, passes by an arched gateway under the west wing. This is one of the emperor's country palaces, which, in summer, is often the scene of gayety and festivity.

However much the palaces in Russia may offend the eye of a fastidious architect, from the *disorderly* arrangements of their design; yet, in a country so remote and uncultivated, the effect is certainly pleasing, and produces one of the most agreeable features in the general sombre cast of the landscape. Gothicism in building is more allowable in unimproved countries, than in the neighbourhood of cities; however much it may detract from the received opinion of the Grecian school, yet, until the standard of beauty is fixed, opinions must ever vary. A traveller cannot avoid remarking, that a Russian palace is an ornament to the country.

We changed horses at Tossna, the second stage from St. Petersburg. Nothing can present a greater contrast than the appearance of the villages from the capital. The one is all splendour, and show,—the others look as so many heaps of rotten wood, the abodes of filth and vermin. These houses are entirely built of wood. The unshapen trunks of trees are laid one above another and dove-tailed at the corners, while a quantity of dry moss is placed between the seams. The gables front the road, and are ornamented by a light gallery, and pent-roof. The only window used, is a small square hole, which is opened and shut like the gun-port of a ship ; and, through which, the bearded head of a Russian is often seen thrust out, as if fixed in the pillory. Every house is exactly like another ; they are built in pairs, and ranged on each side of the high road, which forms the only street. From the scarcity of stones, not only are the houses built solely of wood, but even the court-yards and roads are floored with it. In front of every house is seen a deep draw-well; the bucket is lowered by a rope, fixed to the end of a long crossbeam, having a balancing weight at the opposite end;—this beam acts as a lever, supported by an upright post. The lower floor of the house is generally converted into a store room, and, in the upper apartment, the inhabitants reside. The interior of the houses are dark, gloomy, unventilated, and full of every species of nuisance. Instead of chairs, long benches are fixed to the wall, which, in many houses, answer both as a seat and a bed. The stoves occupy the greater part of the room, and in cold weather afford the greatest luxury to the women in lolling over them. Wrapped in his sheep-skins, the Russ does not seek the comforts of any other bed, than what the floor affords him, and, in the summer months, all places, whether in the house, or under his cart, are alike to him.

All the utensils are made either of wood, or clay, in shape not unlike those dug from the ruins of Herculaneum. One large earthen pot is used to cook the food for the whole family, and, out of which, all eat at once. Their favourite food is a kind of hodge-podge, made of groats and poultry, highly seasoned with garlick, with balls of minced meat and eggs. The common bread is made of rye; it is soft, black and sour. During the fasts, they chiefly live on mushrooms, bread, vegetables, and oil.

In every room is the picture of some favourite saint, called a bogh; before which every person bows and crosses himself, with all the stiffened formality of an automaton. We have frequently seen instances of violent disputes, in the streets, when one of the party would immediately run into the house, perhaps for some weapon of revenge, or to vent his rage upon his own family; but, the instant he enters the room door, the rage of his countenance, for a moment, subsides, and, hurrying over his obeisances to the picture, he, as suddenly, gives a loose to his passions. These pictures are generally of a small size, about eight inches square. Only the face and hands are to be seen, the rest is covered with a drapery of tin; or some are coarsely daubed upon wood. Before the picture is generally seen a lamp, which is lighted on particular occasions, and a vessel of holy water. Every one, before he retires to rest, in the evening, and after he rises in the morning, never omits to prostrate himself before the object of his religious adoration.

Tossna exhibits an irregular heap of miserable huts, with a tolerably showy church in the centre; it has a square steeple, and a dome surmounted by three large globes. It is a singular contrast to observe the elegance of the churches in those villages, and the truly deplorable state of the dwelling-houses. Every labour and expense seems to be sacrificed in adorning the church, in preference to domestic comforts. Tossna is laid down in the Russian maps as a bourg, or borough, and contains about three hundred inhabitants. The people are all clad in sheep-skins, and are noisy and quarrelsome.

The country around is generally flat, and covered with birch, mountain ash and poplar. The soil is sand and clay, without stones, and but little cultivated. A small brook runs by the town, which supplies the inhabitants with water. The high road, leading through the town, together with the greater part of the last stage, is floored with planks of wood. This is one of the principal ways by which the roads, in this part of the country, are made; but only in those places where there are no

stones, and the surface of the country soft and
marshy. To keep these roads in repair is the constant employment of the neighbouring peasants, the
extent and neatness of whose labour deserve the
highest praise. The plantations, on each side of the
road, to a certain extent, are entirely appropriated
to its use, and which the inhabitants are prohibited
from using as fire-wood. The manner of forming
these roads is extremely simple, yet very complete
and even durable, when finished. The planks used
are generally those of trees of a small growth, from
four to six inches in diameter. These are cut about
twelve feet long, and laid parallel to each other,
while their ends are supported upon a row placed
parallel with the side of the road, and fastened
down by sods or pegs. However level and hard
these floored roads may be, yet the unequal and
jolting motion given to a carriage, is perhaps the
most fatiguing exercise, which a traveller ever suffered. It is impossible to endure the pain which is
occasioned, without having a broad belt tied round
the waist. The Russian travelling carriages are seldom hung upon springs, but are furnished with
several leather bags of feathers, upon which the
traveller reposes at full length. These common
stage conveyances consist of a slight open cart, with
four low wheels, called a *kibitki;* they are entirely

made of wood, without any iron, and seem to be the most peculiar to the country. The body consists of a boat shape, and the axletrees generally extend two or three feet beyond the breadth of it, and which form the nave of the wheel, consequently occasion an extraordinary degree of friction. This contrivance is used to prevent the vehicle from being entirely upset.

The Russian couriers are obliged to travel with those carts, in preference to their own carriage, in the event of its breaking down, and thus retard their progress. From the extreme fatigue which this occasions, they seldom survive for any length of time.

The speed at which these postillions drive is astonishing, as well as their uncouth manner of managing the horses, and holding the reins. The horses, however many are used, are always yoked abreast; the outriders draw from a cross beam, which is fastened to that of the carriage, something similar to the yard-arm of the studding sail of a ship. The reins, as well as the harness, are entirely made of ropes. The postillion seldom uses a whip; the cheering sound of music is the only lash he uses, to encourage his horses to proceed. The reins are thrown over his back, and held in each hand, while his arms are widely exten-

ded. At the point of the pole a large bell is fastened; the jingling noise of which is to announce
the approach of the traveller. The bell is used, similar to the horn in Prussia, to warn travellers to give
place to the postillions of the crown. As soon as
a traveller reaches the stage, he is immediately
driven to the post-house, where he is surrounded
by multitudes of idlers, every one requesting to be
employed, yet as constantly refusing. The *poderos-
noi*, or imperial order for horses, must be presented
to the post-master, and who must be bribed to encourage his activity. He procures the horses from
the peasant, and hires them to the traveller, at an
advanced price; but the peasant always drives his
own horses. Every one of the postillions appears
with his bell slung to his girdle, and which he takes
off, when engaged, and fastens to the pole. The
instant he is mounted on the box, and got clear of
the village, he halloos to his horses, and sets off at
full gallop. His gayety never forsakes him, and he
continues to sing his national airs, without interruption, during the stage. Whenever they meet on
the road, they take off their hats, with a degree of
studied formality, but never turn their eyes to each
other. Whenever they pass a church they alight
and rapidly cross themselves; even before they
mount the carriage, they regularly perform their

manual exercise of crossings, and uttering a prayer. Those who furnish the post-horses, are called *yam-shics*, and are exempt from the payment of the poll-tax, and also from being enlisted as soldiers. The rate of posting is so small, that they regularly quarrel among themselves, who shall be employed. Their noise and disputes are always carried to such a height, that the only means of commanding obedience, is by the cudgel. A regular number of horses must always be in readiness, to convey the government couriers, who are compelled to travel at a certain rate, equal to ten miles an hour.

The rate of posting in Russia is fixed at so much a werst, for each horse; but is higher for horses leaving a town or borough, than from the villages. The regulated price is rather less than two-pence a werst* for each horse. The hire of the horses from St. Petersburg, for the first stage of thirty-three wersts, was twenty-eight roubles, the value of a rouble being at present about one shilling sterling. The next stage (being from a village) of twenty-five wersts, only cost five roubles. No travelling can be more expeditious, or cheaper than in Russia.

* One hundred and five wersts is equal to a degree of sixty-nine miles and a half.—or seven wersts to five miles.

The road from Tossna led us through a country extremely flat, and uncultivated. The whole road is laid with planks, and partly covered with sand. On all sides, as far as the eye could reach, forests of fir, birch and poplars were extended; they were however of a very slender and stunted growth, from the barren coldness of the soil. Before we reached Pomerania we passed two small paltry villages, more wretched than any we had hitherto seen.

Pomerania, the next stage at which we arrived, resembles Tossna in every respect; the inhabitants are clad alike, but somewhat of smaller stature. No degrees of rank are here seen, all is one dull, insipid level.

A few wersts from Tossna, we left the government of St. Petersburg, and entered that of Novo-goród. Our next stage from Pomerania, was to Tischoudovo; the road was exactly similar to the former, with two intervening wretched villages of a few huts; also a plain brick house, said to be one of the emperor's hunting seats. Tischoudovo consists of a long straggling range of wooden huts, with a neat gothic wooden church, painted with red and yellow streaks, and green domes. Its population is about one thousand persons.

Between the last two stages, very little of the country is cultivated, excepting small patches stolen from the confines of the forests. The only crops are rye and barley, extremely light and scanty. The corn, when cut, is dragged to the barn on sledges. The plough is of a simple construction. It consists of one perpendicular handle, which forms its body, and to which a forked coulter is fixed at right angles; also two wooden shafts, between which the horse is yoked. From the light sandy nature of the soil, only one horse is used to a plough, and the furrow turned up, is not more than three inches deep. From the forked form of the coulter, the furrows are considerably pulverised. This form of plough is certainly well adapted to a loose friable soil. In the neighbourhood of Tischoudovo, the surface becomes marshy, and is generally covered with brush willows, and sickly fir trees.

The women alone seem to perform the field work, such as cutting down, and threshing the grain. When working in the fields, they only wear a loose shift, fastened round the waist by a girdle, and fancifully embroidered round the skirts and neck, with red threads. The sleeves are very wide and secured at the elbows. The hair of the head is bound up, by a laced bandeau. In features they seem to be even coarser formed than the men, and, in their man-

ners, extremely masculine. In cold weather they
are clad, like the men, in sheep-skins; and, were
it not for the bristly chin of the latter, a stranger
would be considerably at a loss to distinguish the
one from the other.

At Tischoudovo the road forms a slight angle,
and proceeds directly south towards Spaskaia-Po-
liste. The intermediate country is hard and dry,
and the road is made of loose stones, instead of being floored; however little cultivation is seen, and
the stunted appearance of the trees continue. This
village contains about two hundred and fifty inhabitants, and is remarkable only for its similarity to its
former companions both in meanness and filth.

Along the road, we passed one or two large
droves of horned cattle proceeding to St. Petersburg. We learned that they were brought from
the provinces south of Moscow. These cattle are
all of a whitish colour, large, well made, and about
seven hundred weight. Their journey to St. Petersburg generally occupies three months; they
travel about eight to sixteen miles during the night,
and are allowed to pasture and rest, during the day,
on the sides of the road. The flocks are attended
by one or two men, who convey their cooking utensils, baggage, etc. in a wagon, drawn by two oxen;
and, while their numerous flocks, undisturbed, re-

pose under the shade of the delicate birch, they
stretch themselves on the bare ground, and pass
their time in a true Scythian state. Here are also
seen a few sheep, but of an inferior breed, and covered with hair somewhat like that of a goat. This
country is not favourable for the pasture of sheep,
owing to the coarseness of the grass, and quantity of
wood. Little or no attention seems to be used in
the rearing of any other domestic animal, besides
the horse. To him alone the Russ devotes his whole
attention, and from him he derives his livelihood.

Podberezie, the next stage, is marked in the maps
as a bourg, and contains about two hundred inhabitants. The houses are built somewhat different
from those of the former villages. Some are built
in a square form, covered with lime, and surrounded
by a rudely constructed piazza. The country becomes gently elevated, and commands a most extensive view towards the south-west, over an immea-
surably flat country, partly covered with forests and
morasses. Around Podberezie more attention to
agriculture is seen, with an appearance of a few
windmills.

At these different stages, the traveller will regularly find the most violent disputes among the common people, about who shall get the preference of
hiring their horses. The horses are, in general,

hired by the keeper of the post-house, who, in return, hires them to the traveller, at an advanced
price, while the proprietor of the horses makes a
noisy demand to be paid also for his trouble.   They
rave at a furious rate ; but an opposite appearance
of anger, or perhaps a threatened chastisement,
soon puts them to flight.

In the country there is only one class of people.
In most countries families of rank are nearly alike,
from a similitude of education, and a general intercourse with society ; but the order of every refinement, in this remote country, seems to be perverted.
A strong shade of national similarity is observed in
the different ranks.   The polish of education cannot altogether conceal the varying lineaments of a
once rude people.   If it were not that vanity was
more predominant than taste, the appearance of all
would be lost in one undistinguished mass.

The continual recurrence of offensive oppression
renders the common people averse to all improvements of agriculture, and they lead an existence
but ill calculated, either to enlarge the solidity of
the community, or to improve their moral character.
The refinements of taste, the fire of youth, or the
soft emotions of love, are all laid aside, and the
animal senses brought into action.   Minds, capable
of such degradation, exist only in proportion. as the

sources of their indulgencies gratify their appetites; but, no sooner do its streams cease to flow, than they assert their contempt of obedience. Hence that texture of mind, which obliterates the finer feelings of sentiment, and the admiration of virtue.

In a general survey of the surface of this part of the country, nature seems to have left an aspect extremely barren, and cheerless. The warbling of birds is not heard; nor are the gambols of children seen. Their wretched dwellings agree with the character of the country. No garden smiles around their habitations; and only partial patches, stolen from the forests, are seen, bearing a scanty crop. Such is the appearance of a country, in which the peasant resides; his time is consumed in the gloomy retrospect, that he has lived only for the moment, and drags on a sluggish existence. No shady groves, nor cooling grottos, invite his careless steps; no angel woman sooths the anguish of his toils, for woman, lovely and adored in every country, is here considered as an animal of drudgery; and the delicacy and softness of their sex are lost in servile submission.

Approaching, from the last stage, we caught the first view of the scattered remains of the ancient city of Novogorod. The view of the country, toward the south-west, continues most extensive and

23

flat, with partial plantations of trees, and some cottages. The soil is more sandy and arid, than formerly, and the roads are paved with stones, but which seems to be avoided by the postillions, who travel at large, over the extensive plains.

Novogorod stands on a rising bank, on the west side of the Volchova river, while the ancient cathedral of Saint Sophia, and some wooden huts, are situated on the opposite bank. The river is crossed by a long and clumsy wooden bridge, at the east end of which is the market-place, lined on every side, with small square houses, surrounded by piazzas, under which are ranges of shops, on a similar plan with those in the capital, but much inferior in point of elegance. The streets cross each other at right angles, and are tolerably well paved; the houses exhibit both age and decay. The number of churches is astonishing; and, though many of them are in a state of decay, yet none are seen in complete ruin; the religion of the country does not allow a church ever to be destroyed. The cathedral of St. Sophia is one of the most ancient in the country. It was built in the eleventh century, by Uladimir duke of Novogorod; in it are interred the bodies of several distinguished princes of the country. The cathedral of St. Sophia was among the first buildings in this country, after the

introduction of Christianity. It represents a square
clumsy structure, with a gilded cupola; and four
domes covered with tin. The cathedral is surrounded by the remains of the wall of the old fortress.
which also includes the ruins of the palace of the
ancient dukes.

The interior of the cathedral exhibits a most extraordinary display of religious paintings, and carv-
ings in relief. The gate which opens the grand entrance, is particularly deserving of notice; it is composed entirely of brass, ornamented with numerous
figures, representing the Passion of our Saviour.
The roof is supported by twelve massive, round
pillars, covered with numerous scriptural paintings,
of the most uncouth performance. However clumsy these daubs may appear, yet some of them are
said to be very old, and to have been the first rude
attempts after the revival of painting in Italy.

Nothing perhaps can more call the mind back to
distant ages, than the scattered relics of an ancient
city. Here once stood the proud capital of these
northern regions, giving life, activity, and laws to
its surrounding tribes; and, like an old and faithful
parent, watching over, and sheltering, their rising
interests. Now all its former splendour is lost in
its general ruin: one uninterrupted scene of gene-

ral decay encompasses it; and nothing but the wrecks of fallen greatness are visible on every side; and churches and temples are now lost in the mazes of the forest. This is one of the most ancient cities in Russia, and was called Great Novogorod, to distinguish it from Nishnei Novogorod, and Novogorod Severskoi. It is said to have been built as early as the fifth century. In the ninth century it became the metropolis of the north, under Ruric, the first great duke of Russia, and continued to flourish, more as an independent republic, than the capital of a monarchy, until the fifteenth century, when the government was removed to Moscow, and the prowess of Ivan Vassilivitch I. secured his dominions from intestine broils, and the daring attempts of the unsettled Tartars. Novogorod was then the great mart of trade between Russia and the Hanse Towns. Its population and wealth became so powerful, as to give rise to the proverb, *quis contra Deos et Magnam Novogardiam?* At the period of its greatest splendour, it is said to have contained four hundred thousand inhabitants; whereas its present population does not exceed seven thousand. When Peter the Great established St. Petersburg, as the capital of the empire, he transferred the whole commerce of the Baltic, which had continued to flow to this city, to his new metropolis. The present ap-

pearance of this ancient city, ill accords with its
former magnificence. Magnificent ruins appear on
every side, standing as melancholy monuments of its
former greatness. Even the surrounding country
appears to have acquired a degree of barrenness,
which no cultivation could overcome. The little
trade which it now carries on, is done by means of
the Volchova, towards Petersburg and the Mista,
to the junction of the Volga; but occasional rapids,
on this river, render it somewhat expensive, and
difficult. We were rather surprised to find that the
most active persons in trade, were Italians, who
seem to be here, what Jews are in other countries.

The lake Ilmen lies low, and is of a triangular
form. Its circumference is about ninety miles; it is
supplied by three small rivers from the south, while
it discharges itself by the Volchova, which runs to
the lake Ladoga, and the Mista which joins the
Tvertza, which in turn falls into the Volga. By
the junction of these rivers, there is a communication
from the Gulf of Finland to the Caspian Sea.

From St. Petersburg to Novogorod, the distance
is equal to one hundred and twenty-seven miles, with
a population of only two thousand five hundred
persons. On each side of the road extend forests
and marshes, which have scarcely been trodden by

the foot of man. On the west side of the road these wilds extend without interruption, to the great road, leading towards Lithuania. On the north-east it extends much farther, and through a space only known to the animals of the forest. In short, the government of Novogorod scarcely contains more than two individuals to four square miles, or one person to one thousand two hundred and eight English acres! No other part of the country is inhabited, than along the line of the great roads; between the principal cities no individual houses are ever seen, but at the different stages, where they are built together, and only round those spots, is the ground cultivated, while the intervening space is a neglected waste.

In viewing this wide, and almost unpeopled country, we are naturally led to inquire, whence do those mighty armies come, which have been so often, and so successively wielded by this country? The question is solved the moment we throw our eye over the map of the Russian empire. Here we see an extent of country, stretching from the banks of the Niemen to the shores of Kamtschatka; from the bleak and frozen country of the Samoide, to the vernal plains of the Tauridian Peninsula; a space even double that of modern Europe. Yet

the whole of this vast and unbounded empire scarcely contains fifty millions of people!

If agriculture is properly encouraged, the population will be increased in proportion. Were this
country to acquire a population, equal to one-fourth
of what England contains, to a square mile, it would
amount to nearly one hundred and fifty millions of
people.

From Novogorod the road is flat, and laid with
wood. It soon enters a fine forest of larger trees
than we had hitherto passed, and crosses a branch
of the Volchovo, about one hundred yards in
breadth. This is, on the whole, a pleasant and picturesque stage. The road winds, in an irregular
manner, through fine natural avenues of fir, weeping birch, poplars, and mountain ash, without an
object to relieve the woodland scene. At length it
reaches the banks of the Mista, and commands a
charming view of the river and church of Bronnitzi,
situated on the top of a conical mount. The banks
of the river are steep and clayey, and the east part
of the road, loose sand. The river is about three
hundred feet wide, but shallow. Bronnitzi stands
on the south side of the river, over which is a remarkably neat bridge on pontoons. The town is of
an irregular form. The houses are partly made of
wood, and some of brick, stuccoed and white-

washed. There are two fine churches, surmounted
with many domes; one of them is situated on a singular steep conical mount, called Bronnitzkaya-
Gora. Concerning this hill various stories are related. On its summit are two springs, generally
covered with aquatic plants. The peasants ascribe
medicinal virtues to its water. The whole hill is
embellished with variegated flowers, and some
dwarf-elms; except on the north side, which is not
covered by any vegetation. The prospect, from
this eminence over the surrounding country, as well
as the lake Ilmen, is very extensive. On festival
days it becomes the favourite resort of the country-
people. This mount is composed of a loamy soil,
except at its base, where the remains of some large
blocks of granite are scattered. The height of
the mount is nearly two hundred feet; and some
German writers have supposed it to originate from
human labour:* but the very circumstance of the
springs on its summit must rather be a proof to the
contrary. Bronnitzi contains about one thousand
inhabitants; the people are more given to imposition and quarrels, than at Novogorod. The inn is
wretchedly bad.

* Pallas' travels through the Russian empire in 1771, (in German,) Vol. I.

From Bronnitzi the road takes a south-easterly direction, and passes over extensive morasses and brushwood. About the middle of the stage, the wood becomes large and luxuriant. The first part of the road is planked, and, towards Zaiffova, paved with stones. Here for the first time, from St. Petersburg, we saw the country swelled into gentle hill and dale. The soil alters from a sandy loam, to red clay, which is tolerably well farmed and to a considerable extent. Along the road are two or three mean villages, nearer in resemblance to the wigwam of the Americans, than those of the Russians. Ziffova scarcely deserves to be mentioned ; it has neither church, nor any object of distinction, beyond the meanest huts.

The implements of agriculture here are similar to those we had already seen ; except the harrow, which is entirely made from the lateral branches of the fir tree, with its twigs serving as teeth, an evident sign that no improvement has taken place, since the earliest attention to agriculture was practised.

We next approached the town of Krestzi, containing about two thousand inhabitants. The road is loose, heavy sand, partly planked or paved with stones. In some places it is irregular, and becomes a broad track, similar to the sandy plains in Swedish Pomerania. The road crosses a small river, issuing from the lake Ilmen, on which is

24

erected a small sawmill, used in sawing the fir
wood, which is here of considerable extent, on the
west side of the road. On this stage were two
small villages, almost in a state of ruin; they were
surrounded by little gardens, well stocked with
cabbage. This was the first instance of an attention to horticulture we had seen. A singular
custom prevails here, among the labouring people; while engaged at their labour at a distance
from home, they do not seek the shelter of their
huts, but are contented to stretch themselves, on
the bare ground, round a blazing fire, and pass the
night in a true Scythian manner. A traveller is
astonished at the frequency, and number of these
flaming piles, they are generally placed at the
side of the road; and on approaching them, his
astonishment is increased at beholding the savage
appearance of men wrapped up in sheep-skins,
with their faces covered with the most frightful
beards, and dimly seen through the rolling volumes of smoke. The people here are little removed from the grossest barbarism, and may almost
be said to lead a wandering life. The entire face
of the country is covered with natural forests, the
abode of wild animals, and the scene of occasional robberies. While travelling this stage, in the
evening, a large wolf sullenly stalked by the carriage.

Krestzi is a considerable town situated on the banks of a small river. It is throughout built of wood, except at its south end, where a few brick houses appear neatly finished; also a very pretty painted church. The houses are filled with vermin and insects; particularly the cock-roach.

We again proceeded through a sandy country, and reached the bourg of Rachino, about half the size of the former town, but very irregularly built, and somewhat in a state of decay. A small village relieves the dreariness of the stage; yet this part of the country seems more populous than the rest. The women appear alone to cut down the grain, while the men are ploughing, harrowing and sowing, or perfectly idle. The women, while working in the fields, are dressed in long loose shifts, fastened at the elbow by wide sleeves. The skirts are fancifully embroidered with red thread; on the head is worn a silver laced bandeau, or a kerchief rolled round it; the hair is plaited behind, and allowed to hang down the back; after marriage it is tied up, and distinguishes the virgin from the matron. Others wear a blue woollen shift, trimmed down the front with a row of buttons.

The road, from the last stage, becomes more irregular, consisting of numerous broad tracks over deep, loose sand, with sudden declivities and ascents. In winter this stage must be both fatiguing

and dangerous. Few objects are seen, but an ir
regular appearance in the surface of the country;
which loses its former flatn ss, and undulates into
considerable hills and valleys, covered with wood
or washed by spreading rivulets. Towards the
south-east the country becomes somewhat bold
and picturesque; the hills assume an irregular
form, covered with wood, or broken up by falling streams of water. Cultivation is less practised, the soil changes to a greyish clay, considerably covered with loose stones.

During the last stage we observed several ancient sepulchral tumuli. A short distance from
Rachi o we passed four, grouped together of considerable height and covered with trees.

The bourg of Jagelbitzi consists of two long
streets, crossing each other at right angles, with
a population of five hundred persons. The
ground, on which the houses are built, is deeply
rutted by the water, which in winter flows from
the Vaiday hills, over these cuts wooden bridges
are placed. At the south-end of the town is a tolerably large and shewy church, with a square
steeple, between two domes painted green and
red. The church yard, unlike the careful attentions usually paid to those sacred spots, is converted into a paddock for cattle.

The people here seem to have a peculiar character of knavery, and are more lawless than those
nearer to the metropolis.

The person who drove our servants found an opportunity of picking their pockets; but he was luckily detected by a traveller passing at the moment. When challenged with the theft, he fell on his knees before the church, crossed himself repeatedly, and invoked the vengeance of all the saints, if he was guilty. However, on offering a reward of five roubles for the restoration of the stolen property, or in case of a refusal, threatening an application to the police, he was induced to confess that he had seen a pocket-book on the road, which he would endeavour to find. One of our servants accompanied him, and found that the careful Russ had secured the stolen property in a hole in the wall of his hut. He had not examined the contents of the book, and, when it was opened before him, and presented to his sight a considerable number of Russian notes, it drew from him an exclamation of astonishment, and as many oaths and prayers, that he had given us a wrong book! Nothing can excel the arch-roguery of a Russian. On the same stage another stole the cushion from the box of the carriage, and sold it to a third, from whom we were obliged to purchase it, on his assertion that it was the work of his own hands.

We could not but shudder at a most extraordinary instance of immorality, which is still allowed to take place among many of these ignorant and wretched people. A father marries his son, when almost a boy, to a girl considerably older; the son is immediately sent to some distant town, to acquire a livelihood, while the parent cohabits with his daughter-in-law, and often presents his son, on his return, with a numerous family. It is to be hoped, that proper measures will be taken by the legislature to abolish these incestuous marriages.

CHAP. VI.

ON leaving Jagelbitzi the heights of Valday opened to our view, extending across the road in a west and east direction. The road soon began to ascend the hill, and to wind in a zig-zag manner, for thirteen miles. The track is partly paved with stones, or covered with sand. The Valday mountains, so called by the Russians, from its being the only rising ground between St. Petersburg and Moscow, is about one thousand feet in height, and not more than sixteen miles wide at it base, and about fifty miles in length. This rising ground appears picturesque, and affords an agreeable relief to the eye, after passing along the insipid flatness of the country from St. Petersburg. It rises in so gradual a manner, and being considerably broken in its surface, that its heights appear somewhat diminished. It cannot be seen from any great distance. The surface is partly covered with loose stones of granite, a few fir trees, and much brush wood: also extensive tracks of cultivatio . Grain is reared on the very summit of these heights. The soil is a reddish clay,

mixed with sand. Along the side of the road
are seen a few miserable wooden huts. The
people partake of that lawless character, which
the aspect of the country is so well calculated
to impress. No features of mineralogy present
themselves, except a slight appearance of strati-
fication towards the south-end of the hill. On
the summit of the hill we were astonished to
find several tumuli, picturesquely covered with
the green fir trees, which considerably added to
the irregularity of the scenery. From its summit
the prospect was not so extensive as might be
expected. Before us, at the foot of the hill,
appeared the little town of Zimogorie, situated
on the banks of a small lake. On entering the
town we found two long streets, formed of wooden
houses, built on the declivity of a rising ground,
and almost joining to the lake. Each of the
streets is terminated by a church. The one is a
large brick building, with several gilded domes,
the other a clumsy wooden structure. A few of
the houses are built of brick, stuccoed and painted of various colours. The inn is kept by an
Italian, and we had the pleasure of being sere-
naded with the music of several instruments. A
slight difference is remarkable, between the people here, and those on the other side of the hill.
Light hair and light beards seem to be the prevailing colour, and a countenance somewhat

sharper. The hair is cut in the same manner; only that, on the top of the head, it is cut very short, forming a kind of circular bald pate. The women are better looking, and possess a peculiar softness of manner. The lake Valday, which extends along the south side of the town, is about fifteen miles in length, and from one to three in breadth, with several islands scattered over its surface, and some fine peninsulas of wood. On one of its islands is a large and shewy convent, with many glittering domes and turrets, rising above the dark green foliage of the surrounding forest. So retired from the bustling scenes of life is this religious asylum, that the pious enthusiast must find in it a retreat equal to his wishes. Altogether, Zimogorie will present objects sufficiently interesting to detain the traveller one or two days.

The road from Zimogorie to Jedrovo is even worse, than that over the Valday hills. It passes over a rugged and barren country, covered with loose stones, and deeply rutted. This fatiguing stage is surrounded, on each side, by young wood, and several narrow lakes. Slight attempts at cultivation are distinguished, but the crops are very scanty. The stalks of corn no where appeared above ten inches in length : corn stacks are, in consequence, thatched with the twigs of the birch tree. Before we entered Je-

25

drovo we passed a small, but picturesque winding lake, near to which we observed several tumuli, not so large as, but more perfect than, those we had hitherto seen. Here we also observed numerous flocks of wood pigeons, uncommonly tame. These, with the common black and grey raven, were the only birds we had ever noticed. This little town consists of one long street, of mean wooden hovels, more like heaps of rotten wood, than the dwellings of men. The street terminates in a square, in which a large and clumsy church is built. This was the first place where we found no kind of inn, or public house. However we met with a tolerable substitute, from the stores of a Russian traveller, who was on his return to St. Petersburg, from Saratoff on the banks of the Volga, about six hundred miles south-east of Moscow. He was accompanied by his family, and, like every native of the country, moved along with his whole household furniture. Every Russian is so well acquainted with the extreme barrenness of his country, and the filthiness of the inns, that they never undertake a journey without carrying along with them a regular stock of provisions, beds, and the apparatus of cookery.

From the last town we proceeded through a broad, open, and unequal track of loose heavy sand, leading through extensive forests of fir and birch. The last part of this stage is formed of wood. On each side are some fine fields, well laid out, and seemingly well cultivated. The crops were oats and buck-wheat. The burg of Kotilovo is another very long range of mean wooden huts, terminated by a fine church, surrounded by trees. The inn is small, and well stocked with garlic, filth, cock-roaches, &c. &c.

A few wersts from Kotilovo we passed the boundary line of the government of Novogorod, end entered that of Tweer. This was a long stage of thirty-six wrests, over a country, flat, sandy and uninteresting. The soil alternately varied from a light clay sand, to that of a dark black grey. The grass was short and scorched, and the trees small.

The first place we arrived at, was the district town of Vishnei-Volotshok. This is a considerable town, well built, and contains about twelve thousand inhabitants. The streets are regular, and many of the houses are built of brick, and stuccoed. A square is allotted to the shops, which are established on a plan similar to those in the capital. The town is ornamented with three fine churches, besides a variety of smaller religious edifices. From its population and appearance, it ranks as the first from St. Petersburg.

This town is situated on the banks of the river Mista, which discharges itself from the lake

Ilmen, and, after passing, in a circular form, through the government of Novogorod reaches Vishnei-Volotshok, where it assumes the name of the Tvertza, or rather from its being joined to that river by means of a considerable canal and which, on account of facilitating the inland navigation of the country, renders it one of the most important places connected with the capital, The navigation of these rivers united, is upwards of fourteen hundred miles ; a communication is also carried on with Siberia and China, by the junction of these noble rivers. However we could not but observe, that the spirit of commerce seemed, at present, to be considerably abated. This may probably arise from the effect of the late campaign.

We continued our route to Widropouskoe, over a similar flat, and sandy country, but more covered with forests, from which small patches of cultivation were stolen. Near the little stream of Zna we passed, for the first time, a solitary farm house. Widropouskoe is a bourg of mean wooden huts, of the vilest description, yet ornamented with a shewy painted church.

The men still hold that low insipid rank, where all is on one level; and their dress the never varying sheep-skin. The women here are singularly dressed. A silk kerchief is bound round the head, with the ends hanging down the back;

while the body is covered with a green sarsnet petticoat and vest, formed into one, fastened under the arms, and supported by broad bracers, from behind, over the shoulders. The arms, as far as the elbow, are covered with a very wide sleeve, of white linen. A cord is drawn tight across the breasts, which it divides into a most disgusting form. Nothing binds the waist: all, from the shoulders, hangs loose. Some have their dress in front trimmed with rows of buttons, others wear a second sort of short petticoat fastened under arms, and which hangs open, and wide, to the waist. The stockings are padded, and worn as rollers round the legs; which occasions every woman to walk in a very waddling manner.

It was not with regret that we left Widropouskoe, and proceeded to Torjock. Along this stage we were highly compensated, by the appearance of extensive fields of grain. The greater part of the country around Torjock is cultivated. The soil is a light friable loam; the crops are barley, black oats, buck wheat and rye; however the straw is short, not exceeding ten inches. There is more grain raised in this district, than in the whole way between it and St. Petersburg. Neither hedges nor fences of any kind are seen. The cattle are herded in flocks, which are still very few, though in greater num-

bers than any where towards the north. They
are generally black, and of a small size. The
sheep are of a greyish black colour, with very
coarse wool, and *natural* short tails.

Between Widropouskoe and Torjock, we observed the effect of fire on one of those wooden
villages. It belonged to the Count Suwaroff,
and had accidentally caught fire. The houses
being built entirely of wood, and no immediate
supply of water, were burnt to the ground in a
very few hours. Even the very planks which
formed the road, were burnt. The loss was
nearly that of two hundred houses. In cases of
such losses, the peasants are exempted from so
many days labour to their lord, and are partly
assisted in rebuilding of their houses.

It is a matter of astonishment, that every
house in this country is not burnt down, or at
least that repeated instances of conflagration
should not more frequently occur; not only,
because the cottages are built of wood, but from
the common practice of using long slips of lighted deal, instead of candles, and which are carried
through all parts of the house, with the sparks
constantly falling from them. Tallow, or wax
candles, are rarely used in the country; except
in the churches, where the piety of the individual is often in proportion to the number of wax
tapers he fixes on the altar.

Torjock is a district town, and stands upon a fine commanding station, on both sides of the Tvertza, which are connected by a singular floating bridge, made of large planks, fastened parallel to each other. The river is about forty yards wide, and navigable by flat-bottomed boats. It has a direct communication with Vishnei-Volotshok, and the commerce of the Baltic, and also communicates with that of the Volga. Its principal trade consist in the exportation of grain, and the manufacture of leather into various articles of dress and other purposes; particularly boots and shoes, port-feuilles, leather beds, &c. These are neatly stitched and embroidered with gold and silver threads, and are partly exported to Turkey and Astracan.

The dresses of the women at Torjock are particularly remarkable. They differ from their northern neighbours, in the gaudy display of Asiatic finery and flowing robes. The dress consists of a lofty Hessian cap, or *coeffure*, about two feet in height, which covers the back of the neck down to the shoulders, while a fringe of pearls hangs over the forehead. Over the head dress is thrown a large white muslin shawl, edged with broad gold lace, which hangs loosely over the shoulders and reaches to the ground. The petticoat is made of red or yellow sarsnet or damask silk, embroidered with broad gold lace.

The sleeves are worn extremely wide, and of a different coloured silk. The shoes are stitched with silver thread, and worn close up to the ancles. This singular costume is worn by all ranks of women, but finer in proportion to the wealth or rank of the individual. The children are habited in a similar manner, without the head dress. Those who do not wear shawl, have the hair of the head plaited into three plaits, down the back, and terminated by a knot of ribbons.

The houses are partly built of brick, but the greater number of them are made of wood, and exhibit a very mean appearance. The churches are the most numerous and shewy buildings in the town. Every one is surmounted by several domes and spires, ludicrously painted and gilt. The singular variety of characters seen at Torjock, is in consequence of a celebrated spring, which is said to perform wonderful cures. To it flock the vulgar and superstitious tribes of the most distant provinces, conceiving it a general panacea for their pains and infirmities. Here we see the various costumes of different countries, and here are heard their various tongues. All crowd to this hallowed water, as to a baptismal fount, where they could rid themselves of sin, and give a new birth unto righteousness.

We again proceeded on our journey, and found the road, at first, hard and well made, with improvements in agriculture on each side, but which soon changed into a dreary vaste of loose sand. Along this stage we passed the country residences of Generals Karamichoff and Gleboff. The first is a mean plain brick house, with a few trees round it, without the beauty of a garden, or even the advantage of a made road to the house. The other is a large shewy building, with many domes and pillars, and extensive avenues of trees, and distant forests. The scenery is extremely beautiful. A small river passes in front of the house, which is crossed by a rude gothic bridge of three arches. Near the bridge are the cottages of the peasants. We continued to travel along the north side of the Twertza, until we reached the bourg of Mednoe, situated on the south side of the river, which is crossed by a wooden bridge on pontoons. This little town consists of a number of old mean wooden hovels, almost in a state of ruin. In the centre is a fine church and parsonage, with a large dome and spire painted pea green. The contrast between the church and houses is very remarkable. We were driven by a Cossack, who, being a freed man, had the privilege of hiring his own horses, independently of the rules of the post-house. Some of the Cossacks who had served in the late campaign, and chose to settle in this part of the country, received a small portion of land from

26

the Emperor, on which they now reside. No travelling can exceed, in speed, that which is here performed. The roads, passing over extensive flat plains, scarcely present an obstacle to the wheel. The instant the postillion has got clear of the village, he gives the well known howl to his horses, which immediately set off at full gallop, and, after running at this furious rate for a few wersts, he suddenly slackens their pace, until they become somewhat refreshed, when again he starts at a similar speed, and a stage of twenty-six miles is generally performed in three hours; they never halt on the stage, nor allow their horses any water.

A considerable trade in grain seems to be carried on at Mednoe, by means of the river; though less attention is devoted to agriculture than about Torjock.

It was not without considerable satisfaction that we reached Tweer, and found a place where we could command some refreshments and repose, after so fatiguing a journey from the capital. However expeditious the Russian postillion may drive his horses, yet, from the inequality of the roads, and the continued dreariness of flat morasses and endless forests, with scarcely an object to arrest the attention, beyond that of the lowest stamp in the scale of human beings, the traveller must, more or less, catch the kindred

gloom, and become the mere statistical writer.
No living objects excite his mirth, nor wildness
of scenery his sublimity. All is on one dull insipid level.

At every village we see the wrangling group
of sheep-skin clad postillions, whose noise is increased by the jingling of their bells; while,
along the flat and dreary stage, the never ending
song, and howl of the postillion, with the tinkling
of his bell, are the only sounds which break on
the awfully predominating stillness.

The town of Tweer is situated on the banks of
the Volga, which is here joined by the Twertza.
The appearance of Tweer is almost that of the
capital in miniature. The houses are regular,
numerous and elegantly designed. Along the
side of the river are the most finished buildings.
The corners of the streets cross each other at
right angles, and terminate in an octagon square.
The houses are generally painted of various colours, and the spires and domes of the churches
are richly gilt. The town owes its present improved appearance to a fire which consumed it
in 1763, and which was rebuilt under the auspices
of the Empress Catharine. The public buildings
were erected at the expense of the government,
and large sums of money were distributed to the
sufferers, to assist them in restoring their dwellings, on a scale of superior excellence. In con-

sequence of this order Tweer soon became a large
and splendid town, and may now rank, in beauty
and size, superior to any of the provincial towns.
Public seminaries were instituted, in the reign of
Catharine, for the education of the children of the
province and those of the burghers; but, from
some defect in either their genius or industry,
these establishments have greatly fallen into
decay.

Tweer was once the resident city of the Grand
Dukes of Russia, but is now the capital of the
government of the same name. It is advantageously situated, in respect to its communication
with other places. By means of the Volga it
carries on an inland trade with the Caspian Sea
and the intermediate countries, also by the junction of the rivers flowing through the extensive
country of Siberia. The produce of those distant and almost unknown regions are brought to
the capital. At Tweer we were regaled with
sterlets, a delicious fish caught in the Volga.
They are preserved in wooden troughs, and prove
a necessary part of food to the inhabitants, during
their religious fasts.

The Volga is one of the largest rivers in Europe, and carries on a commercial communication
through a greater extent of country, than any
other river. It rises from two small lakes, on
the boundary line between the governments of

Novogorod and Tweer, in latitude fifty-seven
north, and longitude thirty-four east, and, after
traversing, in an irregular direction, to the forty-
ninth degree of east longitude, it takes a southerly
course, and falls into the Caspian Sea at Astracan,
in latitude forty-six north, including a space of
nearly one thousand nine hundred English miles.
It is worthy of remark that the Volga, Dnieper,
and Duna, three of the largest rivers in Europe,
take their rise within a few miles of each other.

This town is three hundred and seventy-six
miles from St. Petersburg, and one hundred and
twenty-two miles from Moscow; and holds, as it
were, the middle link in the chain of civilization.
The streets exhibit that singular contrast of
splendour and poverty, so conspicuous in the capital. It is singular that, only in the cities of
any importance, the appearance of persons of
wealth, rank or education is to be found; while
the extensive plains of the country are entirely
left to the possession of uncultivated boors. From
the effects of a military education and a despotic
government, it is considered as an instance of
degradation, for any branch of a family of distinction to engage either in farming or commerce. They are all educated for the army;
and, in that situation, alone, can they exist. In a
moral point of view, this distinction of rank must
more or less prove destructive to the state. It

encourages a mode of education favourable to despotism, and destructive of commercial, as well as moral improvements. Man, trained from infancy to follow the career of war, loses, all attachments to individual spots, and, only lving in the expectation of meeting the enemy,—the study of the arts is neglected.

The agriculture, in this part of the country, can scarcely be expected to equal that of more improved countries, as long as the present degraded state, in which it is held, continues. An individual proprietor may partially induce his tenants to altar their mode of farming, but, as he seldom resides on his estates, his orders are neglected, and he is led to believe, that the attempt is useless. Until the government itself gives the command, and enforces it as a law, that such means ought to be pursued, and that only the new invented and most approved implements in agriculture be used, the present system will never vary. Plans must be drawn up, and strictly followed. Officers of sufficient knowledge should be appointed to mark the improvements, and to instruct them, as well as to reward individual attentions. All the old machines in use should be abolished, and the native artizan should be instructed in the knowledge of making no others, but those of other countries. Schools should also be instituted, solely for practical farming;

and the young farmers ought to labour as servants, and afterwards be dispersed. as inspectors
and stewards.

The soil is naturally either arid or wet, and
would consequently require considerable attention and care to enrich it. The most irregular
method pursued here, is the promiscuous assemblage of crops. Neither ditches nor fences mark
the extent of a field, nor scarcely are the divisions of ridges used; this perhaps is of very little
importance, particularly in dry situations. The
crops of rye, barley, and buck weat may be seen
occupying alternate spaces, while their seeds are
constantly mixing with each other. Hemp and
flax, which are the greatest source of wealth to
the proprietors of land, in this country, we scarcely observed along this line of our journey. The
fields are ploughed in any direction the horses
chuse to drag the plough, but, in most instances,
the furrow is drawn in an oblique manner across
the breadth of a ridge, while the next space is
done in an opposite direction, and the whole
field appears ploughed in a zig-zag manner. The
furrow turned up is scarcely of sufficient depth
to reach the moisture. After the seed is sown, a
harrow is used, formed of the small branches of
the fir tree, which pulverises the soil so much,
that, with the shallow furrow, it soon becomes a
bed of dry dust. By these means the roots have

not sufficient hold, and the crops are consequently short and delicate. Manure is scarcely ever
used, nor any green crops, such as turnips, potatoes, or even pulse. The common oats in use
are the black kind. Were potatoes more generally cultivated, it might succeed better than the
grain, and prove a more substantial food to the
inhabitants, during their long, and oft repeated
religious fasts.

The rearing of black cattle forms no part of
their rural pursuits, beyond what is sufficient to
supply them with milk. The markets of St. Petersburg and Cronstadt are annually supplied
with cattle from the southern provinces of the
empire, a distance of one thousand to fifteen
hundred wersts; and, in winter, the cattle are
killed at an equal distance, and brought in a frozen state. The calves which are produced here
are killed to supply the market in summer; in
consequence of which no increase of stock takes
place. The great cause of the want of black
cattle, along this line of country, does not arise
from any want of pasturage, which, in summer, is
abundant, but from the impossibility of supporting them during the long winter, when so little
food is raised by means of farming. No part of
the country is more advantageously situated than
the present, to be benefitted by this circumstance. The great demands which the two capi-

tals require, must present a ready market to the
grazier, and those large sums which are annually
paid to those from the neighbourhood of the Crimea, might be retained, and the circulation of
money become more abundant. The first step
towards the increase of black cattle, should be
the gradual decrease of horses. It is well known
that, from one hundred to two hundred horses are
to be found almost at every stage. From this
useful animal the peasant derives his present livelihood, and which consumes, during the winter,
all the food raised by their scanty state of farming, and thus presents an insurmountable barrier
to their keeping any other animals, but one or
two milch cows. It has been already mentioned,
that the immense quantity of tallow exported
from Russia, would be sufficient to shew to what
an extent the rearing of cattle must be carried ;
yet we are here deceived, and can only consider it
as collected from the most fertile of the southern
provinces. The introduction of sheep could not
be attended with so much immediate benefit,
owing to the immense extent of forests, which
every where cover the face of the country ; and
the quality of the herbage is not exactly suited
to the nature of the animal. Another defect,
which ought to be abolished, is the distillery of
spirits from corn. It is carried on to so extensive
a degree, that, scarcely is there sufficient grain

left for the manufacture of bread. This pernicious spirit is distilled chiefly from rye, and the
quantity distilled in the different provinces is in
proportion to the quanty of grain raised.

The greater proportion of the peasants being
slaves to the nobles, the land is portioned out to
them, according to their own interests. Except
the peasants on the estates belonging to the Emperor, and some others, who have been emancipated, the rest still continue, as a part of the land,
and are either disposable with, or without it.
Those who are slaves generally give so many
days labour to their master, in the cultivation of
the soil; and those crops, which the traveller
passes along the road, are not to reward the industry of the peasant, but are reserved as a part
of the income of the noble proprietor and, while
the poor Russ beholds the waving corn, smiling
under the labours of his hands, he knows it is sacred from his touch, and that he may starve in
the midst of plenty.

From the indifference, and even oppression,
with which the nobles treat their slaves, arises
one of the many causes which induces them to
avoid residing, in the country, among them; as
their conduct would soon meet with that fate,
which tyranny must ever dread. The peasants
of the Crown are more independent than those of
the nobles, and consequently more industrious;

their rents are fixed, but the others are compelled to pay in proportion to their improvements. Whether they act as farmers, mechanics, or postillions, they, in proportion, pay from the rate of the emoluments which they receive from their various occupations ; even to that of begging ! With so slight inducements to industry, it is no wonder that we observe such a striking degree of idleness among the peasants, particularly when they have no excitement to become industrious. Those few who, by trade, amass money, are a prey to the needy proprietor, who borrows, but forgets to repay ; and those who are freed-men, meet with a similar degree of taxation from the officers of the government.

During our journey from St. Petersburg, the weather continued extremely hot, varying from sixty-one to seventy-two degrees of Farenheit. The nights were regularly cold and foggy which always increased towards sun-rise.

Taking leave of Tweer we continued our journey towards Moscow. The first stage was through a flat country of light sandy loam. The crops are extensive, but not luxurient. Extensive plantations of dwarf birch and elms cover the surface of the surrounding country, which, in the distance, becomes gently diversified into hill and dale.

Wosskresenskoe is marked as a borough. It

contains about three hundred inhabitants, is built entirely of wood, and exhibits a very mean appearance. From this stage we proceeded through a country still flat and uninteresting. Little or no part of the road is made, but passes, as a track, through loose sand. Before it reaches Zadivovo it crosses the Volga by a bridge of boats; and, immediately after, enters the government of Moscow.

In the evening we reached the district town of Klin. This stage is diversified by one or two small villages, and a paper-manufactory. Round Klin, the country is more allotted to pasture than to grain, and yet few cattle meet the eye, Klin, though a district town, is yet one of the smallest of that class on the road. It consists of two streets of wooden houses, which cross each other at right angles, and form a square in the centre; in which is now building a large brick church. In the square are a few brick houses, and a range of shops. The town stands on an elevated situation on the north side of a small river, which is crossed by a floating bridge of planks.

In the neighbourhood of Klin were some excellent country seats, but they were destroyed by a party of the French army from Moscow. The people do not appear either so well cloathed, as in the province of Tweer. Their features

are sharper, and of a darker complexion. The
hats, worn by the men, are high crowned, with a
broad slouching brim. The dresses of the women are not so rich as those at Torjock, but
equally gaudy and cumbersome. The head is
bound round by a broad gold lace, which is raised
in the form of a helmet, and fastened behind by
a silk kerchief, hanging loosely over the back.
The shirt sleeves are extremely wide, and terminate at the wrist by a deep red frill, embroidered
over the shoulders with a similar colour. The
short loose petticoat secured under the arms,
thickly plaited, and the rolled stockings, with the
addition of cords, bound round the legs, complete their dress.

At Klin we engaged one set of horses to take
us to Moscow; the distance is three stages, or
eighty-one wersts, which was to be performed in
twelve hours. The first stage was rather uneven;
the birch and fir trees were more healthy and
larger, the crops also appeared more luxuriant.
At Pecheki we observed one of those temporary
palaces which Potemkin built for the accommodation of Catharine, when she undertook her celebrated journey towards the Crimea.*

The road from Pecheki to Tschernaia-Griasse,
the last stage, is almost a track through forests;

* Segur's Life of Potemkin.

between it and Moscow, the road is flat, and passes through a waste of uncultivated ground, spread over with birch. Nearer to the city it enters an immense flat common, without either a shrub or a hut to be seen, and which, in many places, is broken up into deep pits, from which a regular supply of sand is carried to the city. Nothing can be more barren and neglected than the appearance of this entry to the ancient capital. The soil is a stiff yellow clay; but, near the city, it becomes fine yellow sand. Over this extensive plain every traveller chuses his own track, until he reaches the barrier gate of the city. The distance from St. Petersburg to Moscow is seven hundred and twenty-eight wersts.* Only three small towns (Novogorod, Vishnei, Volotshok, and Tweer) occur in this long line. Miserable wooden villages occasionally fill up the dreariness of a flat, uncultivated country, mostly covered with forests, and morasses; through which the greater extent of the road passes in a straight line.

* About five hundred and twenty miles.

CHAP. VII.

Moscow, September, 1814.

THE toils and fatigues of a long journey were now to have some repose; the long looked for object of our cares and wishes was approaching, and the spires of Moscow soon hailed our gladdened sight. When the weary pilgrim with tired limbs comes in view of the turrets of Medina, he stops at the distant fonts of the city, and his zeal and strength are awakened. In like manner did we, at view of this holy city, feel refreshed and restored. We forgot our toils, our sufferings, and our cares; and a full and fresh tide of enthusiasm carried us along.

And here we must pause: before us stood the ancient and once proud seat of the mighty Czars; the once grand emporium of the North, where the fates of kings and nations were so proudly wielded; where despotism had so long reared its crest; where vice had so long held her court; and where the tides of wealth and luxury were for ages rolling in as to a common centre. Here was to be seen every thing costly and magnificent; the grand mart of European and Asiatic

splendour, the pride and envy of the northern
world.

This is the spot we now gazed on; what a
change! lowly and prostrate it now lies, its
crumbling towers, falling into decay, its proud
banners torn from their burning walls, and scat-
tering the shivered fragments to the hollow winds
—its temples torn—its gates demolished—its
houses ransacked—its streets laid waste. One
sad and sorrowful picture of desolation is thrown
around: wherever the traveller turns his wearied eye it is still the same; he will yet see the
dæmon of ruin stalking abroad in all the majesty
of devastation, and treading on those mouldering
piles, where perched the proud eagle of the
north; he will still see the sorrowing inhabitant
sighing over the ruins of his roofless dwelling,
and clinging to the yet warm ashes of those sacred shrines, where so lately he had invoked his
fathers and his saints.

Here indeed was a melancholy picture; on
every side we turned our eye, fresh objects of
dilapidated splendour presented themselves;
fresh scenes of falling greatness were strewed
around, and as we gazed on the crumbling heap,
we needed not memory to give outline; we
needed not fancy to give colouring,—the picture
was complete.

And who can look on this sorrowing group

without one sad, one solitary sigh? Who can muffle himself up in his cold-blooded *philosophy* and look on with unconcern? Can his eye be as unmoved as the ruin on which it is gazing; cannot the wreck of fallen greatness shadow it with a cloud; cannot the wail of his fellow-man dim it with a tear? Happy, ye few, if such there be! your feelings may be envied, but ye have them not of nature!

The appearance of the city from the point at which we now were, is not equal to that from the opposite country; however, the innumerable spires and domes glittering in the horizon powerfully arrest and astonish the beholder. The extensive plain surrounding this part of the suburbs occupies nearly ten thousand acres, uncovered either by trees or houses: at a distance it is bounded by forests of birch. Here the army of Napoleon Buonaparte spread themselves, as a lawless band of ruffians, sharing the spoils of this devoted city. To this spot were conveyed every thing that could be snatched from the all-devouring flames; and even the helpless mothers and infants came to beg a covering to their nakedness, but who, as might be expected, were refused at the point of the bayonet. About two miles from the gate we passed the palace of Peterskoff, embellished by Peter the Great, and which he used as his favourite residence when at Moscow

It is a huge gothic brick building, encompassed by a circular wall, with regular bastions. One great and vast feature of desolation surrounds it; the vestiges of war are strewed around its mutilated walls. Here Napoleon fixed his head quarters, when he found the Kremlin no longer a place of security against the raging flames; and here he became the dupe of his own credulity, and brought on himself that contempt and disgrace, which his unwarrantable pretensions so justly merited. From this palace he issued those empty decrees, which trumpeted forth falsehood in all its unblushing colours, while his dastardly soul shrank with fear and meanness from the dangers which surrounded him.

Crossing the first barriers of the city, a small dry ditch, we entered the Sloboda or suburbs, and reached the gate of the second division, where we were received by the guard , who strictly examined our passports, and escorted us to the police, where we left them, and entered our names. Here money was necessary to afford an entry into the town, without delay and vexation, as at the other capital. The entrance to the city exhibits a general scene of ruin, and appears, from those parts of the houses now standing, to have consisted of brick and wooden houses, huddled together without any order or neatness. At present nothing more excites the appearance

of wretchedness and filth; as we proceeded, the
streets began to assume a more regular form, with
the remains of large and splendid edifices divided
from each other by mean hovels and gardens;
churches of the most singular and gothic forms,
with numerous gilded spires and domes, crowd
on each other; it is almost impossible by any
description to convey a correct idea of this singular appearance. All that ingenuity and religious enthusiasm could suggest, have been here
executed, exhibiting more the laboured effects
of rude show and expense, than elegance or utility. At the termination of the street by which
we entered the city, we ascended a gentle elevation, and approached a lofty and massive wall,
which appeared as the bulwark of an interior city.
This is partly supported by an earthern mound,
with a broad open space, through which a muddy
puddle runs, called the Neglina river. To the
right of this wall another immediately appears,
more massive, and on a situation more elevated,
and crowded with gilded spires and domes. This
is the bulwark of the Kremlin, and the central
part of the city.

From the circumstance of having engaged only
one set of horses to bring us from Klin, we found
on our arrival, that the postillion, being a stranger,
and the situations of the hotels somewhat changed,
he had considerable difficulty to procure a place

of accommodation. Every house of this description was crowded with persons, who had no
other place of shelter to enter. After considerable delays we established ourselves at the
Hôtel de Londres, opposite to the Kremlin gate.
In this house we were accommodated with a
suite of unfurnished rooms; a table and a few
chairs were procured, but neither beds, nor even
bedsteads, could be got. These are useless
luxuries where the people find a ready couch,
either on the floor, or on the ground. Every
Russian seems to travel with his household furniture, and from this circumstance, few, or no
preparations are made, at the different stages,
for their accommodations. From these advantages, the state of the country is somewhat an
excuse to those who live in it; but in a city so
long celebrated for its luxury and splendour, the
same apology cannot be offered. The destruction of the city may have made great alterations,
but this custom does not seem to have been affected by it.

Every thing here seems to be on a grander
scale than at St. Petersburg, but more rude and
irregular. The buildings assume a different
form and complexion, and the people a slight
difference of manners. Every degree of restraint seems to be less regarded; manners more
free and unrestricted, and a greater licence given

to every department of life, more conspicuous than in the other capital.

The city of Moscow is divided, like St. Petersburg, by a river, the Moskwa; which, however, scarcely deserves any other name than that of a muddy brook. It rises in the government of Smolensko, eighty miles west of Moscow, and after a circuitous course of two hundred miles, and assuming other names, it joins the Volga at Nichney Novogorod. The river is not navigable; but during the spring season, at the dissolving of the ice, flat barges are floated within the eastern suburbs of the city. It is crossed by a small stone bridge of seven arches, at the south end of the Kremlin; and by another made of wooden planks, at a short distance below the north end of the Kremlin: besides these two bridges, there is another, made of floating planks, in the suburbs, at which the barges are moored. The part of the river which flows along the east side of the Kremlin, is not fifty yards wide, and very shallow: here, during the hot days of summer, may be seen men, women and children, indiscriminately bathing together, in the most indelicate manner; while idlers are stationed on the bridges and walks, to admire, and laugh at an exhibition, so public and gross.

The finest and most commanding view of the city is to be taken from the Kremlin, which is the most elevated spot in Moscow. The view to the east is the most varied and the most beautiful: here the finest churches are seen, and the most regular buildings, while the surface of the ground is gently undulated. On the west side fewer churches are seen, but many magnificent palaces and gardens fill up an extensive space. The town is almost of a circular form, while the river forms the figure of the letter S on its southern boundary. From the Kremlin, a ridge of considerable height runs north and southeast, which gives the buildings on it a more elevated appearance than those on the west side of the river, which evidently appears to have originally been a morass. Frequent open spaces occur in various parts of the city, where gardens are laid out, and even corn fields. In many places the houses are built in such a scattered manner, and surrounded with trees and bushes, as to exhibit an appearance from a distance, not unlike the grave-stones in a churchyard—in other places small lakes and ponds are seen; from one of these, the Neglina river (as it is called) takes its origin, and used to fall into the Moskwa, at the south end of the Kremlin. The length of this river was nearly two miles; it is now completely dried up, excepting at one place where a puddle is formed for a few ducks. Another stream, called the Yauza river, is somewhat larger than the Neglina, but equally useless. None of the streets are intersected by canals, and the range of shops being situated near the river, the merchandize is conveyed by means of it to and from the city.

The most remarkable feature in the construction of Moscow is in its churches. It is said there were nearly one thousand six hundred churches in this city; every one differs from another in size, form, and ornaments. Few of them are large. Some are built purely gothic,—others Asiatic;—some European,—and others Tartarean.—In short, the most irregular combination of discordant architecture is every where exhibited. Many are mean paltry houses, others are really superb and magnificent. Still more numerous and fanciful are the spires and the domes which ornament the churches, and which point out many places of worship, that might otherwise be passed unknown. The number of spires and domes were calculated at between five and six thousand; these are either painted white, yellow, or green, or gilded with gold or silver, or covered with sheets of tin iron. Each spire or cupola is ornamented with lofty crosses, entwined with wires, in the form of a broad fringe. The crosses are divided by two transverse bars, the lower is always placed in an inclining manner. Over the crosses a huge figure of a spread eagle the emblem of the empire, is placed, and in many instances under the eagle is seen the Tartar crescent, marking the city to have been under their protection. The spires are much lower than those of other countries: some are not more than thirty feet high, and few above seventy to one hundred and thirty feet; except the spire of St. Ivan in the Kremlin, which is nearly three hundred feet in height. The filagree work and numerous little pillars, and architectural excrescences on every spire, take considerably from their height, and give them a very heavy, yet rich appearance. This is one of the most singular features in Moscow. A church may be seen with an insignificant body, not more than twelve feet high in the walls, yet supporting five to nine gilded or painted domes and spires. Every principal spire has from one to three tier of bells, and frequently nine bells are seen in one of the divisions. The continual jingling of the bells of different churches is heard throughout the day, and even the greater part of the night. The outside of the body of the churches is generally covered with large representations of the Virgin Mary, and of different saints. Over each door is seen an enormous painting of the Virgin Mary and the infant Jesus. Over the great entry of the cathedral of the Assumption of the Virgin Mary, in the Kremlin, is seen this particular representation of an extraordinary size, the infant in the mother's lap is nearly five feet in height! The paintings of other saints are yet more preposterous—before these the superstitious Russ is constantly seen offering up his prayers.

The interior of the churches are richly ornamented with paintings and precious jewels. The roof is generally supported by massive pillars, covered with figures of saints, and historical representations from the sacred writings. These pillars divide the body of the church from the sanctuary or shrine. The screen and folding doors, which divide the sanctuary from the body of the church, is the part most ornamented. Nothing can exceed the brilliancy and riches of these shrines. The many donations from pious christians are generally exhibited here. The most precious jewels and stones are carefully placed around the different saints, and revered with a degree of religious enthusiasm. In the centre of the skreen the folding doors are placed, which in many instances are entirely made of pure silver, independent of the valuable and precious ornaments, which on every spot add to its splendour. These doors are denominated the *holy doors*, which, during the service, are thrown open by some concealed mechanism, and the high priest appears before the altar in his richest robes, and the consecrated elements of their re-

ligion. This part of the service is very imposing.
The melodious tones of the concealed choristers
gently swell through the vaulted aisles. The
enthusiasm of the moment is raised to the highest
pitch, and the whole audience fall prostrate on
their faces. On the north side of the holy doors
the pictures of the Virgin is always placed, and
that of our Saviour on the south. The next is
that of the Saint to whom the church is dedicated.
Over the folding doors is seen suspended the
dove, as a symbol of the Holy Ghost. Before
the images of the Virgin and of Jesus, wax tapers
are suspended, and in many churches kept constantly burning. Each painting is crowned with
a glory, which, in many instances, is so richly
ornamented with precious stones, as to dart forth
the most sparkling rays, while the drapery glit-
ters over with jewels. The most valuable pictures are generally very old, and coarsely painted ; only the face, hands, and toes are seen. The
rest is always formed of a gold drapery, fringed
with pearls, emeralds, rubies and diamonds. Every
representation of the Virgin and the infant Jesus
are painted of a dark brown colour, while some
distinguished saints are painted with the most
light and delicate colours. Although there are
so many churches in Moscow, yet it is said that
a magnificent new one is to be erected by the
Emperor, in commemoration of the destruction
of the French army on the plains of Russia.

Such is a short description of the churches of
Moscow, which certainly is its most characteristic
feature, and particularly so at the present moment, when contrasted with the ruinous appearance of the other parts of this vast city. Many
of the churches were injured, some almost destroyed, but the greater number of them escaped
the dreadful effects of the conflagration of the
city. From being entirely built of brick, with
little or no wooden work connected with them,
they could not be so easily destroyed, as the
wooden houses, or those churches partly built of
wood. The whole city appears as one group of
spires, cupulas or domes. From being painted
in light colours or gilded, their appearance is remarkably shewy. If the spires had been loftier,
the effect would have been inexpressibly grand.
From the present state of the churches, the appearance of the town is but little altered. At a
distance, Moscow must present nearly the same
form that it did before the conflagration. But
what a sad and melancholy difference is seen when
passing along the streets; scarcely a house is
seen that escaped the all-devouring flames, except a small portion of the buildings in the division of the Bielgorod. The walls of the houses
are still standing, and in tolerable preservation;
from this the original form of the city might be
imagined, but all that singular contrast of wooden

huts and mean hovels are completely destroyed.
The blank places are therefore the greater, and
more numerous. The walls of the houses now
remaining shew them to have been of a most extensive and superb form. Every other house
seems to have been a stately palace in size and
structure ; but now only broken walls, roofless
houses, and gaping windows, remain in solitary
and deserted grandeur.

All the houses seem to have been stuccoed
and washed with different colours ; the roofs were
either of wood, or iron, or tin, and generally
painted green. Almost every house is surrounded with endless tiers of pillars and piazzas. No
view can be so truly diversified, nor more astonishing and wonderful than that of this city. To
admire Moscow it should be viewed from a distance ; from thence the churches, with their numerous glittering domes and painted spires,
seem to cloud the horizon. The appearance of
the city from the Kremlin is truly fascinating.
Hundreds, nay thousands of spires and cupolas,
varying in size, form, and colours, and grouped
in the most picturesque and irregular manner,
strike the eye with admiration and delight : added to this, the solemn and constant tones of the
ponderous bells, echoing through the vaulted
canopy of heaven, like the distant thunder !

What must not this great city have been be-

fore the infamous invasion of the French. Before that unhappy period, it was said to have
contained upwards of three hundred thousand inhabitants, with the greater part of the Russian
nobility, and the merchants of wealth, besides a
promiscuous assemblage of foreigners from all
quarters of the world. It was the scene of luxury
and parade, but never of elegance, taste, nor literature. Vice took the sway, and virtue was
lost in one general wreck of morals. The city
was frequently stiled the *Holy City;* from the
number of its religious edifices, and the imposing
appearance of the priests and mode of worship,
it might not unjustly be looked upon as such
But here the extremes of religion were contrasted by the extremes of vice. Here it is held too
common, and becomes only a mechanical duty,
which is no sooner over, than all restraint is removed. Profligacy of manners, and a promiscuous hostility to all the refinements of virtuous
delicacy, too often deadens the religious feelings,
though the routine of its duty is mechanically
performed. The depravity of manners, and the
vices of Moscow, could scarcely be credited,
were it not presented before the very eyes
of all!

It is impossible not to contemplate even the
external character of this city, and its hallowed
temples, without a certain degree of reverence

and religious feeling—there is a kind of scenic grandeur around it highly imposing; and on no other human constitution, perhaps, has this more effect than on the Russ. A stranger would here say that the Russ, and his religion, were formed for each other, but he would be puzzled to say which was formed first; both are simultaneous; both harmonize with each other; and in forming an estimate of Russian character (either as it is, or as it has been,) this is the most faithful and important guide we can have.

When the human mind becomes, from various causes, so gross and unenlightened, as to totally do away with religious toleration, it becomes necessary to appeal to the common senses; " outward and visible signs" must be exhibited, in order that " inward and spiritual grace" may be formed. The Russ must have his eyes and his ears excited; his saints and crosses must be gaudy and gilded; his bells must ever jingle; his incense must burn around him;—this is the manufactory of his enthusiasm; these are the ingredients of his adoration; and without these he cannot " walk in the holy way."

Hence it is, perhaps, that this city has afforded so perfect an illustration of that connection, which subsists between extremes of religious zeal and extremes of vice—between fanaticism and profligacy.

As all the principal buildings, &c. were destroyed by the late fire, it cannot be expected that any description of what they were can be faithfully given. The houses appear to have been extremely large, and generally terminated at each corner with large wings, or circular colonnades; pillars of every description, and statues, every where appear to have added to the general effect. Painted railings, playful fonts, and cooling grottos, on each side invited the attention of the stranger; while numerous and really superb china vases contained the most delicate exotics and fragrant shrubs : but now all these are strewed around in silent neglect, and their mutilated and withered forms bespeak the confusion and horrors of an invasion.

From the regularity of the divisions of the city, and that of the streets, the whole town might be superficially seen in one or two days, but it would require a residence of many weeks, to form a correct judgment of the whole. Every day opens new and pleasing scenes; the singularity of its churches gives an endless variety and beauty to the general scene. It is perhaps one of the most extraordinary cities in the world, and must impress the mind of every stranger, with lasting remembrances of its singular features.

The scite of the town is by no means a level.

The ground on which the Kremlin stands is nearly one hundred feet above the level of the river. Another ridge, equally high, crosses it at right angles. Towards the suburbs, the buildings are widely scattered, the surface of the ground more flattened, and divided into extensive fields of growing corn, tracts of wood, convents, monasteries and palaces. The view up the river is remarkably beautiful, and perhaps one of the finest seen from any part of the city. Its banks are richly cloathed with the delicate birch, while numerous gilded cupolas, in every avenue, contrast their gay and glittering forms, with the green foliage of the forest.

In this charming landscape is situated the nunnery of Devitchney. We visited this religious establishment the evening of our arrival; an aged nun invited us to prayers the following morning. Here we saw the sisterhood assembled in the chapel. Their devotion was calm and solemn, but whether sincere or not, a less fastidious observer might have construed certain looks and signs, as evident tokens of love of life, beyond the cold embrace of the altar; and piety and virtue might have blushed to own many of the fair recluses of Devitchney among their votaries. The service being finished, the lady Abbess honoured us with her conversation; and we had the pleasure to breakfast with our former acquaintance. Here we were treated in a cell, after the manner of anchorites, with milk and fruit. The nunnery contains at present upwards of an hundred nuns. Its rules are neither strict nor particular. It admits wives, widows, and unmarried females, who only are permitted to take the veil. They reside in cells ranged under the wall which surrounds the buildings; their dress is entirely black, with a long train. The nuns who have taken the veil are distinguished from the rest, by wearing on the head a high conical velvet helmet. The building of the nunnery is that of a large and shewy gothic structure, without much design or neatness. It consists of a large square wall with regular towers, encompassing the churches and other buildings. The gateway through the wall is remarkably fine. There are two churches covered with numerous gilt cupolas, in the centre of the square, besides an elegant minaret—the spots selected for the interment of the dead, are placed immediately opposite to the windows of the nuns' apartments. From the circumstance of our presenting a small donation of money to the establishment, our names were written on a slip of paper, and placed before a distinguished saint, and a certain number of wax tapers were ordered to be lighted in respect to the gift.

The interior of the churches was completely destroyed by the French, who converted them

30

into hospitals for the sick and wounded of their
army. One of them is nearly restored to its
former splendour, while the other remains in a
state of ruin. We could not avoid remarking,
with what detestation the *nuns* mentioned the
name of Frenchman!

There are several other nunneries and monasteries in the environs of the city—none of them
appear to be so rigid in their laws, as those of
Catholic countries. In the chapels of those nunneries, the service is always performed by one
of the priests, and the chanting by the nuns,
which has a very impressive and delightful effect.
Instrumental music is not permitted in the Greek
church of this country, but which is admirably
substituted by the finest singers.

Moscow is regularly divided by walls and
ditches, into five divisions, *viz.* the Kremlin—the
Khitaigorod—the Bielgorod—the Semlainogorod—and Sloboda. From the regularity of these
divisions, it is impossible for a stranger to find
any difficulty in traversing all parts of the city.

The Kremlin, which is nearly the central part
of the city, stands on an elevated ridge of ground,
on the west side of the Moskwa. It is the citadel
or fortress of the town, and easily commands all
parts of it. This was the first part of Moscow
that was built in the twelfth century, more from
accident than any design in its noble foun-

der, to lay it as the foundation of a future capital. The beauty of its situation and the surrounding country, induced the future sovereigns of the country to strengthen its situation, and fix in it the royal residence. From that time the infant city gradually increased in size, and swelled around, until Peter the Great removed the seat of government to St. Petersburg, and after that period it became more the residence of discontented nobles, and those who did not chuse to be eclipsed by the superior splendour of the Court. From the singularity of so many parts of the town being walled in, one within another, it bears marks of those ages of feudal despotism, when every chief lived within his fortified castle, while his numerous dependants sheltered themselves under its bulwarks. As the retinue and followers augmented, the buildings increased to such extent, as in time to require a similar bulwark, and thus became an enclosed city. Without these walls, new suburbs would be raised, which would increase in extent to the former, and ultimately require a similar fortification, and so on. This appears to have been the cause of the present outline of Moscow (the Kremlin forming as it were the kernel of the nut;) and, probably had not St. Petersburg been reared, what is now the exterior boundary of the Sloboda or suburbs, might have been raised to a wall, and new suburbs, and a larger circumference taken in. The extent of the wall which surrounds the Kremlin is about a mile and a half—that which encompasses the third division, or Bielgorod, is about five miles, while that of the Sloboda is nearly twenty-five miles. Only the Kremlin and Khitai-gorod are walled in—the third division or Bielgorod appears to have been surrounded by an earthern rampart, but which has been partly levelled. The external boundary of the suburbs is a narrow dry ditch, about three feet deep.

Of these different fortified parts of the city, that of the Kremlin is the most conspicuous, and the most singular. Here the ingenuity of the artist has been displayed to its utmost extent, and the riches of the state deposited. Within the once sacred walls of this spot, the mighty monarchs of the empire held their court; and here the most dignified ministers of the church shared the pomp and splendour of the Imperial court. The most prominent buildings in the Kremlin are the churches, the imperial and patriarchal palaces, and the arsenal. The great cathedral does not equal the expectation of a stranger; it exhibits an oblong square, lost in the disproportion of the height of the wall; the roof is surmounted by numerous large gilded cupolas, each of which supports a magnificent cross richly ornamented, with curious devices. The

interior of the church is extremely rich in gildings and colours, but heavy and badly arranged.
Opposite the cathedral is seen the cathedral of
the Assumption of the Virgin Mary. It is larger than the other, but similar in design. In it
are seen suspended from the roof nine massive
chandeliers of silver, and some very beautiful
paintings. Among the most valuable of these
paintings is a head of the Virgin, richly studded
over with jewels and precious stones, and kept in
a gold box, near the altar—this venerated picture
is shewn to every stranger by one of the officiating priests, and who regularly demands a dona
tion for the miracles which it wrought. In this
church are seen the tombs or stone coffins of the
patriarchs, covered with black velvet. In this
cathedral the Czars are generally crowned ; and
interred in the other. Between these churches,
and nearly in the centre of the Kremlin, stands
the spire of St. Ivan, the highest building in Moscow. The body of this church was completely
destroyed by Napoleon's order, but again nearly
rebuilt on its former plan. The spire is built of
a circular form, and about 300 feet high. The
top terminates by a large conical shaped cupola
richly gilt, and surmounted by a huge plain cross.
The present cross is a substitute for the former
one, which being made of pure silver, was seized
by Buonaparte. From the height of the build-

ing, and its ruinous state, it was thought a dangerous attempt to take it down. Napoleon offered a reward to any one who had sufficient courage to accomplish it. A native Russ it is said performed the sacrilegious deed, and the silver cross became the property of the invader, but which was recovered before his flight from the city. From the vile manner in which it was taken down, the present gilt one has been substituted. The spire is divided into three apartments which contain the bells; in the lower division are eight large bells, nine in the second, and thirteen in the third. The largest of these bells fell to the ground at the destruction of the church, but fortunately without any injury. This is the largest bell in Moscow, except what is called the *great bell*, now buried under the ruins of the church. From the upper division of this spire the most commanding view of the city is taken. The whole town, suburbs and surrounding country are distinctly seen spreading around in every direction, like a vast map, studded with the most grotesque buildings, while the Moskwa in all its winding, appears as a flat, muddy stream, meandering and struggling through the endless avenues of the city. Perhaps no sight can equal the diversity and grandeur of this. No smoky atmosphere clouds the trasparency of the azure canopy of heaven—all is bright and resplendent.

Near to the belfry of St. Ivan is seen the top of the great bell, which was cast in the reign of the Empress Anne. Many descriptions have been given of this extraordinary bell; only its top can now be seen, the pit in which it lay being completely filled up with the ruins of the church. The next bell, in point of size, to this, fell from the belfry of St. Ivan during the burning of the city : it received no injury. Its size is fourteen feet in length, twelve feet in diameter at its mouth, and about twenty inches thick. Its outside is richly relieved by historical representations in bas-relief.

This bell was presented by Boris Godono as a mark of his piety, and which was accordingly measured by the magnitude of the offering. It has always been considered a profound act of religion to present a church with bells ; the tongue or clapper of the bells are slung by means of leather bands, and are moved by ropes, so as to strike the sides of the bell.

Besides these churches, there are the convent of Ischudof, and the church of the Holy Trinity, and some small chapels. The church of the Holy Trinity forms the principal gateway, or entry to the Kremlin from the Semlainegorod division of the city. In this church the body of a distinguished saint is placed ; and in respect to his remains, every individual passing under the

portal is compelled to uncover his head. Besides the churches, convents and monasteries, the
Kremlin contains the palaces of the Czars and of
the patriarchs, with the arsenal and some other
modern buildings. None of them are particularly grand. Within the walls of the Kremlin
there are no less than one hundred and eight
spires and cupolas : of these forty-five are richly
gilded, the rest are painted either green, red, or
white.

The house in which Napoleon lodged is the
most modern and elegant building in the Kremlin. The view from it is most extensive. In
front of the house are ranged the guns taken
from the French army during their retreat from
Moscow. They are placed on the ground parallel to each other, with tickets affixed to each
division, marking the time and place where they
were taken. The first line comprehends sixty
beautiful pieces of light artillery, with Napoleon's initials on each ; the other divisions contain the guns of all the kingdoms and states of
Europe, of various dimensions. Altogether
there are eight hundred guns, the glorious trophy of the Russian conquest ! Among these guns
are seen some that have long been the object of
the traveller's notice, as part of the curiosities of
the Kremlin, but which do not (more than the
bells) deserve those vain eulogiums, which have
been repeatedly applied to them.

It is impossible to give any particular description of the palaces or riches of the Kremlin, it is only the bare walls, ruinous and deserted, that now invite the stranger's curiosity. When all hopes were banished from the ambitious and discontented mind of the French ruler, and when he found that he could no longer maintain his usurpation of the seat of the Czars, he determined on destroying what he had not the courage nor strength to defend. The beautiful church of St. Ivan fell as the first sacrifice to his revenge. The walls of the Kremlin were next mined : the explosion took place, but from its immense thickness, only a part of it was destroyed. The north-west angle with two fine spires was completely destroyed, occupying nearly one hundred yards in extent. On the east side, next to the river, are two considerable breaches. The rest of the wall is perfectly entire. Many parts of the wall are nearly forty feet in thickness, and in general from twenty to thirty feet in height. The top of the wall is divided into a number of gothic loop-holes, and at regular distances by gothic spires. There are six gates by which the Kremlin is entered, though only two of them are used. A new and elegant promenade was lately finished between the east wall and the river, which adds greatly to the beauty of the Kremlin, from what is represented in old drawings. The Kremlin

31

has long been considered, by those who have
not beheld it, as a spot of uncommon magnificence and extent. It certainly does not answer
that high description which the traveller is led
to expect. The buildings are numerous, but
they are heavily constructed, and grouped together without order or design—every thing is
sacrificed to mere shew of gildings and useless
cupolas.

The annexed drawing of the Kremlin is copied
from a print of *Guerard de la Barthe*, done in the
year 1799. At that time the present pier was
not built along the side of the river ; and which
contained a row of trees. From the rigid strictness of the police, we were not permitted to take
any drawings of the city ; in consequence of it,
I have given this copy with the addition of the
pier, and parts of the wall destroyed by the
French. It is also to be regretted, from this circumstance, that so few views of Moscow are
given. The other drawing, of the churches,
was taken from the window of our hotel, and on
its accuracy the reader may rely.

Around the north side of the Kremlin is placed
the Khitaigorod, or second division of the city.
From the singularity of its buildings, it has been
called the Chinese town, or Tartars' town ; from
the circumstance of being either built during the
usurpation of the Tartars, or from the number of

Chinese merchants, who settled in the vicinity of the Exchange. It contains numerous churches, besides the range of merchants' shops, with the ruins of the university, several public buildings, and the printing-house, which last has been again repaired. The size of this division is nearly double that of the Kremlin, and is divided into regular streets, with the houses closely built together. The Khitaigorod, like the Kremlin, is encompassed by a massive wall and dry ditch, and entered by five gates. The most singular features here are the tradesmen's shops and market place. The Exchange fronts the Kremlin, and is calculated to contain six thousand shops, which are ranged on a plan similar to those at St. Petersburg, but on a smaller scale. During the sacking of the city, this part suffered the most, and which has been the only part of the buildings repaired—and these are but temporary erections. The conflagration of the Exchange and shops is described to have presented a spectacle of the most frightful description. The shops are ranged under covered piazzas, and lighted from the roof. From the number of these shops, a stranger might imagine the space which they occupy to be very extensive ; the reverse is the case : instead of seeing rooms of houses, containing the various articles of merchandize, we here behold paltry stalls, or centry-boxes, sufficiently large to hold the shopman, with his goods arranged around him in little covered boxes.

Every thing here is coarse and rudely fashioned; except the various attempt at imitation,—ingenuity and taste seem to be stationary, and have not changed for ages past. The street appropriated to the rag-shops and tailors is the most extraordinary sight in this department of trade; the street is covered with women, dressed in tattered silks, squatted on the bare ground, sewing, mending, cutting-up, or selling. The sellers have the rags and old garments fastened around their bodies; while ribbons and thread are suspended from a pad fixed on the head. All the various costumes of the nation, and from the east and south, are here displayed;—tattered garments of gold lace, ragged cloaks of velvet, and petticoats of coloured silks, hang around the filthy bodies of these women. In short, the court dresses of the Sultan—the finery of the seraglio —the rich robes of the priests—the uniform of the warriors—the sheep-skin tunics of the Kalmucks—the thick furs of the Baskirs, &c.—all are here exposed to sale. The manner of working and idling, sleeping and gambling, are wonderfully contrasted;—one man may be seen, with several tiers of boots fastened around his body, playing at chuckfarthing with another laced up in furs and silks;—again, another, like a portable kitchen (with tea and coffee-pots slung from his neck, over a charcoal grate, with cups, sugar, &c. stuck into a leather belt fastened round his waist,) is attentively engaged at chess;—or, profoundly crossing themselves, before some gilded picture of a saint. Idleness and sloth, knavery and superstition, are the offensive appearances of this singular place.

This division contains the greatest number of gothic churches, and between the cupola and cross of many of them is seen the Tartar's crescent. One of the most singular churches in Moscow is situated in this division, exactly opposite to the north gate of the Kremlin; it is named the church of the Holy Trinity, or the church of Jerusalem; it was built in the reign of Ivan Vassilievitch II, in the fifteenth century. The wall of the church is scarcely twenty feet in height, while the roof supports a massive steeple, and ten domes, variously painted, gilded, or covered with small pieces of green tiles. Each of the cupolas differ in size and design: some of them are shaped like an inverted balloon; others of a globular form—some are painted green; others doubly gilded. The interior of this church corresponds in irregularity with its exterior arrangement. Though situated near to the scene of the greatest havoc and destruction, yet it does not appear to have been in the smallest degree injured. The printing-house, also situated in this division, has been repaired.

The Bielgorod, or third division of the city, entirely surrounds the two former divisions. The only building of importance is the Foundling Hospital, which stands close to the banks of the river, at a short distance below the wooden bridge, as represented in the drawing of the Kremlin; it was intended to have been built of a quadrangular shape, but owing to the increased number of foundlings, and consequent expenses, only two of its sides have been finished. The present building seems to have entirely escaped the destruction which the rest of the city suffered. It was converted into an hospital for the wounded soldiers, and the children were dislodged; at present very few of them have returned, and, from late events, the institution has been prevented from admitting an equal number of children, or attending to those already under its protection, with that strict regard to their health and education, which it had formerly done. Before the invasion of Moscow the hospital contained nearly four thousand infants, they were divided into different classes, according to their ages, and received an education scarcely inferior to the students of the academies in St. Petersburg. A most singular custom is allowed to prevail in this hospital, and indeed in many parts of the country, that of rearing the infants from the lacteal food of animals, instead of that from its natural parent. When the increase of children became so numerous, it was found impossible to procure a sufficient number of nurses; as a substitute goats were used, and the infant was placed under the animal to draw its nourishment.

Since the institution of this useful hospital, there has not been known a single instance of child-murder in the country. Whether it tends towards encouraging infidelity and vice, has been a subject of dispute; but which of the two evils is the worst, that of immorality, or murder? In few countries is this last crime carried to a greater extent than in England, and no where perhaps are the morals of the people more correct. Would a similar institution in England not remedy the evil complained of? The present morals of England are nearly as perfect as ever they can arrive at; nor is it likely that the principles of the people of Britain will ever become so immoral as that of their neighbours on the Continent.

In this division are situated the public baths, which are formed on the same plan with those already described in St. Petersburg, but less commodious and clean; the same indiscriminate mixture of all ranks of people are here seen, and both sexes seem to bathe, though in different apartments, yet without any delicacy or restraint. Nothing can be more odious than these public exhibitions; independent of the warm baths, the open river is one of the most frequented places by all classes—here men, women and children, promiscuously blend together in the muddy stream.

The remaining divisions, *viz.* the Semlainogorod and Sloboda, encompass the others by a vast circle. The buildings are very irregularly constructed, and often divided by broad fields and gardens, filled with trees, which give a delicate and refreshing appearance to the light coloured and painted walls of the churches. In these divisions many distinguished convents and nunneries are seen, and many mean hovels. Here the greater bulk of the common people reside, and their dwellings are generally in character with their rank.

Through all the streets a great part of the rubbish and ruins of the houses are cleared away, but extensive tracks of desolation yet cover many places. A few of the houses are partly repaired, and many new wooden ones are put up. In twenty years the greater number of the houses may be restored to a habitable state, and the town (from the preservation of the churches and spires) may appear as beautiful as formerly; but the splendour and magnificence of Moscow is perhaps for ever gone ! From the annexed drawing the reader will observe the present state of the churches, &c. which was taken on the spot, from the window of the hotel in which we lodged, without the least alteration. In this view the body of the houses are concealed, and only in particular parts are they distinguished as ruins. Nothing can be more astonishing than the general effect of the conflagration. From the local situation of the houses they must have been individually set on fire, as there are many instances of houses now standing, without having received the least injury, though all around them remain a mass of ruins ; even the trees in the gardens, &c. have recovered their foliage. At the destruction of the city, most of the principal inhabitants fled to the country and neighbouring towns, while the greater bulk of the common people remained, and many foreign merchants. It is computed that the present population of the city amounts to one hundred and fifty thousand.

The amusements of the city are at present very limited, the theatres being completely destroyed, also the public walks. A wild savage exhibition of wolves and bears, are every afternoon presented to the people, in different parts around the exterior circle of the suburbs. The teeth of these animals are drawn out, and they are made to fight against each other—occasionally

32

a poor horse is fastened by a rope, and a certain number of bears let loose upon him.

Such was the extent and situation of Moscow when Napoleon Buonaparte first beheld it, and such is its present state. What a melancholy contrast between former splendour, and present ruin! Can future ages forget the infamy of such a deed? Can the historian plead for a conduct so base?—Impossible! The names of Buonaparte and horror, will ever be translated by each other.

Whether the destruction of Moscow was the effect of unbounded patriotism, or matter of policy, is a speculation that will long interest the politician. It certainly filled the minds of every individual with horror and revenge; but from the previous unshaken loyalty, and unabated courage of the Russians, it was scarcely a necessary act to stimulate them to further feelings of revenge against a foe, who had already given too many insults. The city might have been saved, and the same fate would have pursued the followers of Napoleon. If the provisions and storehouses had been destroyed, the French could not have remained longer than they did. It was entirely from the want of provisions that the retreat of the French army became necessary. Very few of the churches were destroyed; from the nature of their structure they could not be burnt, though considerably injured—these alone were sufficient to have contained one hundred thousand men. Besides, many of the public buildings and palaces were entirely built of brick, and many of the rooms arched with the same. Of these, only the roofs and windows were destroyed—and which could have been easily renewed from the neighbouring forests. It was the original intention of the Russians, only to destroy the magazines of provision, in the event of the enemy gaining possession of the city.—The stores were in consequence kept un-removed, until too late; and when the order was given to set them on fire, the frenzy of the moment carried the flaming torch to every house, and which cool judgment now condemns. The Exchange and store-houses were set on fire the morning of the day on which the French army entered. It partly communicated with the con-tiguous buildings, and all those houses and hovels constructed of wood, soon fell a sacrifice to the flames.

During the evening a violent storm arose, which continued during three days, and occa-sioned a rapid expansion of the fire—still these wooden houses were the only part of the city that suffered, with some occasional streets, where the houses were closely built together—but all those palaces and magnificent buildings, which stood in isolated situations, surrounded by gardens, so characteristic of Moscow, were all *individually* set on fire. It is reported by the present inhabitants, who remained in the city during its occupation by the French, that every afternoon at a certain hour, the flames burst out with increased vigour; and at those times, numerous reports of pistols were heard, which is asserted to have been used in firing phosphorous balls into the houses, and thus, setting them on fire. One part of the Bielgorod entirely escaped the flames, and is the only spot in the city that appears in its original state—otherwise every house, and every street, exhibits one continued ruin. All the walls remain, and many of them without much injury—but every house is roofless, and without either windows or doors. Many superb houses are completely demolished, particularly the theatres. None of the houses are as yet completely repaired, though a considerable number of wooden houses are building. It is improbable that Moscow will ever be rebuilt on a scale equal to its former magnificence. The sister capital is too favourite a rival, and it is a matter of policy in the government not to increase Moscow, in order to draw its wealthy inhabitants to St. Petersburg. Another obstacle against the immediate restoration of Moscow, is the increased extravagance of the nobles, and the immense expenses and sacrifices they have lately

undergone, in expelling the French from their
territory, and assisting in the security of a general peace ; this has greatly limited their incomes,
which depending on the production of the soil,
varies, according to the necessities of the times—
added to this, a strange antipathy to repair a
house once destroyed, or even to live in a palace
where a relation has died. This is one of the
causes, that many superb palaces are seen deserted by its noble owner, and filled with tradesmen.
It is now impossible for many of the nobility to
raise such superb palaces, as what their forefathers
have done. In those feudal times, the nobles
scarcely ever quitted their own country, and the
means of adding to the public and private debts
of the nation were less; and the rage of building
palaces and churches were more in fashion then,
than at present. The inhabitants were certainly
lulled into a belief, before the battle of Boro-
di o, that the French could not enter the city,
and it was not until after that eventful day, that
the destruction of Moscow was decided upon.
Dismay and confusion became general, the aged
and the weak immediately sought their safety in
flight, leaving behind them the greater part of
their wealth; had not this false security been
allowed to prevail, the properties of individuals
might have been removed, and the store-houses
alone destroyed. If this had been the case, the

French army could not have remained longer
than they did, and the city might have been
saved; except that Napoleon, in a fit of disap-
pointed ambition at the failure and disgrace of
his plans, might have ordered the city to be
blown up, as he did the Kremlin.

However, if we put aside our feelings of terror,
we must say, that the deed itself boasts of such
bold and frightful heroism, and furnishes such a
noble instance of the pure and wild passion of
patriotism, that future ages will mark it as one of
those acts, " which can never be wearied out by
time."

Unhappy and ill-fated city! may thy sufferings and thy sorrows plead not in vain, at the
altar of Him, who looks down from on high ;—
may thy vices and thy crimes be no more remembered—may they perish with thy ruins and
mingle with thy dust—may thy flames ne'er
cease to throw their lights around, till distant nations catch the spark, break their bonds, and be
free—and, as the winds, the hollow winds of
night, sigh along the grass that shadows thy
tombs, may they wander up to heaven, and
breathe thine orisons!

CHAP. VIII.

Moscow, September, 1814.

It is a much easier task to describe the boundaries and divisions of a country, than to investigate the origin and progress of its history. The latter is the province of the historian—the former that of the traveller. The extent of this immense empire, including the islands of the Eastern Ocean, is upwards of seven thousand miles in length, and its greatest breadth two thousand three hundred and sixty-three miles.

The Russian empire is generally divided into Russia in Europe, and Russia in Asia. This division is marked by the chain of the Uralian mountains, which extend from the fiftieth degree of north latitude, near the confines of the Kirguisian Desert, and stretch, in a north-western division, to the Arctic Ocean, opposite the island of Nova Zembla. The Asiatic division contains the greatest extent of surface; and the European the larger number of inhabitants. These great divisions are again divided into the southern, middle, and northern tracts, and they again are subdivided into fifty governments. In such a

vast extent of country, and, hitherto, so little
civilized in its most remote provinces, it must necessarily present a varied race of people, as rude
and uncultivated as the wilderness in which they
wander.   The mixed race of Fins, Poles, Muscovites, Tartars, Cossacks, Tchouwashes, Votiaks,
Ostiaks, Voguls, Kalmucs, Baskirs, Tunguisians,
Samoides, Kamtschadales, &c. in part tend to fill
up the population.

When we investigate those principles on which
the fabric of society is reared, those principles
which form the basis of political economy, by
which governments are structured and nations
connected, we are naturally led to consider the
feelings which actuated them towards each other,
and, consequently, to trace the effects resulting
from them.

It is not more than two hundred years ago, that
Russia began to emerge from a state of abject
barbarism, towards the first step of rude civilization.   Except on the western frontiers, where the
people had become somewhat civilized from frequent wars and predatory excursions, the greater
bulk of the people continued enveloped in all
the darkness of ignorance and barbarism: but
the seeds of Christianity began to grow apace,
and, from the more general intercourse with
other nations, and the introduction of the arts,
this great and almost unwieldy empire begins to

assume a more characteristic form, and may yet
become the mediator of Europe in physical,
though not altogether in moral strength.

Nothing has tended more towards the improvement and civilization of this country, than the
wars in which she has been engaged with the
neighbouring nations. The late campaign was
the means of sending thousands of the natives
into the fairest portion of Europe. Here they
beheld every thing new, every thing superior to
their own, and the height of civilization. Their
attention was excited; they could not but behold, and admire the superior excellence of
France, compared to their own rudely formed
country. Its effects have not been altogether
lost: many individuals have already given specimens of their imitative talent; and the country
at large may yet derive a benefit from its late
misfortunes.

It is not the object of the present pages to delineate the political history of this great country;
what is here detailed, relates in a more cursory
manner to the natural productions and advantages of the country at large, and in its relation
with others.

The vegetable productions at St. Petersburg,
and a slight observation on those in the intermediate country between the capitals, have been
already mentioned. In the neighbourhood of

Moscow, vegetables are raised in greater abundance than at St. Petersburg, and the fruits possess a richer and more delicate flavour. Both
the climate and soil, in this middle tract, are
more favourable to vegetation than in the more
northern latitudes of the country. Melons,
peaches, pine-apples, &c. are very plentiful, besides apples and pears of a most delicate flavour.
All the varieties of woodland berries, are very
common. The gooseberry alone seems to reach
the least perfection. The most delicate fruits
are all reared under glass. Hot-houses are remarkably numerous and extensive. It is not
unusual to see them, of several hundred feet in
length. Dwarf cherry-trees, &c. are planted in
pots, and in the season of bearing fruit, they are
placed on the tables of the nobles, and the company regale themselves with fruit from the tree.
The potatoes are in general round and small, and
do not appear to be cultivated with so much assi-
duity as some other vegetables, particularly cucumbers and garlick. These seem to be the
chief food of the poor people. The heaps of cucumbers and garlick exposed to sale in different
parts of the street, are almost incredible, and far
exceeds the quantity of potatoes or turnips. A
peculiar small yellow turnip with a smooth shin-
ing rind is very common; also a small apple,
which when ripe, becomes semi-transparent; but

which, when removed to another climate, loses this peculiar character.

Among the many singular customs of this country, that of blessing the apple, before it is allowed to be eaten, is a regular religious ceremony. As soon as the apples are known to be ripe, the high priest solemnly blesses the fruit in the most public manner, and not until after this ceremony can it be eaten. Cabbages and medicinal herbs are in considerable quantities; particularly the latter, which form the chief ingredients of the druggists' shops.

Vegetations in general is very rapid in this part of the country; but the soil does not appear of a rich nature, and the crops, in consequence, do not seem luxurious. The market is supplied with astonishing quantities of poultry. The common fowl, ducks, geese, and turkies, with wild water-fowls, and snipes, &c. are very numerous and remarkably cheap. The woods abound with several species of *tetrao*, or grouse; they are larger than those found in the highlands of Scotland, with a plumage more variegated and beautiful; but their flesh is tough, dry, and without flavour. This may arise from the nature of their food. Although many parts of the country is covered with a short heath, yet those birds seem entirely to frequent the forests. A peculiar species of snipe is also found here, nearly as large as a woodcock, and accounted a great delicacy.   Beef or mutton is less used at table than poultry.   In this respect it is of little importance what sort of food the table is covered with, as every dish is invariably cooked in a manner to destroy the natural taste of the food :—the whole, more or less, floats in oil.

The black cattle are supplied from the neighbouring provinces south of Moscow.   They are of the same breed which is forwarded to St. Petersburg; and are generally sold at two hundred rubles each.   The sheep are of a small, yet beautiful form; not unlike the figure of the fallow deer.   They have short tails, and hair instead of wool, and are remarkably large in the loins.   In the southern provinces the fine lamb's fur is obtained by cutting the young from the side of the dam.   Hogs are not numerous, though the ham cured here is superior to that of any other country.

Horses are in great numbers; they are uncommonly hardy and tractable.   They brave, without the slightest pain, the severity of the winter climate, which would be almost death to an English horse.   The common horse of the country is a picture of ugliness—a short bony animal, with a hollow neck and large head.   The larger horses are the result of a breed introduced by Peter the Great; they partake much of our Suffolk breed, but are more fiery and active.

No trait in the Russian character is so amiable as his humane treatment of his horse. Here, this noble animal seems to meet with that kindness and attention which his usefulness deserves. In no country perhaps in the world, is more attention paid to the breed of horses, than in England, and where they may be said to stand unrivalled ; yet it is a melancholy fact, that in no country does this useful animal receive such cruel and unmerciful treatment. The humane Russ knows not the use of a horse-whip. The soft sound of music is the only lash he uses to propel his horse forward : with him he is domesticated ; and the animal, by instinct, knows him to be his friend, and instead of avoiding, courts his acquaintance !

What relates to the natural history of this extensive country, will be found described with great care by many authors, and to whose works the reader is referred, also for an account of its geological history. In this last respect, so little characteristic of mineralogy has come within the observation of the present remarks, that no apology is requisite for the slight manner in which it has been treated. A country so uniformly flat and marshy offers but few features in geology; and, to enlarge on what is not particularly prominent, nor what cannot be brought to the advantages of man, is only an idle waste of time. Agriculture is the sole object which ought to in-

terest the legislature of this country. By it will
the wealth and population of the country be increased, and from its sources can the country be
enabled to maintain an increase of population.
Many obstacles, at present, prevent the gen ral
cultivation of the soil, but the natural advantages
which this country possesses will yet overcome
them all.

The facility of transporting the various productions of the soil, from one place to another
is so general throughout this country, that the
farmers and merchants must always command
an independence, unknown to the inhabitants of
those inland countries, deprived of the different
ramifications of rivers. Russia at present is more
of a military, than a commercial character, and
her warlike attitude is certainly very imposing ;
but it is possible that her population may yet
become unwieldy from its bulk ; and without the
aid of commerce and wealth, must, sooner or la-
ter, tend to demolish the fabric of her government.

No part of Europe is, naturally, better adapted for commerce than Russia. By means of the
extensive rivers, which flow through all parts of
the empire, the productions of the north can be
exchanged for those of the south, with the greatest facility.   The Baltic has now a direct communication with the Caspian and Black Seas ; and
even the connection with those to the Northern

Ocean has been found practicable. If the Island of Zealand were under the power of Great Britain, and in friendly alliance with Russia, the general productions of Turkey, Persia, Syria, &c. might easily be brought there, by vessels adapted to the navigation of these rivers, and thence exported to England. The shortness of the voyage, compared to the circuitous and dangerous navigation round by the Mediterranean Sea, and the Atlantic Ocean, independently of the security against dangers by storms and enemies, is a matter of the greatest importance to the commercialist. How much more valuable would this communication be, were the fortress of Gibraltar to fall under the power of any other nation, and the passage of the Straits become an object of dispute. A vessel, properly constructed, might sail from any port in Great Britain up the Baltic to Memel, thence ascend the Niemen to its source, and, by a canal which now joins that river to the Dnieper, at Pinsk, pass down its stream to the Black Sea. The whole of this voyage may be performed without an obstacle.* From London along this course, by the canal of Tonningen, the computed distance is about two thousand three hundred miles; and under favourable circumstances, the voyage may be performed in from

* The cataracts, near the junction of the Samara, being now almost removed.

two to three months. The other voyage, by the
Mediterranean, is nearly four thousand miles,
and liable to all the dangers of storms, and those
enemies which line both sides of the Mediterranean coast. Besides the junction of these rivers,
we have already noticed the junction of the Volga at Vishney Volotshok, to the Neva, forming
an uninterrupted communication between St.
Petersburg and the Caspian Sea, also from Riga
to Odessa, by the junction of the Duna to the
Dnieper, by the Beresinski canal. The Caspian
and Black Seas will also be united, when the canal of Kamushinski, which joins the Don to the
Volga, is completed.

To a commercial nation, like Great Britain, it is
a matter of the greatest importance to cultivate
the friendship of Russia ; both may mutually depend on each other. Their local situations greatly preclude them from any grievous aggression ;
yet, in a war, this nothern empire would be the
greatest sufferer. The advantages of Russia to
Britain is almost like those of America ; and, if
Great Britain were under the necessity of wag-
ing war with the one, the other could supply the
British markets with the necessary commodities
of these countries ; but if Russia and America
were to form a warlike league against Great Britain, the prosperity of our commerce would receive one of its most severe checks : even were

such an event to take place, still the immense and almost unknown riches of New Holland might be brought into more general use, and a substitute could be drawn from that country, equal to the loss of what is now mentioned.

The principal wealth of Russia depends on the natural productions of the country, and her riches are regulated by her internal commerce. Between the northern and southern divisions of the empire, is situated the largest, and the most valuable, extent of territory. In this middle division, the greater bulk of the population is to be found; the soil is better cultivated, and its returns are more certain. In this tract also, both the productions of the other two divisions are to be found, exclusive of the large quantities of grain, hemp, and flax, which form its staple commodity. Hemp and flax evidently, at present, appear to be the principal source of wealth to the proprietors; being more easily transported than grain, and better adapted to the climate, it becomes an object of attention and profit.

The great annual fair held at Makaroff, four hundred miles east of Moscow, regulates the prices of manufactured goods throughout the empire, and to which the interest and speculation of all the merchants are directed. This fair is the grand depot of trade between Europe and

34

Asia. It is held towards the end of July and
beginning of August. The silks and teas of
China, the productions of Persia, &c. are exchanged for those of Russia and the west of
Europe. The merchants of the east generally
exchange their goods for woollen cloths, and it
is a singular fact, that British manufactured cloth
alone is the most valued, while those of the Russian loom are generally refused. This year considerable discontent prevailed among the Chinese and Persian merchants, from the want of
British fine woollen cloth; in consequence they
sold their tea, silks, &c. for cash, and thus tended
to drain the Russian people of their specie.
However severe the Russian laws are against
the introduction of English manufactured cloths,
yet we find its use to be almost general in the
country, and so highly valued by the eastern
merchants as to be an object of considerable demand. This is one, among the many proofs,
how necessary it is for Great Britain to hold an
amicable commercial alliance with Russia; and,
if possible, to overcome the scruples of that
country against the introduction of British manufactured goods. This is a point of great importance to our manufactures. It also proves with
what facility we may acquire the rich productions
of Asia, regardless of the monopoly of the India
Company. Tea, silks, &c. are annually brought,

by the caravans, from Persia and China, to Makaroff, which is situated on the banks of the Volga; whence there is a direct communication by water to St. Petersburg and the ports of Britain. In short, through Russia, the commerce of the eastern nations could be carried on, without the protracted and circuitous navigation of the Atlantic and Southern Oceans. From London to Pekin in China, by the Cape of Good Hope, the voyage is upwards of fourteen thousand miles; —through Russia, the distance is about eight thousand miles : besides, the goods are brought by the natives the greatest part of the journey, free from all risks and dangers.

The Angora river takes its rise near to the north-western corner of the great lake Baikal not unfrequently called the sea of Baikal, from its size, being nearly three hundred and fifty miles in length, and about fifty in breath. Irkutsk, the capital of a Russian government of the same name, stands near the source of the Angora, and the lake Baikal. This is a large commercial town, said to contain nearly ten thousand individuals, and is the see of a bishop. It is the first great stage for the caravans, passing into Russia, from China. From this town there is a communication by water, to the Arctic Ocean, by means of the Angora, which joins the Yenessa. From the mouth of the Yenessa, through the straits of Waigate, to the longitude of Archangel, is not more than one thousand miles. From the lake Baikal to the mouth of the Yenassa is under two thousand miles. British ships trade regularly, in the summer months, with Archangel, and it is well known that the season is sufficiently favourable to extend the navigation to the eightieth degree of east longitude, to which the natives of Irkutsk might forward their merchandize. The river Oby, with the junction of the Irtish, &c. at the same time offers an easy conveyance for the productions of the extensive districts of Tartary thro' the same course. The communication and advantages of these rivers are pointed out, exclusive of the overland trade by the numerous caravans. Thus we find that the Yenessa, the Oby, the Volga, the Don, and the Dnieper, all have an uninterrupted communication with the Arctic Ocean, and the Caspian and Baltic Seas, and, by means of canals, &c. are more or less calculated to convey the various commodities of the countries through which they flow. The land carriage, between Moscow and China, is also facilitated by the lateral branches of these rivers, and established towns; particularly Ca-an, Tobolsk, Tomsk, Enisesk, and Irkutsk, which connects the great road from China to Europe, and is daily frequented by travellers.

Nothing tends to cramp the spirit and regular standard of commerce, so much as private mono-polies ; and, were the present suggestions more enquired into, and, in any manner, found prac-ticable, it might be unnecessary for the other commercialists of Britain to urge a termination to the charter of the India Company, as a com-mercial intercourse might be opened, through the medium of Russia, with our East-India pos-sessions, and those rich and productive nations. It is evident, that the expenses of fitting out large vessels for the India trade could be avoid-ed , also, the heavy insurances attending it. Be-sides, the exchange or barter of manufactured goods could be more easily accomplished ; as here the productions of various countries, and numerous individuals of all nations, meet at one spot, and at one time. The manufacturing towns of England might establish agents in various parts of Russia, export their own manufactured goods, and receive, in return, those valuable producti-ons of the East. If private jealousy, on the part of Russia, should prevent the establishment of such agents, it might be better secured in giving Russia a leading interest in the trade ; by which means the specie of Britain would circulate thro' her dominions, and add to her wealth, indepen-dently of her resources from her own producti-ons. The commercial relation between the two countries would be reciprocal; and the merchants of Russia would be dependent on the British markets. In the present state of things, the Russian nobles and landholders depend on their merchants, for the sale of their agricultural produce and their government; on both, for the revenue. When Russia, therefore, becomes acquainted with the advantages resulting from a commercial relationship with Great Britain, every class would firmly unite to maintain it; for the prosperity of Russia must, in a great measure, depend on that of the commerce of Great Britain.

Wollen cloths are in great request among the Tartars, Persians, and throughout the north of China. In all those countries, though at certain seasons of the year extremely hot, yet their nights and winter months are generally very cold, and the inhabitants require a warm, yet light dressing, and which only the productions of the British, or French looms, will answer. The woollen cloth of Russia is of too coarse and heavy a texture for those regions, and consequently does not meet with general demand. In this respect Russia cannot easily overcome the British m nufacture. We have seen that the breed of sheep, throughout the country, produce a wool extremely coarse, and unfit for general use: nor is it likely that an improved breed can be introduced. The present state of cultivation of the country prevents their increase, as well as the immense forests, and a long and severe winter.

The list of exports from Russia includes nearly two hundred different articles, in which are comprehended many of the productions of the East; and Great Britain alone seems to be the chief market.

" It appears that nine hundred and ninety-two ships cleared out from St. Petersburg in 1814, whose valuable cargoes were brought to Great Britain, with the exception of a small part carried to Ireland and some other quarters. The quantity of iron was 567,733 poods, of 36lbs. English, each; of hemp 1,261,765 poods; of flax, 405,723 poods; of tallow, 1,693,209 poods; of potash, 269, 089 poods; of diaper linen, 782,777 yards English; of sail-cloth, 34,833 pieces, 38 yards each; of ravenducks, 71,197 pieces. Of these commodities Ireland imported direct to

	Poods of Iron.	Hemp.	Tallow.	Potash.
Dublin	7,560	11,750	11,323	1,033
Londonderry	7,245	6744	8,219	246
Newry	1,115	3,794	9,548	960
Belfast	3,150	10,920	8,918	——
Cork	1,480	7,222	1,507	——
Limerick	5,040	1,575	329	——
Total	25,590	42,005	39.844	2,239"

These suggestions are the result of many inquiries from different merchants in Moscow, who
have been in the habit of trading with the eastern
merchants, and who have performed the journey.
We, who live in so insulated a manner, and hold
but little communication with these countries, are
apt to look upon any attempt to mingle with them,
as a task of a difficult and insurmontable description.   There is no country where an individual
could travel with greater safety, and facility,
than in Russia ; difficulties of travelling to Casan
and Tobolsk are only imaginary ; the roads are
open, and the stages regularly established.

The attentive observer cannot shut his eyes to
the advantages, which this country must derive
from her commercial relation with those countries.   There are few subjects which have crea-
ated greater perplexities and wealth, than the various systems on which our commerce is conducted ; and the suggestion of any mode whereby
such embarrassments could be obviated, and any
advantages gained, must surely be highly important, and well worthy the attention of our commercial legislature.   Even in a moral point of
view, these advantages would extend into those
remote provinces of Russia.   A spirit of cultivation and commerce would take place, and those
parts of the country, at present almost barren,
might become improved, the inhabitants more nu-

merous, and their fortunes enlarged. Even in this land of proscription, there must be many individuals, who, in the exercise of commerce, might ameliorate the pains of captivity, forget his absence from his native land, and his separation from his dearest relatives. While we congratulate ourselves on our elevated station in civilized society, we ought to look with an eye of pity on the sufferings of our fellow-creatures.

Several great roads lead from Moscow, towards the east, south and west. That towards the east passes by Makaroff to Casan, and towards Persia and China. The other, by Kaluga, stretches towards the Crimea and Constantinople. This is accounted the best road in the empire, and which passes through the finest provinces. The other great road is by Smolensko, to Warsaw. This was the route of the memorable track of Napoleon, and which we are to pass over, and detail in the order of travelling. It is accounted the least frequented path; couriers, &c. generally pass by Riga.

Before a traveller can arrive at Moscow, he must necessarily pass through a great part of the empire; and become more or less habituated to Russian manners and characters. He observes his fellow man fettered by despotism, humbled by slavery, and blinded by superstition.

Probably, from the disastrous effects of the

35

late war, the character of the inhabitants may be
considerably altered, particularly in this part of
the country. In Moscow, the nobles and persons of wealth, and their dependants, are gone;
also two-thirds of its population. The shops are
only temporary sheds—the streets exhibit a
gloomy range of ruined houses; and an air of
deserted melancholy, every where pervades the
city. This alone is sufficient to change the character of Moscow from what it originally was.
When the Earl of Carlisle came here, as ambas-
sador, it was the most magnificent and splendid
city in the world: at present it is the reverse.

The manners and characters of the Muscovites
are considerably different from those at St. Petersburg. Here they are more careless and less
ceremonious; and, not being under the controul
of the court, indulge in a ruder and more expensive magnificence.

Every thing bears the mark of age, gothicism
and rudeness; change of manners no more oc-
curs, than change of dress; in this respect they
seem not to differ: they are all clad alike—one
uniform costume is seen, only differing in quality
from those of the country—the one is a sheep-
skin tunic, fastened round the waist by a girdle;
the other of cloth, plaited behind like a woman's
petticoat. The hair of the head is cut according
to one shape, while the lower part of the face is

hideously disfigured by a goatish beard. The
women retain all the display of Asiatic finery
and gaudy robes; in their countenances they are
inanimate statues and highly daubed with paint;
in their figures unshapely, appearing as those
" wish to be, who love their lords."

The capital and the country present a strange
character of the nobles, and peasants or slaves.
The last is what particularly arrests the attention,
and are the most characteristic. The common
Russ, laying aside his filthy appearance, is often
a prepossessing creature. He is good-humoured,
lively, and submissive; seldom complains of any
hardship, and quietly bears every treatment.
He is however cunning and imposing, addicted
to thieving, knavery, falsehood and deceit. Many
of the Russians are seen in the streets, disgusting-
ly intoxicated; though many of them never taste
spirits. As an instance of this, we often could
not prevail on the postillions to take a glass of
brandy, though travelling all night. This is a
class of people who profess religious sentiments,
somewhat different from the established church;
in regard to drink they are strictly prohibited.
The offensive fumes of tobacco rarely annoy the
sense of smell; how different from that obnoxious
and detestable practice in Holstein, Hamburg,
and Prussia. The Russians are prevented from
smoking tobacco, lest they should carry it to

their churches, and soil the images of their saints
—as a substitute, they take snuff, but not generally.

A Russian's character is soon known, and by
proper means, may be used to advantage. Prevent him from imposition, and excite not his attention by too open a display of wealth; treat
him with occasional flattery, and particularly
allow him the freedom of speech, and he becomes
obliging and indefatigable. Like untutored sa-
vages, their passions are strong and uncurbed;
they will grossly abuse each other, vent their
rage in the most shocking and indelicate expressions, spit in each other's faces, but never fight;
in this respect they have a tender regard to their
feelings, and are finished cowards, yet they make
admirable soldiers, and do not hesitate to march
to the field of battle, or put a foeman to death.
They quietly submit to be beaten or caned without resistance, and which they daily receive from
those who have power. Money here is scarce,
and of high value, and hath a charm over the
Russ, more than over any other nation. For a
trifle his services may be commended; and, for
that trifle, he is most grateful. A postillion who
drives six horses for thirty miles, is content to
receive forty copecks, equal to six-pence. If a
rouble is given, about one shilling in value, he is
most animatedly thankful. He bows to the

ground, which he kisses, crosses himself and re-
peats a prayer. For so small a sum, what other
nation would be so thankful? A Prussian is never
grateful; the more he receives, the more avaricious he becomes. If he is offered a dram, he
takes it most greedily, but never expresses the
least sign of thanks. How different is the poor
Russ. I would sooner deal with one hundred
Russian postillions, than with one Prussian,
Saxon, or even Englishman.

Here, if a beggar accosts one, it is done in a
suppliant manner; if they receive the smallest
donation, they prostrate themselves before the
charitable donor, and mutter a prayer; but the
extent of their gratitude is always in proportion
to the value of the offering. All the postillions
regularly cross themselves, and offer up a short
prayer, before they mount the box; and regularly, as they pass a church, they take off their hats
and cross themselves. If it is a church of importance, they alight and perform their duty to the
Virgin.

When not actively employed, they immediately fall asleep, and the instant they are awaked,
they are ready to act. Beds they never use, the
pavement of the street, the floor of the stable, or
between the wheels of a carriage are all alike to
them. If a postillion has occasion to wait for
travellers, during any part of the night, he quits

his horses and lies down on the bare stones under the carriage, with his hat placed under his head as a pillow, and thus sleeps like a dog. All hours are alike to him; the rising of the sun neither awakens his indifferent soul to animation nor to delight; nor its setting, the softened melancholy of a departing day. The varying seasons of the year equally pass on, unnoticed, beyond the effects of its temperature. When it is hot he basks in the sun, almost destitute of clothes: in winter he enjoys the warmth of his sheep-skins, and the tide of his existence passes on, as that of a living machine.

They live both simply and frugally. A Russian is seldom observed to take a regular meal. They are passionately fond of garlick, onions and cucumbers, which they eat raw, similar to apples. The first thing he does in the morning, is to put a root of garlick into his mouth, which he considers as an excellent stomachic. The market-place is covered with garlick, and their food highly seasoned with it; and when they are met in the streets, the smell of garlick is most offensive. They rarely keep provisions in their houses. Every street has a number of bread-stalls, where it is exposed to sale; attached to the stalls is a grate of charcoal, over which is boiled different beverages; such as milk seasoned with herbs, mead beer, a kind of punch, and

sour quass. To such a spot the Russ retires
when the calls of hunger invite. There he pur-
chases bread which is covered with a little salt
and linseed oil, and receives a ladle full of the
beverage. In this manner he takes his daily
food, which occupies the smallest space of time.
Every morning the workmen, coachmen, and in
short all the common people, stop at the first of
these portable eating places, and appease their
hunger: little satisfies them. In the one hand
he holds his brown bread, and in the other the
ladle of sour beer. During the day they are always seen gnawing a raw onion, or cucumber.
In their living, they differ little from the brute.
Whenever they are hungry, they resort to a
bread or vegetable stall, where they immediately
settle their hunger; whenever they are wearied,
they lie down on the bare ground and fall asleep.

At all times, it is an unpleasant, as well as a
disgusting subject, to describe the effects of inat-
tention to cleanliness: here the stranger will remark it in various degrees:—the striking contrast between splendour and filth, &c. will, every
hour, present itself before his eyes; but, from
every intelligence which our military friends
have given us of the degraded state of filth, &c.
in Portugal and Spain, the Russians must be,
comparatively speaking, void of such nuisances.
Were it not from the structure of their houses

and dress, the Russians might be as cleanly as
their neighbours. A Prussian or German peasant's house, in the country, is as offensive to the
external senses as they are here, independent of
the fumes of tobacco.

To prevent the uneasy sensation of the attacks
of vermin, which crowd in their wool dress, the
common people are in the habit of rubbing their
bodies over with a quantity of greasy ointment.
The ointment is put into a bag, and each performs the operation of unction to the other; by
this means their skin becomes impervious to the
bite of these animals.

Though they are partial to music, yet they are
seldom seen to partake in the amusement of
dancing; this appears to arise rather from indolence, than from any aversion to so graceful an
exercise.

Though labouring under every degree of ser-
vitude, the Russian frequently displays the most
unbounded generosity. Many instances are
known, where the noble proprietor, being compelled to offer his estates to be sold to pay his
gambling debts, that his slaves have purchased it,
and restored it to him; this has been repeated in
the same family twice, and on a third ignoble
failure, the poor peasants purchased it again, and
with a degree of generosity scarcely paralleled,
presented it to a young noble of a highly distinguished, but poor family.

What is here mentioned entirely relates to the common peasant or slave. Those who are free, and are more independent, by commerce, become avaricious and less generous. The common peasant is a faulty character, in many respects; but this may be attributed to his station in life, his ignorance of learning and religious superstition; otherwise he is the most amiable character in the community. Those who are engaged in traffic, generally amass money. They dislike all foreigners, and consider it meritorious to cheat them. In short, cheating is not more considered here as dishonest, than honesty and honour, in England, is considered as a common thing. Every piece of goods, to be bought, must be bargained for, and can always be purchased at one half the sum the seller demands. I have frequently known them ask an hundred roubles, and afterwards give it below fifty. It is a rule always to offer less than the half of their demands, and they will even rather run into the street after the customer, than lose his offer.

The Russians cannot be said to possess any inventive genius; but their imitative powers stand almost unrivalled. The most perfect copies have been executed, both in paintings and in jewels, and which is often carried to such an extent as to elude every possibility of detection.

It is impossible to contemplate the Russ, without remarking the astonishing influence of climate and soil on both his physical and moral constitution. Not only do they give it its character,
but they seem even to create it : they seem to be
the mould in which it is stamped.

Although the moral constitution of a people
must always arise from its government, laws and
religion, yet we often find that this is but a se-
condary process, and that, if we trace the springs
of their constitution to their original source, we
discover them to arise often, though indirectly,
from the operation of climate and soil. Of this
we have the most perfect example in Russia.
The Russ is almost the very being of climate and
soil, both in his moral and in his physical character, and thence his government, laws, and religion,
borrow, in a great measure, their original traits.

Here the moralist will have a fine study.—
He knows that, although the external senses are
the original stock, from which the faculities of
the mind, whether active or passive, arise; yet,
that our intelligence indeed would be very gross
if it were confined to them. Here he will see
this strongly illustrated, and first, of *climate*, he
knows that the growth and produce of mind is
greatly under its influence. Although he may
highly extol the doctrines of its immateriality,
still he knows that its nature is often mechanical

—that it has its periods of contraction and relaxation—that these periods must follow each other; and that, like the sun-flower, on which night's breezes blow, it must, at times, sink within itself and retire to rest. He knows that, in proportion as we exercise our external, we diminish the delicacy of our internal senses. Here he will see the latter almost subordinate; he will see them, as it were cramped up for want of temperature, and without one genial ray to expand them. The poor Russ must live, for the sake of living.— With him the business of living is the businss of life. His winds and snows render his means of subsistence scanty; for these alone he wishes to provide; for these alone his external senses are sufficient; these alone he uses. His mind, from relaxation, droops, decays and dies, and one sad night of darkness overshadows its tomb.

No less interesting is the picture which the moralist has to contemplate on the effects resulting from the influence of *soil*. He knows how strongly the faculties of the mind may be influenced by it, and that, even the qualities of the one, may have a correspondent relationship with those of the other. Of these faculties there are none more strongly marked, none more beautiful than that of *imagination*. The tints of imagination must often be borrowed from landscape, and the tints of landscape, must be borrowed from the soil, that is the face of the country.

What an abundant influence then must these
have on moral character! From no source does
the picture of man derive such lights and shades;
from no source do his pleasures or pains more a-
bundantly flow. Hence he often dates his brightest joys, or his darkest sorrows. He knows that
it is not in flats or plains that this gift abounds in
man. It cannot grow among their low-born weeds,
it is along the towering cliff, and the cloud-
capt-hill; it is with the native of the mountain
or valley, he is to find it. Here, o'er these wide
and far stretched plains, as level and as countless
as the sands of the desert, no object will he see
by which this gift can be created or revived.—
No mountain throws its giant form over the wide
land; no rock flings its rude surface o'er the desert waste—all is flat, lifeless and insipid.

Here are no objects to bind the poor Russ to
his native soil. His imagination cannot be created, or if created, it cannot be revived. His memory cannot recal those past *images* on which his
younger days have often rolled; and thus he is
deprived of the largest sources, on which his
happiness or his misery depends. His cheerless
course knows not their extremes. His stream of
life is dull, coarse, and unjoyous—the sink of
agony does not lower its tide—the swell of rap-
ture does not ruffle its wave. For him, no more
does the light of heaven throw around its morn-

ing dawn—no more does the sun of science gleam
on his mind—all around him is dark and dreary.
Wrapped in his furs, his ignorance, and his snows,
he treads along his sad and weary path. The
mere creature of his senses, he looks abroad from
his den to gratify them. For these alone he
thinks he was born, he blesses his altar, eats,
drinks and sleeps; and thus goes on his life's insipid round.

It would indeed seem here, that in the chains
of animated nature, the links assigned to man and
brute are not separated by distinct spaces, but
that they gradually run into each other. If so,
it is here then, the solitary Russ holds his link,
assuming the character of either, and mingling
the actions of both. Indeed Russia is not the
only country in which we are taught, that the gift
of reason may be so debased, as completely to
lose its true qualities, and thus, no longer, present those barriers by which the class *mammalia*
is otherwise partitioned. We see that the constitution of animated nature has been wisely formed,
in adaptation to the various necessities of its various countries, and that the grand end in view is to
preserve and continue the species. In like manner then as the polypus, which connects the
animal and vegetable tribes, a *theorist* would here
suppose that he saw a class of beings holding an
intermediate rank between the human and the

brute creation ; he would find that there is an in-
terchange of qualities which assimilate them together.   Where reason is deficient, cunning will a-
bound ; where intellect fails, instinct will predo-
minate. There are no qualities more truly characteristic of the brute than cunning—if it is found
in the well organized systems of society in refined
nations, it is the result of what has been *acquired*,
not of what is natural, and the individuals in whom
it exists are always, more or less, degenerate.—
Another quality, most illustrative of animal character, is *sloth*. The operations of reason and
intellect are too active and two subtle to allow
such gross particles to insinuate themselves between them.   They are only to be found in the
parts of our constitution purely physical. Perhaps there are no properties more immediately
manifest in the common Russ than these two, and
their operations seems to follow each other successively. By his cunning, he gratifies his senses ;
by his sloth, he puts them to rest ; he wakes from
his torpor, and his cunning is again exercised.—
His periods, between waking and sleeping, are
none. He has no mental operations to throw
their veil between them. To him is unknown
that elegant dusky film, which, like the grey twi-
light overshadows our morning hours, and drops
on our eyelids its visionary seal. When his nature is refreshed he instantly awakes ; his vigi-

lance is on the alert, he looks abroad from his den, and thus begins the business of the day.

To attempt inquiry into the nature, causes and extent of this animal character, is not the business of these pages. It is the province of the moralist. How far climate and soil have their operation, we have already hinted, and how far this operation has been promoted, by the effects of government, laws and religion, is only for the political economist to investigate.

If however we narrow these inquiries, and take a closer view, we may perhaps gain some light ; and here, we cannot but notice a fact, no less curious than illustrative of it, *viz.* that the lacteal food of goats is sometimes substituted for that of the natural parent; that the infant is placed under the animal, to draw that nourishment, which from a mother, is the greatest source of delight. This is a most singular circumstance, indeed almost a melancholy one, and scarcely to be found in the history of any other modern nation. To give it its full range of influence I shall not attempt. The physiologist has here a fine field of speculation ; but at present we must turn aside from such, although we cannot shut our eyes to it.

We need not however, have recourse to so solitary a circumstance, in illustration of that character so truly possessed by the natives of this country. Many and various are the sources which contribute to it. If we look to those which are not *natural* but *acquired*, we shall find there is none more abundant than that of *slavery*. Of this the poor Russ is the most perfect creature. He is a slave to his appetites, to his religion, and to his government. From his cradle to his grave, is one incessant series of thraldom and pressure. The current of his life resembles a kennel, struggling betwen two dunghills; it rolls along its muddy stream in sloth and fatness; its banks are steep, filthy and dark; by these alone its waters are directed; by these their ebb and flow must be regullated; and, beyond these, they never can wander.

He cannot think for himself, his rulers save him the trouble; by their fiat he is ruled, by their frowns he is moved, and, on their will, hang his destiny. If the Almighty has infused into him a rational principle, he can scarcely exercise it.—It is, by his cunning, not by his reason, that his wishes and his wants are provided. The despotism, under which he moves, presses and clogs every thing around him; it narrows his views; it gives him his prejudices, and the clanking of its *manacles* ever dins in his ears; he has no stimulus for exertion; no reward for improvement. Bound down to one dark and lowly path, it is here he delves his weary way, and here alone he must tread, where his father has trodden before him.

No less enslaved is the poor Russ, by the rites of his religion. This the traveller cannot but immediately remark; of this he will be constantly put in mind; this is the general veil which he will see wraped around almost every object and under which alone he can get a real insight into its true colours. It is with his idols and his saints that the Russ hols communion : with these he is domesticated ; to these he addresses himself in all his troubles. These are the objects of his constant solicitude, and hereon hangs the interest of his concerns, whether spiritual or temporal. To them his morning hours are devoted; with them his vespers are passed, and, without their invocation the business of the day cannot go on. Not more idly play the sunbeams around his drifting snows than does the light of reform over his benighted soul. All is dark and dreary; his spirit of devotion is cold and cheerless ; it cannot stray beyond himself; it cannot touch his fellow-man, and, if once the warmth of humanity can draw towar ls him its cheering ray, the spell of his soul, like the *Demophoon* of old, will shiver at the spark and blot it out for ever.

37

CHAP. IX

We were now to bid adieu to the ancient seat of the Czars, and gaze no longer on its hallow-ruins. The last chime of its bells was to ring on our ear, the last glitter of its domes was to fade on our sight, and, as their tints stole away into the horizon, our minds mingled with their dying hue, and left us at peace with a jarring world.

And now lay before us the dark and dreadful part of our journey, the most interesting, but the most melancholy. Hitherto its picture was calm and serene; whatever dark spots it had belonged to the canvas, not to the pencil, and we gazed on a country, on which God and man had bestowed many choice gifts. Far different now were the scenes before us. On all sides lay vast and dreary wilds, their only tracks the bloodstains of war, their only companions the sad remnants of its desolation. No longer was the cheering warmth of humanization to be felt; all was dark and dreary: one wretched map of misery "threw

its listless length around." Wherever we rolled
our wearied eye, still it was the same, nothing
to catch, on which it could sweetly gaze, nothing
discernable, on which it could fondly linger; and
wherever our fellow creature gave colour to the
scene, it added interest, but it added melancholy.
The tear of the widow was to awake our sympathy; the cry of the orphan was to din in our ears,
and send its echo to the listening waste, their hus-
bands, their fathers, and their friends no more!
their alters insulted, their homes polluted, and
their wretched, houseless, figures stalking abroad,
like the genii of famine and despair, and clinging
to the yet reeking embers of their roofless dwellings.

Let not the enthusiast roam here. Far different are those scenes, where the bright fancies of
his boyhood plumed their eagle wing, and took
their gay and glittering flights. The cup from
which he has taken his draught will be dashed
from his lips; the dream, from which he is awakened, will add to its bitterness; the spell will be
broken, and he will turn away with disgust. No
more; for him, will the lovely features of nature
smile; hideous and distorted they will " rack his
gaze." He will see his fellow-creatures in all
the varieties of wretchedness and despair, steal-
ing away, from the scanty boon of nature, where-
with to support their miserable existence.

The road from Moscow passed out at the West-
gate, after crossing the Moskwa by a long wood-
en bridge. It then enters on a flat plain, partly
diversified with clumps of trees and numerous
ruins of wooden huts, &c. and it continues flat
until it reaches Perkouchekovo our first stage.—
This place presents a miserable group of wood-
en hovels, about thirty in number, and scattered on each side of the road. A large green
painted church, partly demolished, stands in the
middle: it is a fine bourg or borough and belongs to the Emperor.

This was the first stage which the French army reached on their retreat, and, while we were
changing horses, we could not but shudder at the
sad relics of their devastation. Paltry and simple
as it was, it could not escape their all devouring
firebrand. Scarcely a vestige of its once neat
form survived, except the church. The wretched inhabitants fled, partly to another village and
partly to their woods and wilds. A few have
returned, and are still fondly lingering over the
ruins of their once beloved homes, with scarce a
rag to cover their wretched forms, and hardly a
roof to shelter them from the pitiless blast.—
Mothers and orphans crowd together, mingling
their sighs and their sorrows; clinging to the shelter of a few hurdles, and hanging over each other
in famine and despair. Here they are to face the

howling winds and winter snows, until tired nature puts an end to the measure of their sorrows. Unhappy country, is it not enough that the depravities of thy ancient mother have called down Heaven's vengeance on her bleeding form? Is the scourge of war to crimson, with its blood stained lash, those peaceful vales, where thy simple offspring draw their little store, and where, like the lowly flower, which droops its head to the blast, their humility, and their innocence should have sheltered them from desolation?

From the last stage, our road continued tolerably good and flat; partly made with planks and partly a track through an extensive plain, level and fit for pasturage, and brought us to a wretched village, or rather a heap of rubbish, which, like the former, is free and belongs to the Emperor. A similar mass of devastation presents itself. The inhabitants received fifty roubles for each house from the Emperor, in the former they received an hundred roubles for each house, being in proportion to the extent of the destruction committed, and to their indigence. The inhabitants of this place are mostly Poles; they are robust and with fair complexions. The men wear a large slouching hat, and sheepskin jackets; the women are clad in rags; in short, misery and wretchedness seem to abound here. This village is called Koubinskoe and contains about sixty persons.

We continued to proceed through a flat and insipid country, without any object which could interest the attention, and soon reached the village of Chelkovo, similarly wretched and ruinous with the last, and containing a few temporary sheds on each side of the road. It shared the fate of the others; but this, it is said, was owing to the Cossacks, more than the French. A small quantity of grain seems to be raised around this part of the country. The soil, from Moscow, is yellow sand and clay, cold and sterile. The pasturage is scanty and bad, and the crops light. The common flail of Scotland is used here; the women thresh out the grain on a platform, in the field. The common plough of Russia is still in use; but the rudely formed harrow of the northern provinces is somewhat improved. This country is more barren, both as to nature and art, than that lying between the capitals.

The road continued flat, cheerless and insipid, irregularly formed and often deeply rutted. We passed by the ruins of three villages, which were laid waste; two of them are entirely spept away from the face of the earth, and now bushes of nettles mark the spot on which they stood. This, in many places, was the only mark by which we could observe where houses had formerly been. It is asserted that the Russians destroyed these villages during the advance of the French Army.

We soon gained a view of the town of Mojaiske pleasantly situated on the south-west of a gentle declivity. Mojaiske is a small town of about one thousand inhabitants. The buildings are partly of brick and wood: a fine Gothic church stands on a high and rugged bank, surrounded by a deep natural ditch, over which a communication is made, by arches. There are also two smaller churches, besides a monastery at a short distance from the town. The ground on which the town stands, is high and deeply rutted, by a small brook, which flows into the Moskwa, on the north side of the environs. The irregularities of the ground, give the town a very romantic apperance, and occasion an endless task, to the inhabitants, in toiling from one ridge to another. This is a district town; but it appears to have little or no trade. After the battle of Borodino, Buonaparte retired to this place and halted four days. The churches were converted into hospitals for the wounded soldiery, while the town became a prey to the firebrand. Many of the houses are again repaired, though several poor families still reside under the shelter of a few branches of trees, stuck into the ground, and knotted together at the top. The people appear to be extremely simple, quiet and inoffensive. A considerable quantity of barley and black oats are cultivated in the neighbourhood. The soil continues a hard stiff clay. Very few cattle are visible ; the horses are small but active. Here, for the first time, we observed the common black rook, the *corvus frugilegus*. A similar plough is used here—it has neither stilts, nor beam—the horse is yoked between the shafts, which are joined by a cross bar, and used as a handle—from this the coulter descends in an inward curved manner.

Leaving Mojaiske, we entered on a rising and extensive plain, partly covered with brushwood and dwarf oak. About ten miles from the town we reached the monastery of Bolgin, situated on the plains of Borodino, where the memorable battle between the Russian and French armies was fought, on the 7th September 1812. As we came in view of the village we could not but gaze with horror, at the scene before us ; one complete mass of destruction and desolation presented itself. Wretched mothers and naked orphans immediately surrounded us, and their extreme eagerness in intreating, and their unbounded gratitude in receiving the smallest donation, too plainly bespoke their distresses, and could not fail to excite sympathy in the coldest heart. Nothing but the sad remnants of its desolation now remain ; the whole is almost a desert. The ruins of the monastery and village are situated on a gently rising ground, on the west side of a small river, which is crossed by a temporary floating bridge of planks. Not a single house of the village is capable of sheltering the wretched inhabitants from the inclemency of the weather.— The walls of the monastery and roof are still standing, though otherwise in a state of ruins; the Popes have left it. The surface of the ground, on the south side of the river, is flat, but gradually rises up to a plantation of fir, in front of which is the breast work of the French battery, on which it is said nearly one thousand pieces of artillery were placed, during the action. On the opposite side of the river, and on each side of the road, is seen the spot on which the Russian cannons were placed. The monastery stood almost in a line, between them, and was taken and retaken three times successively. No spot could have been better selected for the operations of a battle. The country is in general, flat and cultivated: the river, which waters the valley, is not above ten yards wide: its banks are steep and partly covered with brushwood. It flows into the Moskwa. Here we learned that the Russian army lost thirty five thousand men and that of the French somewhat more. The bodies of the killed were burnt on different parts of the fields— layers of trees and bodies were piled alternately above each other, to a considerable height, and thus consumed. The Russian Commander in Chief, Koutousoff, had made such excellent prepara-

tions to oppose the enemy, that the army of Napoleon was foiled at every attempt, and after
three days continued fighting, both armies retired from the combat. The Russians waited for
a supply of men, while Napoleon took the advantage and pushed an advanced guard on to
Moscow. The victory was claimed by both parties. On the first and second day the French
were completely beaten; and after the third the
Russians were only prevented from renewing the
attact, from the want of men. Nothing can be a
more convincing proof of the ardour with which
they fought, than the number of the enemy which
was killed.*

From the great magnitude and importance of
the battle of Borodino, and its forming so remarkable an æra, not only in the annals of this
campaign in particular, but in the history of modern warfare—there needs no apology for giving,
to its account, more detail than what, otherwise,
the nature of these pages might admit of, we

* The day after we had passed the plains of Borodino, we had the
honour of procuring the acquaintance of a Russian nobleman, who was
travelling from Smolensky to Moscow. He had fought on the plains
of Borodino, where his father fell. He gave us some interesting par-
ticulars on the fate of the day of Borodino. From him we understood
that the Russians occupied the field so admirably, that Napoleon could
not bring up the whole of his army to the attack. The height on
which the French battery was placed, perfectly corresponds with that
stated in Napoleon's bulletin.

shall therefore extract a summary of it from the pages of a French officer,* who was present on that occasion......

" Worn out with fatigue, we felt the want of sleep. There were many among us, so enamoured of glory, and so flushed with the hope of the morrow's success, that they were absolutely incapable of repose. As they passed the wakeful hours, and the silence and darkness of midnight stole upon them, while the fires, now almost extinct, of the sleeping soldiers, threw their last rays of light over the heaps of arms piled around, they gave themselves up to profound meditation. They reflected on the wonderful events of our strange expedition; they mused on the result of a battle, which was to decide the fate of two powerful empires; they compared the silence of the night with the tumult of the morrow; they fancied that death was now hovering over their crowded ranks, but that the darkness of the night prevented them from distinguishing who would be the unhappy victims. They then thought of their parents, their country,—and the uncertainty whether they should ever see those beloved objects again, plunged them into the deepest melancholy.—Before day-break, the beat of the drum was heard, the officers cried to arms, the

* La Baume.

men eagerly rushed to their different stations,
and all, in order for battle, awaited the signal for
action. Such were the feelings of the army,
when a radiant sun, bursting from the thickest
fog, shone for the last time on many of us.—At
six o'clock the firing of a cannon, from our principal battery, announced that we were engaged.
The thirteenth division marched upon the village
of Borodino, to which the Russians had already
set fire. Orders had been given that they should
confine themselves to the occupation of this position; but, carried away by the enthusiasm, natural to Frenchmen, they crossed the river Kolo-
gha, and took possession of one of the bridges,
which connected the village with the eminence,
—while the thirteenth division possessed itself of
Borodino, the fourteenth, crossing the Kolagha
under the eminence, lodged itself in a ravine,
near the principal redoubt, whence the enemy
poured a horrible fire. This position being carried, our artillery crowned the heights, and seized the advantage which, for more than two hours,
the Russians had over us. The guns, to the
destructive fire of which we had been exposed
during the attack, were now turned against the
enemy, and the battle was lost to the Russians,
when they imagined that it was but just begun.
Part of their artillery was taken, and the rest
withdrawn to the rear. In this extremity, Prince

Koutousoff saw that every thing was lost. Yet determined to make one effort more, and to maintain the reputation which he had acquired, by the service of half a century, he renewed the combat, and attacked, with all his forces, the strong positions he had just lost. Three hundred pieces of cannon, now arranged on these heights, spread devastation and death among his ranks, and his disheartened soldiery perished at the feet of those ramparts, which they had themselves raised, and which they regarded as the bulwark of Moscow their venerable and sacred city. The thirtieth regiment, French, attacked, on every side, was unable to keep the redoubt, which it had carried, not being supported by the third division, scarcely yet drawn up in order of battle. The enemy, encouraged by the success he had just obtained, brought forward his reserve, with the hope of striking a decisive blow. It was partly composed of the Imperial guard. With all his forces concentrated, he attacked our centre, on which our right had wheeled. For a moment we feared that our lines would have been broken, and that we should have lost the redoubt we had gained the preceding evening ; but General Friand, coming up with twenty-four pieces of cannon, arrested their progress, mowing down ranks at a time. Both parties continued two hours exposed to a fire of grape shot, neither daring to advance nor willing to recede. The Viceroy of Italy seized this decisive moment, and flying to the right, ordered a simultaneous attack of the grand redoubt by the first, third, and fourteenth divisions. Having arranged all these in order of battle, they advanced with cool intrepidity. The troops approached even the intrenchments of the enemy, when a sudden discharge of grape shot, from the whole of their artillery, spread destruction and consternation through our ranks. Our troops were staggered at this fatal reception. At the same instant a division of cuirassiers, from the centre of the army, rushed on the redoubt, and offered, to our astonished sight, a grand and sublime spectacle. The whole eminence, which over-hung us, appeared, in an instant, a mass of moving iron; the glitter of the arms, and the rays of the sun reflected from the helmets and cuirasses of the dragoons, mingled with the flames of the cannon which on every side, vomited forth death, gave, to the redoubt, the appearance of a volcano in the midst of an army. The enemy's infantry, placed near this point, behind a ravine, kept up so destructive a fire on our cuirassiers that they were immediately forced to retire. Our infantry took their place, and, turning the redoubt to the right and left, recommenced a furious combat with the Russians, whose efforts rivalled our own. The

Viceroy advanced, with Broussier's division, followed by the thirteenth and thirtieth regiments. They advanced on the redoubt, and entering it by the breast-work, massacred, on their pieces, the cannoneers which served them. Prince Koutousoff, who had witnessed this attack, ordered the cuirassiers of the guard to advance and endeavour to retake the position. The shock between their cuirassiers and ours was terrible; and one may judge of the fury with which they fought, when the enemy, in quitting the field, left it completely covered with dead.—The interior of the redoubt presented a horrid picture. The dead were heaped on one another ; the feeble cries of the wounded were scarcely heard amid the surrounding tumult. Arms, of every description, were scattered over the field of battle. The parapets, half demolished, had their embrasures entirely destroyed. Their places were distinguished only by the dismounted cannon. All the Russian soldiers, in the redoubt, chose rather to perish than to yield.—On our left, our attention was directed to a grand movement of cavalry, directed by the enemy, on that point. Being unable to penetrate the square formed by the brigade of General Delzons, the enemy advanced to the extremity of our left and commenced a brisk attack on the Bavarian light cavalry, which were, for a moment, thrown into disorder.—During this memorable period, the Emperor remained constantly in the rear of the centre, and made, on the extremity of his right, several grand manœuvres with the Westphalians and the Poles, to support the Duke of Elchingen* in his repeated and desperate attempts to turn the position of the enemy. On this point, the Russians obstinately withstood all our efforts, and repulsed, with considerable loss, the Westphalians and the Poles. Although we had taken two redoubts, the enemy had still a third, situated on another eminence, and separated by a ravine. The fourth corps which, since ten o'clock, had intrepidly sustained the attacks of the enemy, was not the only one which had losses to deplore. Although the battle was not yet concluded there was not a corps which had not to mourn the death of one or more of its chiefs. Advanced as was the day, the fate of many an unfortunate being was yet to be decided. The cannon roared with unabated fury, and continued to overwhelm new victims. In the evening, the firing was so briskly maintained, that the legion of the Vistula was forced to kneel down, behind the grand redoubt. The enemy, at length, became móre quiet, while the silence gave us reason to believe that the Russians were preparing to retreat on the road to

* Ney

Mojaiske.—The weather, which had been very fine during the day, became, towards evening, cold and damp. The whole army bivouacked on the ground it had gained.—The next day (September 8th) we returned to the field of battle. What had been predicted the preceding evening had actually taken place. The enemy, seeing the intrepidity with which we carried his redoubts, despaired of maintaining his position, and resolved to evacuate it during the night. As we passed over the ground which they had occupied, we were enabled to judge of the immense loss the Russians had sustained. In the space of a quarter of a league, almost every spot was covered with the killed or wounded; on many places the bursting of the shells had promiscuously heaped together, men and horses. The fire of our howitzers had been so destructive that mountains of dead bodies were scattered over the plain, and the few places, not encumbered with the slain, were covered with broken lances, muskets, helmets, and cuirasses, or with grape-shot and bullets, as numerous as hailstones after a violent storm. But the most horrid spectacle was the interior of the ravines; almost all the wounded, who were able to drag themselves along, had taken refuge there to avoid the shot These miserable wretches, heaped one upon another, and almost suffocated with blood, utter-

39

ing the most dreadful groans, and invoking death with piercing cries, eagerly besought us to put an end to their torments."

On this occasion we cannot withhold the greatest praise due to Koutousoff, the indefatigable and heroic defender of Russia—a warrior who had saved his country from bondage, and struck at the root of the tree, no longer of liberty, but of despotism, and who destroyed the devoted legions of Napoleon, which, for twenty years, had foiled almost all its opponents, and crushed the independence of most European states. As early as 1769 he distinguished himself in the service of his country. At the storming of Otchakoff, under the command of Prince Potemkin, he received a ball, which passed through both his temples. The preservation of his life must have been almost miraculous, and the cure prevented his active service for a long time; but even before it was completed, he joined the banners of Russia, and, under the great Suwarrow, commanded the rear guard at the bloody storm of Ishmael.

No General among the nations of the continent since the overwhelming superiority of the French, had so evident a claim to such a distinction as the old hero who was selected for that occasion. Such a deed, effected by the unbounded perseverance and valour of a native host, unassisted by any active allies, and under the guidance of a native general, whose fortunate success has proved equal to his military capacity, calls on all for admiration, gratitude, and every mark of acknowledgement. Here Napoleon met an army, on equal terms; neither his briberies nor intrigues could insure him success, because they were equally spurned, and treated with that contempt which they deserved. It should not be forgotten, though a kind of negative merit, that the battle of Austerlitz, and the subsequent slavery of the continent, was principally owing to the entire neglect of Prince Koutousoff's advice, though he had the nominal command—in consequence of which he refused to sign the general report. The retreat to Moscow is acknowledged to be, at least, equal to that, which immortalized the name of Moreau; and every disposition the host of Russia acted upon, proved him to have been a consummate master of the art of war. Before him, the genius of Napoleon shrunk and was foiled; before his warriors the long glory of the French army withered, and the laurels, which they had so long been accustomed to boast, have only served to glorify those, which the host of Russia has won. No praise can be too great for this departed hero,—no mark of distinction can exceed his deserts!

We proceeded from Borodino, through a rugged road, and soon passsed the boundary stones, between the government of Moscow and Smolensko, and changed horses at the little village of Gridneva, consisting of a few ruined huts and about fifty inhabitants. Hence, to Iatzke, the country is somewhat undulated.; the road becomes more irregular, partly a track, and partly made by bunches of birch twigs.

Iatzke is a considerable town, and seems to have been a place of great beauty. It stands on the banks of a small river in a flat country, beautifully surrounded by woodland scenery. Here are several plantations of birch and extensive fields of pasturage; indeed the whole scene, although flat, is beautiful. A luxuriance of culture prevails every where; at a distance it appears like a fine large English village. The town consisted of several good houses, churches and wooded huts; but now, nothing besides a sad skeleton remains. All was the prey of the firebrand. Its population was formerly rated at three thousand men. The inhabitants are of somewhat a superior class to those of the other villages, more lively and animated. Few men are to be seen, but wretched mothers and orphans are wandering about, in all direcrions, or issuing from the most miserable huts. Two hours before the arrival of the French army, the bridge was destroyed by the natives; and it took a day's labour, on the part of the former, to repair it, in order to get complete possession of the town. All the goods and properties of the inhabitants had been previously removed. The French halted four days, and on their retreat, finished the destruction of the town.

Leaving Iatzke, we proceeded through an open flat country somewhat cultivated, and exposing the sad relics of three villages, until we arrived at a wretched mean village called Teplouka, consisting of about a dozen miserable ruined hovels. Here we changed horses as well as our dress, and breakfasted; but were obliged to do so in the open fields near a small brook. There was no shelter, except that afforded by one solitary dwelling, which had been erected since the invasion, and was inhabited by a few sick women. The scene of our shaving, &c. in the open field, was a high source of amusement to these poor creatures. Our breakfast consisted, of our Moscow ham unboiled, and bread; this, with some excellent milk, which they provided, regaled us heartily. Their kitchen utensils are all of earthen ware, and filthy beyond description.

The soil from Iatzke consists of a white hard clay. The natives are dark in their complexion, with black beards. The women are generally dressed in coarse woollen frocks, with short

sleeves, ornamented on the shoulders with red
embroidery; the head is bound round by a napkin. This part of the country belongs to Prince
Gallitzin. Every house in the villages has a deep
draw-well in front, into which the straggling
French soldiers were often tumbled, by the irri-
tated inhabitants. In this manner, we were assured by the postillions, nearly two thousand
were destroyed during the retreat from Moscow
to Smolensko. What a horrid death! and how
much must this rack the soul of him, who gave
occasion to it!

After a pleasant day's journey, through a country agreeably diversified with woodland scenery,
we arrived at the beautiful town of Wiasma, situated in a low vale, and on the sides of two gentle
hills facing each other. Here we had the unpleasant intelligence that we could not procure horses
for some time; but from the interesting picture
which the town presented, we did not much regret a delay which might enable us to glean
what was either amusing or instructive. It was
Sunday; the day was warm and delightful, and
all the gay dresses and fineries of the lower orders were sported around, and all were busily arranged or employed at their stalls and shops.
The higher ranks were strutting about, in all the
gaudy colours of their national costume; the men
wrapped up in cloth great coats; the women,

with vast embroidered petticoats. In this article
of dress their whole taste and attention seemed
to be concentrated—each woman resembled a
walking petticoat; over it is worn a short vest of
black velvet, which is fastened under the arms,
and tightly secured about the neck, from which
it hangs loosely down. The neck and arms are
covered with a loose white shirt, terminated at
the wrist by a deep frill of red thread. On the
head, is worn a gold laced helmet with a silk
napkin tied over it, and hanging down the back,
the hair is plaited into three plaits. All the women are dressed alike, only that the colours vary
in each. Nothing can equal the glare and gaudi
ness of the petticoat : the highest ambition and
care of the women seems to consist in shewing it
to advantage ; but, to such an extent is this car
ried, that this otherwise bewitching piece of ap
parel, which naturally excites the most delicate
and magic associations, here loses all its charms
Their whole costume is rude, shewy, and inele
gant in the extreme ; totally devoid of those
graces, which give to woman her proud pre-emi
nence, or her soft endearments !

The town of Wiasma is built in an irregular
and straggling manner. Almost every house is
surrounded with a garden, so that the whole presents the appearance of a town in a forest. It is
a singular circumstance, that, though the houses

were generally consumed, the trees around them seemed to have sustained but little injury. There are twenty fine Gothic churches and about sixty spires and domes. The churches are particularly shewy, the roofs are painted pea-green colour, and the body white or red. The streets are regular, and the houses appear to be generally built of brick, and in a neat manner. The market place forms a large square, in the centre of the town, through which the Dnieper river flows, dividing the town into equal parts. The whole town presents to the traveller a most interesting and picturesque group; and if he could forget its devastation, it must naturally cheer him after his fatigue.

But alas! the cold grasp of devastation has torn away every thing, and this beautiful town, once the prototype of Moscow in brilliancy, is now its prototype in ruins. Here the French Autocrat fixed his infernal seal—on his approach to Moscow, finding the town totally deserted, he set fire to part of it, and finished his work on his return.—It is now little more than a mass of ruins. except a few houses which have been repaired. Most of the churches escaped the flames, on account of their size and strength. The population, before the French entered it, was about twelve thousand inhabitants; it is now about two thousand, and a great part of these are lodged in temporary hovels.

It is easy to conceive that, in this country, the mere name of Frenchman is held in the utmost execration and horror. We felt it ourselves in a most unpleasant degree; being mistaken for such we were laughed and hooted at in the streets, with vile epithets of *Franksowsie!* The women laughed in our very faces, others sneered and desired us to look what we had done! Apples were thrown at some of our party, and at last we deemed it prudent to retire from the impending storm, and left the town, quietly, at midnight. Such a strong impression have the French left on these unhappy beings, that they know no distinction between them and other nations—every stranger is considered a Frenchman, and never will that name escape from their lips, or their memory, without just and savage indignation.

The good effects of the subscription raised in England, for the relief of the suffering Russians, have been here felt. Already money and cloaths have been distributed to several, and small charitable donations, in the name of England, have been granted to the lowest orders, and their warm expressions of gratitude plainly denote what they feel for her bounty.

We now bade adieu to these melancholy scenes, and pursued our journey, over a rising ground planted with birch, and soon arrived at the miserable village of Semlevo, consisting of a

40

few ruined huts, and about forty inhabitants, alike
the victims of ruins and desolation. Here we
made no delay, but passed on, through a most
agreeable and well planted country, until we arrived at a solitary stage-house, situated in a large
valley, where we changed horses. From this,
the road lies through a picturesque, open, and
pleasant country, affording extensive plains of
pasturage and cultivation, and presenting a pleasing aspect of hill and dale and woodlands. The
road is hard and smooth, and is lined, on each
side, by the graceful birch, which however too
often shews the sad vestiges of war in its mutilated trunk.

The surrounding country here, and from the
last stage, somewhat resembles the southern
counties of England. It is generally relieved
by large inequalities, and prodigious plains of
pasturage, shaded with birch and fir. The soil
is one continued light coloured clay, hard and
dry, neither marshes nor springs; and but little
grain reared. Notwithstanding the large masses
of grazing ground, we only observed one small
herd of black cattle and a few sheep. Among
the latter we remarked some with long tails and
better wool. this seems to be the first attempt at
an improvement of the breed; at least it was the
first we remarked. We were assured that, before the invasion, there had been a considerable

quantity of black cattle; but, during that event, they had all been consumed by the armies.

Here we passed the monastery of Bolgin, a large and massy edifice, surrounded by a high wall, and near a small lake. On both sides of the road were strewed numerous earthen mounds, the silent tombs of many a gallant soul, and plainly indicating that it had been the scene of an action. The road winds along an immense morass, on the south covered with brushwood, while, on the north, it becomes considerably elevated and neatly divided into fields. This ridge is about one hundred and fifty feet high, and is the greatest elevation we observed since we left Moscow, notwithstanding the beauty and apparent cultivation of this country, we could not but behold, the sad traces, which war had scattered over it— near the monastery they are quite fresh. This fine monastery, we understood, had been occupied and plundered, but not destroyed by the French. Along this stage remained the marks of several decoy fires, which the natives had kindled; and, whenever a party of French stragglers observed and approached their cheering warmth, they fell upon them and committed them to the flames. For this cruelty the Cossacks were ordered to punish the peasantry. A French party were encamped here for eight weeks, and committed every species of barbarity, to which their insatiate lust could prompt them.

The whole of this country belongs to Prince Sacolnisky, who resides in the neighbourhood. Near this place, is the source of the Dnieper* which is here merely a deep ditch. After crossing it, we came within sight of Dorogobouge, which, from its elevated situation and churches, has, at a distance, rather an imposing appearance; but, when entered, is found to consist merely of a wretched collection of hovels partly built of brick or wood. The Dnieper divides the town; the population of which is reckoned at four thousand souls. The inhabitants are lively and comely, with fair complexions and dark beards. Here the French remained six weeks, but did not completely destroy the town.

On leaving Dorogobouge the road led over a large flat common, partly along the banks of the Dnieper. It soon improved and shewed marks of cultivation, particularly in corn, barley, and buckwheat. A mean, solitary hovel was observed, named Mikailouka, too worthless to merit description. The circumjacent scenery is very extensive, generally flat and covered with forests of small growth. We passed several tumuli, where were interred the remains of Poles, who

* The Boristhenes of the ancients.

had fallen in the battle, many ages ago, in the
early wars between them and the Russians. The
country gradually improves in cultivation: but
the mode of farming is the same: neither fences
nor ditches mark the boundaries of fields, all is
one confused mass, blended together—one ridge
of grain *here*—another ridge of hemp *there*. The
land is not ploughed more than three inches
deep; the soil is most excellent, and is capable
of the highest state of cultivation. A considerable quantity of hemp is raised here. It
grows strong, from three to four feet high. The
forests are very extensive but the trees are remarkably small—most of them, near the sides of
the road, have suffered from the desolating axe,
and many only shew their ashes strewed around.
The greater part of those, cut down by the
French, are replanted, and are used as sign marks,
in winter, where the country is covered with
snow.—These *sign* trees are planted on each side
of the roads, at regular distances.

From the last stage we entered on a road of
loose heavy sand, through one uninterrupted
forest of birch, without a glimpse of the surrounding country until we again reached the
banks of the Dnieper.—Here we saw the remains
of a plantation, where the French army had halted for some time. Nothing can be more sad
than the spectable it presents—the relics of

horses' bones, &c. old shoes, broken china, ac-
coutrements, books, remain untouched! The
space of wood cut down, is about ten acres—the
trees all appeared to have been cut down breast
high, and burnt on the spot. The name of this
spot is Caronoviksy—close to it, we crossed the
Dnieper, which is here about four yards wide,
with steep clay banks, and came in sight of the
little village of Pneva, standing on a fine flat
plain on the north side of the river. This plain
is covered with earthern mounds, the tombs of
those who fell in battle, during the passage of this
river.

Here indeed was a spectacle at which forlorn
nature seems to yearn; the memory of the horrid scenes which this spot witnessed makes the
mind shudder. Before us lay those plains, on
which a brave and injured people opposed a
cruel and ruthless invader, and shed their sacred
blood for their nearest and dearest ties; now alas!
what a scene—all is tranquil, melancholy and still
every where around are the marks of burning ruin and devastation. Through these, in soft mean-
ders, steals the gentle Dnieper, calm, serene and
unconscious of that storm which so lately tossed
its waves—untinged by that blood, which so lately stained its waters. Its banks, strewed with the
yet crumbling remnants of slaughter,—no kindred
spirit breathes its requiem to the departed souls;

but where the raven's croak sends around its hollow wail, or where the moaning wind sighs along
the tombs. What a dreadful picture of morta-
lity ! Here once stood, in proud array, the
banners of kings, princes and armies; and scarcely has that day gone by—here were stretched
the giant forces of mighty empires, struggling for
conquest, and scarcely has the tomb covered
their yet warm ashes—still as the grave, where
these ashes lie, and cold as the sepulchre which
will hand them down to posterity. Scarcely
have a few months elapsed since Buonaparte and
his desolating legions crowded around this spot,
obliged to retrace their blood-stained steps from
Moscow, a prey to poverty, hunger, wretchedness
and cold ! Here; surrounded, on all sides by in-
terminable forests and wilds—sheltered by the
sky's bare canopy—pillowed on the drifting
snows, and rocked by the scowling winds, they
passed their wretched nights ; and, as their watch
fires gleamed along the sky, the crackling flames
gave, to the savage picture, the true light of horror and desolation. It seems as if this destroying
dæmon resolved to leave the whole country an
everlasting monument of vengeance; he drew,
from every quarter, as Burke says in the case of
Hyder Ali, " whatever a savage ferocity could
add to his new rudiments in the art of destruction, and, compounding all the materials of

fury, havoc and desolation into one black cloud, he poured down the whole of its contents.—Then ensued a scene of woe, the like of which no eye had seen, no head conceived, and which no tongue can tell.   A storm of universal fire blasted every field, consumed every house, destroyed every temple."

We now turned away from these melancholy scenes, and pursued our journey.—The road from Pneva, towards Smolensko, is generally hard, but uneven; it crosses over a small river, by a floating bridge of planks.   The country gradually becomes hilly, and partly covered with wood and cultivation.   Indeed, altogether, it presents the finest aspect of landscape we had seen in Russia.   No longer were we traversing wearisome flats, immense commons, boundless forests and extensive marshes—hills, varying in shape and cultivation, arrest the traveller's eye, many covered with woods and shewing all the warmth of industry.   Continuing our track by this road, which led us along the north bank of the Dnieper, we soon came in sight of the turrets of Smolensko. The view was striking and picturesque: an irregular ridge of hills, about three hundred feet high, rises up, on each side of the Dnieper; on the south side it forms an isolated height, whereon is seen in the centre, the great church, and, along the brow of the hill, the walls of the town.—

The walls, at regular distances, are divided by towers, and, between them, are smaller ones. Opposite to the town, and on the north side of the river, is a similar hill, surmounted by a large white church with a green roof. On approaching the town, the road agreeably winds along the bank of the river, and passes between two pyramidal pillars, marking the extent of the suburbs. After passing through the suburbs, we crossed a temporary wooden bridge, and entered the city by the north gate.

Smolensko is a regularly fortified town, and capital of the government of the same name. Its distance from Moscow is three hundred and seventy-eight wersts, or two hundred and seventy English miles. The walls are partly built with stone and finished with brick. Their circumference is about three miles, their height from twenty to forty feet, and their thickness about fifteen feet. They are surmounted by round towers, placed at the angles; between which are others of a small square form. The wall is defended at different corners, by large earthern bastions, which support a few guns. The north side of the wall runs parallel with the river about half a mile, when it suddenly turns at each side of the hill, and joins at its summit. The top of the wall is divided by loop-holes. The gates by which the city is entered, are

41

through the round towers. The north gate is
neatly ornamented with a small dome, painted of
a purple colour, covered by gilded stars and surmounted by large crosses. The city is divided
by one long street, which ascending from the
north gate, and passing the great church, extends
to the top of the hill and joins the south gate.
On each side the ground sinks into deep ravines,
covered with fruit trees and mean hovels. The
upper junction of the ridges is flat, and is laid out
into a large square, surrounded with avenues of
trees, and formerly adorned with large and elegant brick houses. Across the ravines, which in-
tersect the buildings, wooden bridges are thrown
in several places, from one precipice to another,
while intricate walks wind here and there, and
the roof of a wooden cottage occasionally peeps
through. The ridges are adorned with large
and shewy churches, the streets seem to hang on
the edge of precipices. In fine, nothing can present a more singular and eccentric appearance,
than the structure of this town. The alternate
rising and sinking of the walls, from the inequality of the ground; the grotesque towers and
their rude gothicism; the steeples, mingling with
the branches of the trees, and the trees concealing
the view of the houses; the number of gardens,
orchards and groves,—altogether form the most
picturesque and irregular group which can be
conceived.

This singular town, previous to the invasion, is said to have contained five or six thousand inhabitants; at present scarcely half that number is here. The French had possession of it for three months, and, on their departure, set it on fire and consumed all the principal houses, particularly those towards the south gate ; however there are many places which appear to have escaped. The principal square, consisting of elegant brick houses, suffered most. It presents one mass of ruin, and is covered with the remains of the French ordnance, carriages, tumbrils, &c. Most of the churches escaped entirely, or with very little injury—they were chiefly, converted into barracks and even stables, which wounded the religious feelings of the Russians to a most extraordinary degree. How little did Napoleon seem to know the means of interesting the people in his favour. Had he respected their religion and their altars, he might have escaped part of that vengeance which his unrighteous conduct so justly deserved. The towns and walls are destroyed in many parts. Never did the hand of destruction press more heavily, than on this ill-fated city. Every thing bears the mark of the French devastation. The inhabitants have mostly fled, and nothing but a melancholy and horrid picture of ruin is distinguishable. In walking through the town, the stranger must wade through crumbling masses of ruin, and, at every step, he treads on its mouldering dust.

The people are simple, quiet and stupid : they are very plain and coarse in appearance, particularly the women; they all dress in the plainest manner, and seem to profess that humility which results from affliction. The remembrance of their past and present fate, naturally throws a melancholy tinge over them, which, in a more intellectual people, must naturally create great interest. Not so here, however; their general course of life is too dull, too filthy and too moderate, to admit of those fine extremes, from which the pleasures or pains of memory have their source. Their joys arise from their senses, not from their intelligence, consequently they are gross—their sorrow is dull, and consequently does not always excite that sympathy, the offspring of extreme sensibility.

CHAP. X.

Grodno, October, 1814.

AFTER a short delay we proceeded on our journey and took leave of Smolensko; a city, whose sorrows and sufferings will be long remembered, and whose fate, like that of Moscow, must ever darken the page of history. The road led us through a country extremely beautiful, well cultivated, and diversified with plantations, somewhat resembling English park scenery:—only one house is seen, the residence of a nobleman; and it was the only house we had observed, since we left Moscow, which was built entirely in the country. Both sides of the road are beautifully lined with birch, until it reaches the solitary station-house at Koritnia, where we found some little difficulty in procuring horses. From Wiasma, the horses gradually diminish in size, strength and activity, and which became more observable as we advanced from Smolensko. We neither travelled so expeditiously, nor could we procure horses so easily along this road, as between St. Petersburg and Moscow; however, considering the ruined state of the country, we had seldom occasion to wait more than fours at any stage. The mode of driving is the same as on the great north road—the horses are all yoked abreast. From the weight of our Russian carriage it constantly required six horses, which, in this part of the country, were so weak as to be scarcely able to drag it up the slightest ascent. The rate of posting is the same from Moscow to Smolensko, as from St. Petersburg to Moscow. Here we passed a considerable detachment of French prisoners, on their return to France. There were about seven hundred of them—regular relays of carts and horses were stationed at the different stages, and they were conveyed at the rate of seventy miles a day. Nothing could exceed the miserable appearance of these men—they were the pictures of wretchedness and filth; yet they still retained their gaiety of spirits, and some remains of tattered lace. Many of them also shewed their gallantry, in being accompanied by some poor Russian females.

From Koritnia we proceeded to Krasnoi, through the avenue of birch; but the country suddenly loses that hilly irregularity, which so abounds in the vicinity of Smolensko. Even the character of the people somewhat changes, and the true Russian character begins to lose itself, in that of a different one, less interesting and more artificial.

Krasnoi is a district town, and contains about eight hundred inhabitants. It has two churches; is situated in a south-west direction from Smolensko, and within a few miles of the boundary between the governments of Smolensko and Mogilew. This spot has acquired celebrity from Napoleon having here deserted his panic-struck legions, and taken to flight on horseback. A few miles from Krasnoi, we entered the government of Mogilew, and reached the village of Liadi, inhabited by a colony of Jews. The general aspect of the country is very pleasing, extensive flat, open, dry gound; neither marshes nor forests; the only trees are the graceful birch, which continues to line each side of the road. From the extreme flat and open state of the country, these avenues seem to stretch as far as the eye can reach. In the warm months of summer no road can be more agreeable to travellers than the present. The wheels of the carriage pass over a smooth turf, without the least noise, while the delicate branches of the birch produce the most delightful shade. The sides of the road are thus planted to point out their track in winter, when these flat countries are covered with snow. In those parts of Sweden, where there are no trees, stakes are fixed along the side of the road, to designate its track.

The commencement of *ancient Lithuania* is passed at Liadi. Lithuania was, formerly, an independent country, between Russia and Poland, governed by its own dukes. It extended three hundred miles in length, and two hundred and fifty in breadth, and is watered by the Dnieper, Dwina, Niemen, &c. In 1401 it was joined to the kingdom of Poland; in 1772 Russia compelled the Poles to cede to her those parts bordering on the Russian frontier; and, in the last unhappy division of Poland, in 1793, she extended her dominion over the whole of Lithuania. At one time Smolensko was the frontier town of Poland, at Present Warsaw is almost that of the Russian Empire!

Here we lost the Russian character—the lively and boisterous mirth of the poor Russ became changed for the cold, calculating silence of the other—even their countenances and costume were altered; the classic form of the hat and cloak, the cut of the hair, &c. were no longer seen, and every feature of their character indicated a change of tribe. We could not avoid remarking, even at Koritnia, this transition, in a manner most unpleasant to us; in short, we perceived we had got amongst a people, whose ruling practice was knavery, and with whom, *money* was

the *sine qua non* of obedience. Wherever we
find these two traits strongly prevail, and keep
pace with each other, we generally conclude,
(and that, too, from principles of association not
very remote,) that we have got in contact with
some near relatives of the very ancient and pro-
lific family of the *Israelites*, whose branches have
shot out so far and wide, and whose root will ever
flourish, as long as commerce continues. This we
found to be the real case ; Jews were the principal
inhabitants of this part of the country ; indeed
much more so than might have been expected,
so near the frontiers of ancient Russia, a country
in which a Jew has never attempted to enter.
But here the *Jews* have fixed themselves in all
the original purity of their sin, and with all those
characteristic traits, for which their tribe is so
notorious.

From Liadi we travelled over a flat, open country, the road excellent, and the avenue of birch
trees still shading it. We changed horses at
Koziani, a solitary hut, kept by a Jew, and proceeded to Doubrovna, by a most delightful road,
finely shaded with birch, and a well cultivated
country. Doubrovna is a *bourg* of considerable
size ; it has two large, open, round spaces—the
one mostly built with brick houses, the other with
wooden huts ; they are connected by cross streets
of wooden hovels. One of these squares is front-

42

ed with piazzas. The Dnieper divives the principal part of the town from a long irregular village of mean huts. The population is about
two thousand five hundred inhabitants. It has
two Greek churches, a Catholic chapel, and a
synagogue. The inhabitants are partly Jews.
The common Lithuanians are poor miserable
abject creatures, and are servants to the Jews.
The Jews are all dressed alike, in long tunics of
black silk, with a broad silken sash tied round
the waist; on the head they wear a small velvet
cap, and over it a huge one of fur; they neither
shave nor cut their hair; in their figures they are
lank and squalid; they all speak the German language, but are deplorably ignorant. Although
it was little more than twenty months since the
French army retreated from Moscow, and partly
destroyed their town, yet they did not know the
month in which it took place. How different
from the Russ, who never passed a spot or a
well, where any event had taken place, without
minutely detailing it. However the Jews inform-
ed us of the dreadful distresses which their invaders had suffered, on their return, and the miserable plight in which they appeared; they only
burnt seventeen houses here.

From Smolensko to Orcha is about seventy
English miles; the road from Doubrovna, to the
latter, resembles the former stages, and is shaded

by rows of birch; it is however more sandy. Before entering Orcha, the Dnieper is crossed by a ferry. The river here is about sixty yards wide; but its stream is dull and quiet. The town of Orcha is pleasantly situated on the west bank of the river, on a gently rising ground; it is large and straggling, with eight churches, partly built of brick and of wood. The greater part of the town has been burnt : its population is about two thousand, and consists mostly of Jews; a more despicable, artificial, mercenary set of wretches cannot be seen; they are without character, without patriotism, and without manners. No more are heard those generous bursts of execration against their invaders, which constantly issued from the lips of the poorest Russ. The women are yet more disgusting than the men; they are clad in a most ridiculous and gaudy dress of silken rags; on their head is a large white napkin rolled round, with three tails hanging over their shoulders; and, under this head dress, a kind of flapping cover of pearls, with dangling steel ornaments, hangs over the ears and forehead. The body is covered with a loose silk vest, and a large petticoat of the same; the arms are hid in long, loose, shirt sleves, terminated with a deep worked frill. The shoes are made without leather at the heels, and every one appears *slip-shod.* Over their dress they wear

a large silk gown, (and in some instances even
two), the sleeves of which hang down the back;
a fur cloak is suspended from the neck. All this
superfluity of dress is huddled on, in the most
careless manner, and the hands seem constantly
employed in detaining it on the body. They take
peculiar pride in their head dress of pearls; the
more valuable denotes the distinction of wealth.
In other respects their dress seems a bundle of
dirt and rags; there never was a more perfect
antidote to love and the graces, than a Lithuanian
Jewess. They command the men, and reign
without controul. The mistress of the house
reads her prayers every morning; but at the
same time walks through the rooms, and in the
midst of her devotion, observes checks, and round-
ly scolds at the faults committed.

The *native* Lithuanians generally wear a white
flapping hat, and a white woollen shirt; their
legs are wrapped up in peices of sail cloth tied
with leather strings—the shoes are clumsy, and
made of the bark of the birch tree. They are a
small class of men, with light hair, fair complexions and little or no beard—they are abject,
gross, indolent and disgusting, both in appearance, and in their habits.

At Orcha, the French, on their advance, fought
a short battle, and crossed the river, by two
bridges, below the town. In this affair the Rus-

sians only lost thirty five men. With the great
est difficulty and vexation we contrived to procure horses from the imposing Jews, after seven
hours delay. We continued our journey from
Orcha, by a very pleasant country, on a fine
road beautifully ornamented with birch trees,
until we reached a small bourg called Kokanovo,
chiefly possessed by Jews.—The next stage was
Tolotzin, straggling in a zig-zag manner over a
rising ground. The houses are partly built of
brick and wood: but extremely mean: the inn is
kept by a Polish nobleman. The country here
is generally flat, with a small quantity of irregular plantations of fir and birch—the soil is whitish clay and sand. It is tolerably cultivated,
but has neither green crops, nor fences.

Leaving Tolotzin, the road becomes hilly, and
the beautiful avenue of birches, which had continued from Smolesko, nearly one hundred miles,
here terminates, and the country assumes a cold,
flat, uninteresting appearance. We reached
Kroupki early in the morning, after having rode
through an immense gloomy forest of fir and
birch. Kroupki is a small bourg, built on a flat
space between extensive forests, and near to a
small lake. The houses are entirely of wood,
with a population of about three hundred Jews.
We were detained the whole day before the Jews
would give us horses. They disregarded the Rus

sian order for horses, and nothing could equal
their knavery and extortion. In most countries
Jews are perfectly alike; but in none perhaps do
they excel more, in knavery, than here. Every
traveller must bargain for what horses he re-
quires, and is sure of being imposed upon:—
there is no appeal, and he must be at the mercy
of these impostors. The instant he arrives, he
is assured that there are no horses to be procured
—shortly after he is asked what price he would
give for them, and a price is demanded in proportion to the haste of the traveller to proceed.
At night they invariably deny having horses, in
order that the traveller might be detained, and
pay lodging money, or more likely, be robbed.
Indeed, throughout Russia, and Lithuania in particular, the carriage and luggage must be carefully watched; if lost sight of, even for a moment, something is stolen. From Moscow to
this place, there is not a single house in which a
traveller could pass the night.—The different
stages are merely places to procure horses, and
their hovels are full of filth and vermin. Provisions must be taken in the carriage, as nothing
but milk can be got. Bread, butter and salt are
very scarce and very bad—the butter is always
sour and rancid. The traveller cannot halt, day
or night, for any length of time, beyond that required for examining places worthy of remark.

Along this route we found our Russian carriage of the greatest use to us; in it we could both sleep and write, and had sufficient room to carry a stock of provision. At Moscow we had procured some excellent cured *ham*, and which we found the most convenient to carry ; however, as we mingled with the Jews, its appearance always excited the utmost disgust and overcame their feelings. Plates, and spoons, &c. were always removed from the polluted touch of the vile ham. If either were used by the Christians, it was instantly scoured, or even broken, and a charge made for it. They never eat from a plate at which a Christian has eaten ; we of course could only get the coarsest and the meanest—a separate fire-place even is allotted for the Christian's use, and here we were obliged to kindle our fire and cook our meals. Though the ham excited so much horror, yet the chocolate often attracted their notice. One of the Jews requested a cupfull, which one of our servants readily gave him, but secretly slipped into it a piece of the pork —the Jew gladly swallowed the draught ; but, discovering the *poison*, he was perfectly inconsolable.

From Kroupki we entered the government of Minsk, and, travelling through a large forest of fir trees, we reached the little village of Lochenitzi. This part of the country is diversified

and somewhat hilly; the road is generally an
unequal tract. Lochenitzi is a singular instance
of a most irregular and scattered town; there
are upwards of an hundred wooden huts,
not more than fourteen feet broad, by twenty in
length and seven in height, and which cover a-
bout one hundred acres. It is called a *bourg*
which is a degree above a village; it has neither
church nor inn nor any Jews. The inhabitants
are mean and dejected. The interior of their
houses is a sad specimen of filth and sickliness.
The soil is a mixture of clay, black loam, dry
and marshy, with some peat-moss. It produces
oats, barley, and two kinds of grass seed used
in the feeding of birds. A singular method is
used in drying and preserving the crop. A
couple of woden posts, about twenty feet in
height and as wide asunder, are fixed into the
ground; between them a certain number of cross-
bars are fastened, similar to the steps of a ladder.
Between these divisions, the sheaves are securely
fixed, with the grain downwards; the sheaf a-
bove always covering the one below, and thus
securing each other from the rain. The appearance of these frames from a distance, and the scattered state of the houses, presents a most singular picture. This method of drying the grain is
both simple and efficacious, and might be adopted with some advantage on the west coast of Su-

therland, in Scotland, where the climate is so changeable. Their agricultural implements are as rude as the structure of their houses. The cart consists of four small wooden wheels, each made of a single piece of wood—the sides, the bark of tree bent round—and the shafts a couple of fir-branches. The plough and harrow are also made from the branches of the fir-tree, without either iron or ropes. The fir-tree is almost as useful to the Lithuanian, as the camel to the Arab.

Leaving Lochenitzi, we pursued our ride through the forest of fir, and reached Borisoff in the afternoon.

Nothing can be more distressing to behold, than the dreary and desolate tracks through which the French army retreated. The avenues of birches which lined this part of the road, are entirely burnt down, and every tree scorched, not only on the road side, but in the very depths of the forest. It would appear that a fire had been placed at the root of each tree, as every one seems half burnt through, or rather scooped out.

This town is built in an irregular manner, though less so than the former. In the centre of an open square stands a heavy wooden church; the population is about two thousand and partly Jews. It is a district town, and is the residence

of a governor and a troop of Cossacks. During
this stage, we passed several detachments of Cossacks and Baskirs; their wild appearance in these
solitary and gloomy forests was indeed terrific.
Though the road was only an irregular track,
yet, at every corner, these troopers were scam-
pering through the forest, like so many huntsmen
in the chase. This was the stage the French
army passed on the day before the battle of the
Berezina. What hardships they must have undergone, in those dreary scenes, and surrounded
by the horrors of a Russian winter, may be conceived, but cannot be described. We observed
the ruined vestiges of their route; fire and destruction marked its progress, and the genius of
desolation hovered every where around. Here
they passed their dreadful nights, a prey to hunger, misery and cold—their only canopy the leafless tree—their only lullaby the drifting snow,
which rocked them to their wretched sleep!

The celebrated dreadful battle of the Berezina
was fought about nine miles above the town of
Borisoff. The French had collected stores and
magazines at Minsk and in Poland; but which
the rapid advance of Admiral Tschikakoff, from
Volhynia, cut off. The river was frozen over,
the ice too thick for the passage of boats, and not
sufficiently strong to bear the artillery, &c. Napoleon was confused; he made many false manœuvres, and crossed the river at a place where

no one could have believed it possible. In this
dreadful scene of confusion, it is here reported
that twenty-two thousand men were drowned in
forcing the passage of the river, and the whole
baggage of the French army was taken. As
soon as Napoleon passed the bridge, leaving his
devoted victims, he pulled off his hat and exclaimed " *the field is won!*" and putting spurs to
his horse escaped by flight to Wilna. Had General Wittgenstein arrived at Borisoff, from the
Dwina, at the time Admiral Tschikakoff did, it
is not improbable that Napoleon Buonaparte and
the remnant of his army would have been taken.
Admiral Tschikakoff deserves great praise for
the expeditious manner in which he conducted
his troops from the Turkish frontiers; but as a
sailor, we could not expect that perfection of
military tactics, sufficient to cope with the genius of Napoleon. This battle completed the
destruction of the French army. Only six
months before, upwards of four hundred thousand chosen soldiers crossed the Niemen, to sub-
vert the independence of Russia. They entered
her territories, unprovoked, with fire and sword,
and plundered and destroyed wherever they
came. Of that number only twenty-four thousand re-crossed the Berezina. Multitudes of prisoners have expiated their rashness, in a climate,
very different from their own; and still greater

multitudes have fallen by the sword, lances and
bayonets of the Russians, or by hunger, cold and
fatigue, and every privation man could undergo
—but the towering pride of France has been
quelled, and her ruler has received a punishment
—though not adequate to his presumption!

Before we left Borisoff, we procured a guard
of Cossacks from the Governor, as a security in
passing through these immense forests, and which,
at this time, were crowded with these irregular
warriors. We could not but admire the lofty
mine of these men, their uncommon politeness,
and mild disposition. We could glean no information from them, as their language was unintel-
ligible to our interpreter. They were dressed
in all manners of uniform, and were armed with
the pike and pistol. Their horses are extremely
small; but very fat and round shaped—their gait
is a quick trot. The whole of their baggage, &c.
is carried on the saddle, over which the rider sits,
in a very elevated manner. By means of this,
the head of the horse is completly out of the
range of his fire-arms. From Borisoff, the road
crosses a country little cultivated, very moist,
covered with forests and most dreary. This
part of the road was excessively bad. We reached a miserable collection of wooden hovels
scarcely deserving name or mention, and some
other stages equally wretched and forlorn—in-

deed there cannot be, perhaps, in any country, more miserable specimens of architecture than the Lithuanian villages present. The huts are about twelve feet square, the walls formed of the unshapen trunks of trees, laid parallel, one above another, with the ends projecting over, and forming a most clumsy angle. The roof is covered with large shapeless boards; the window is a small hole in the wall,—it answer a double purpose of giving ingress to the light and egress to the smoke. No less miserable are the wretched inmates of these hovels, both in person and manners. They are hard-boned, and sallow complexioned. The men wear coarse white woollen frocks, and a hat of the same, without a brim.— The hair of the head is not cut; it hangs loose and is generally of a flaxen colour.

The difference between a Russian and a Lithuanian village, in their structure, is very remarkable. The former is built in a neat manner, and regularly along each side of the road. The latter consists of a straggling head of huts, without order or arrangement, and separated from each by large spaces of ground.

Along this immense forest we still continued our journey over a dark and gloomy road. The fir trees are about sixty feet in height, but very slender. The country between Orcha and Minsk is one immense forest, and, useless in some open spaces, round the towns and villages, is perfectly compact and thick. It bore frequent marks of fire and the *bivouacs* of armies. We noticed several wooden platforms attached to the trunks of the trees, about thirty feet from the ground, which are used to place beehives upon, in order to collect honey and wax, during the summer months.

The approach to Minsk is by a sandy road; the view it presents is shewy and grotesque, from the number of clumsey churches it contains. The town is entered by a wooden bridge, over a small river, and along an avenue of trees and shrubberies. This street rises to a considerable elevation, and terminates in a large open square of grass and mean wooden huts; from this another street goes off at right angles, containing large houses, and joining with a second square. Here the principal buildings are both of brick and wood. From this square several streets branch off, and enter a crowd of wooden hovels irregularly huddled together, and covering a large space of ground.

Minsk is rather a fine town for Lithuania; but is very dirty and very irregular. The buildings in the square are large churches very heavily constructed, without any elegance. Their gable ends front the street, are terminated at each corner by a square spire, with a low dome be-

tween them. This kind of church is peculiar to
Lithuania. The religion is partly catholic and
partly Jewish. The population is about seven
thousand, of which about three thousand are
Jews. Of the lower classes, the Jews are the
most filthy and the most annoying; it is impossible to avoid the pestilential intrusion of these
groveling reptiles. The moment a traveller arrives, he becomes haunted by them—he cannot
stir without being watched. Every Jew employs a vagabond to ply in the streets and so-
licit the custom of the stranger; his house is
ready on all occasions, for an hotel, or any thing
else, no matter how base!

On entering the town, we had great difficulty
in finding an hotel to breakfast in, every house
being crowded by the military. Jews innumerable flocked around and invited us: one of them
begged us to enter his house, with the utmost
obsequiousness; but at the door demanded sixteen roubles for the use of a room. Fortunately we found a German, less imposing, and here
we were lodged in a common billiard room, and
slept on the long benches, amidst all the noise,
filth, and vociferation of gambling Jews and
Lithuanians. The people are rude, unpolished, vulgar and noisy. As an instance of their
rudeness, we were often asked to mark the game
for the player, they not being able to appreciate

that good breeding and politeness, which is due
to strangers, in civilised countries; and as an instance of their unparalleled and acknowledged
dishonesty, the billiard balls were not allowed
to lie on the table unless when the game was
playing; and in every room a spy is placed, to
watch lest any moveable article should be taken
away.   In all public rooms and companies, also,
are busy, prying, inquisitous characters, seeking
for some words which may drop from a stranger
as to the government, laws, &c;—in short, men
who appear to be employed as informers, and
report at the police office what they collect.
Such is the dreadful effect of that powerful engine of depotism, which this vast empire weilds,
and which forms so prominent a feature in its
character.

In so small a town it presented rather a lively
spectacle in its equipages, dresses, &c; but the
most interesting part to us was the exhibition of
four or five thousand Cossacks, Baskirks, &c.;
fully equipped. They were stationed here to
receive the Emperor Alexander, who was on his
way from St. Petersburg to the Congress at
Vienna. As in Russia proper, a vast deal of
shew, parade and costliness is exhibited; but it
has all that boldness and barbarity about it, so
peculiar to rude, unpolished and powerful nations. The ladies sit in open carriages, without

any head dress, although the weather is now so
cold, that the common people are all wrapped
up in their sheep-skins. There are many nobles
here, both Lithuanian and Polish. They are a
remarkably fine made class of men, and their
dress is extremely graceful. They wear a long
silken or cloth tunic, with loose sleeves—a broad
silken sash is knotted round the waist, the head
is closely shaven, and on it a Hessian cap is
worn. It is said that Charles II. attempted to
introduce this dress into England. The common Lithuanians exhibit the most abject and
palsied appearance—man can scarcely present a
more degraded picture. Their looks are squalid and haggard, their gait heavy and lifeless;
their dress can scarcely merit description, for it
scarcely deserves the name of dress ; it is more
like an irregular bundle of rags. The horses
somewhat resemble the men in poverty and
wretchedness, they seem half starved are unshod,
and without strength : six of them could scarcely
drag our carriage.

The effects of the French invasion, on this
town, were not so conspicuous, as in the others
through which we have passed. On their retreat, being obliged to change their route towards Wilna, they did not reach Minsk, and it
thus escaped their flames. The capture of the
French magazines, by the arrival of Admiral

44

Tschikakoff, may be said to have sealed the fate of the tyrant; and hence his retreat became a perfect and wretched flight. The only trace of invasion, now presented, is in the poverty of the people, who were plundered by the soldiery on their advance to Moscow. The houses were not touched. After the battle of Berezina, it became a depôt for French prisoners, and held about twenty thousand, who mostly died.

From this neighbourhood vast quantities of ship-masts are sent down the Niemen; from the different sources of the river, the land carriage is about thirty miles. A large quantity of hemp, flax and grain, is also sent from this country. At present the price have fallen considerably; what formerly sold for thirty roubles, is now sold for three.

We were detained two days at Minsk for horses; the post-house could grant none, as every thing was in hurry and bustle, on account of the arrival of the Emperor. What also contributed to our detention was, it being the Jew's Sabbath, and his unwillingness to do any business on that day: at length we overcame his religious scruples, and for thirty-eight roubles we procured six horses for the next two stages. The Jew would not receive the money into his hand, but held up the flap of his cloak for it!

The road leaves Minsk, over a large and

beautiful common, which forms a kind of open circular space about the town, while, beyond it, one uninterrupted circle of forest binds the view. In one part of this common is seen a magnificent burying ground of the Jews. The country, for the first stage, continued partly open, but in general covered with distant forests; the road was excessively bad. We baited the horses at a solitary station-house, about seventeen miles from Minsk, and travelled the next stage during the night. We had not proceeded far when one of the Jews fell asleep, the horses strayed to one side of the road, and the carriage was overturned into a ditch; fortunately no injury occurred to our persons excepting a slight contusion which one of the servants received on the knee; but our carriage was severely damaged, and all our light baggage was tossed out. We procured a torch and after a careful search recovered all our books, &c. A scene like this in a dark, cold, rainy night, in the midst of Lithuania and the inhospitable Jews, was by no means agreeable. Early in the morning we reached the small village of Koidanovo, containing about eight hundred inhabitants, and built in a tolerably neat manner. Here we were driven into a large stable, similar to the different stages throughout Holstein and part of Prussia. At every stage we began to remark a change of manner, strongly indicating a change of people. All traces whatever of the Russians we had long lost sight of, and that of the Poles began now to mingle with the Lithuanians. We were detained at this place several hours to repair the damages our carriage had received, and met with several traits of the Jewish character. For the next stage they demanded as many roubles as what we had agreed to give for the former ones ; this is a common piece of imposition with the Jews, a charge was also made for the time the carriage had occupied the stable, and a still more extraordinary demand was made for a few blows which one of our servants had given the Jew at the time he overturned the carriage ! The greatest confusion and vociferation prevailed. The Jews had just quitted their morning prayers, and entered the stable in a body. One half spoke the Hebrew tongue, another the Lithuanian dialect, and German, French, and English, added to the noise. The glimmering rays of the carriage lamp were feebly thrown over this motley group, and never did a scene of such confusion prevail. At length the dispute was settled by money, the only power the Jews would submit to.

The road from this is heavy, boggy, and mostly through one continued forest. Komeli is the next stage ; it is a solitary station house, situated in a picturesque opening of the forest ; the land-

lord is a civil Pole. Leaving Komeli we proceeded to Novo Svergino through a beautiful avenue of trees, and surrounded by a deep forest,
the greater part of which seemed to have suffered from the enemy's fire The trees are still
alive, though much scorched at the trunks. The
road is flat and sandy ; and, in many places,
passes small lakes and little hamlets. Novo
Svergino is a small bourg, consisting of one long
irregular street of wooden houses, and about
five hundred inhabitants, mostly catholics. The
country, to the east, is an extensive morass, which
is divided by a small branch of the Niemen; it
is the property of a Polish nobleman.

This part contains the finest fir wood we have
hitherto seen, and the best improvements in agriculture. The fields are extremely large ; the
crops are rye, wheat, oats and buck wheat. The
soil varies, from a fine light to a black heavy
loam, yet the crops do not appear luxuriant, and
very few black cattle are to be seen. The people are very plain, coarse looking, and shabby in
their attire ; the women are dressed in coarse
woollen coats like the men, with a napkin tied
round the head; over it is fastened a white band
of linen, which hangs down the back with three
ends. The people are chiefly Catholics, and the
road too often presents the spectacle of a small
wooden figure, dressed up in rags, to represent
our Saviour.

In the countenance and costume of the people, in several parts of this district, we could not but remark a great similarity with the lower orders of the Irish;—the cast of the countenance and complexion are exactly alike—the ragged coat, and flapping high crowned hat, with a cord tied round it for a band, are also similar. This resemblance, however, is only external; the moment the mouth is opened the simile is lost; and, instead of hearing from it the varied expressions of wit, genius, and passion, so peculiar to the one, nothing but the language of wretchedness is delivered by the other;—for the hospitality and soul-speaking welcome of the one, we discern the vile, cringing approach, of the other;—for thought-less, hurried generosity, is exchanged cold, calculating cunning;—for wit and imagination, craft and dullness.—Ages must roll over their night-shaded history, time must improve in the tardiness of its course, governments must be changed, and soil must alter, until that day and hour arrive, when the bards of Sclavonia shall be enlightened with the spirit of a Sterne, or its temples consecrated with the genius of a Burke! But never will that day arrive, never will human nature, here, shine out;—like where, at north, the grey denuded steep points its chill brow to shade the Polar wave, ever will it be lifeless, dreary, and still, in these inhospitable, melan-

choly regions. Not more impotently does that
weak winter sun, which lights them to their lot,
throw down its unwarming beam,—not more idly
does the summer's wave play around the base of
Zembla's isle, than does the light of soul around
these benighted beings. But to proceed with our
journey.

On taking leave of Novoe-Svergino, we had,
as usual, to proceed through some fine forests of
fir. The country, however, soon opened, and
appeared to be extensively cultivated. The
fields are very large. We were now on the
borders of the government of Minsk, and were
about to enter that of Lithuania. From Novoe-
Svergino the road goes south to Nevisge, one
stage, and thence north again to Mir. These
two stages form fifty-four wersts; but, by crossing from Novoe-Svergino to the latter, along the
base of the angle, a very short cut is made, by a
bye-road, which is excellent. The country
around is flat and well cultivated. The town of
Mir stands on a gentle eminence, on the west side
of a small river. It consists of a collection of
wooden houses, with a large brick church in the
centre of an open square ; the population is about
one thousand persons. Close to the town are the
ruins of a palace of the Duke Radgiwiloff. Along
this part of the country we could not avoid remarking the extreme speed with which the horses

are driven. The postillions are generally boys; they are clad in a loose frock coat, without shoes or stockings, and constantly ride without a saddle, Leaving Mir, we entered on an excellent road, and passed through a fine extensive grain coun-try; on all sides, as far as the eye could reach, there were neither trees nor waste land; every acre seems to be under the influence of the plough; the soil is a light black loam, but the crops do not appear plentiful. Single oxen are yoked in small wains, and driven by women, who also assist at the plough and harrow, &c. Large flocks of horned cattle and horses were herded together; but we observed neither sheep nor hogs. It is worthy of remark that, along the country, from Moscow, the harvest was comple-tely finished; here it is generally finished by the middle of September, when the rye is sown.

Pursuing our road we came to a small bourg, named Korelitzi, consisting of mean wooden houses, thatched, very small and comfortless, and resembling their inmates. The streets are execrably paved, and filthy. It is impossible for any one to walk through the streets of the Lithu-anian towns, without wading above the ancles in dirt. Here was stationed a large depôt of Russian artillery and Cossacks. At sunset we left this village, and had not proceeded more than seven wersts, when, on descending a steep hill, we felt

one of the carriage wheels giving way, in consequence of the damage it had received the night
before, and the rapid manner in which we had
been driven during the day. Shortly after we
had procured a light, and examined the extent
of the damage, a band of Lithuanian Jews arrived, and offered their assistance. The wheel
was taken off, and the carriage dragged to a solitary house named Pollanna, in a lonely, wild and
sequestered vale; here our perplexities were increased, for no sooner had the Jews and their
associates got possession of the wheel, than it was
stolen;—neither threats nor reward could induce
them to restore it. Hitherto we had travelled by
night, as well as by day, among hordes of Cossacks, through endless forests and marshes, over
hill and dale, and never met with an obstacle
which could retard our progress; but such a
check given to our speed made us feel the inconvenience of being in the wilds of Lithuania,
among Jews, whom we knew both by report and
experience would rob us, and who had been accustomed to attack and plunder the wretched
French soldiers. In Russia we had often been
warned of the dangers of travelling; advice which
we disregarded: the reports of dangers we treated with ridicule, and never found ourselves, in
the least frequented parts of that country, in any
manner insulted by the people. In this dilemma
45

we entered the house. Instead of finding in it
the few men who had come to our assistance, we
discovered the hall of a common drinking house,
full of Jews and Lithuanians. It was not the
lively face of the Russ we beheld; but the haggard and vicious look of intoxicated miscreants,
dimly exhibited by the light of a torch. Noise
and tumult now ensued, and every means was attempted to perplex us; numbers collected around,
while drink stimulated and encouraged their
rudeness. We were twelve miles from Novogrodec, the next stage, and, as we learned, the
greater part through a forest. The women of
the house were particularly anxious to know
whether we would proceed, or remain until morning: as we decided they wispered the men, and
treated them with drams. We resolved to drag
the mutilated vehicle, on a long pole, to Novogrodec; but which plan we relinquished, in consequence of our friendly interpreter overhearing
that they had sent off a band to the forest, to
waylay our approach. We had no alternative
but to remain until morning. The carriage was
secured, and having armed ourselves, we set at
defiance the repeated insults levelled at us, and
guarded our property until six o'clock the following morning. The night was clear, yet excessively cold; each minute seemed lengthened
by the wish for its departure, and never did

morning dawn with more delight. As the night advanced, our antagonists passed from the quarrelsome state of intoxication, into the most harmless stupidity of complete drunkenness. We now dispatched our servant to Korelitzi, for the assistance of the police, and had, during the night, agreed to all the exorbitant demands of the Jews, who demanded sixty-three roubles for the horses standing in the stable, and ten more for the use of the posts which supported the carriage! When the police officer arrived every one had disappeared, and the Jew was most submissively contented to receive seven roubles, and to permit us to retain the plank which supported the carriage.

After a day's labour we reached Novogrodec; the country is partly cultivated, and its surface is finely undulated into gentle swells and plains; the prospects are boundless. Novogrodec is a district town; it stands on a high ridge of ground, and is seen from a considerable distance. As in all the towns, in Lithuania, it has a large square, from which a number of dirty lanes branch off. In the centre of the town are a few means brick houses, also the remains of an old castle, or citadel. The people are coarse, mean, and dirty, and consist chiefly of Jews; the women however are more attentive to their dress, and have the most pleasing countenances of any of the Lithuanian females we had seen. There is little or no trade carried on beyond the traffic of the Jews

The scene of our entering Novogrodec, with the carriage supported on a plank, and with only three wheels, was a source of infinite amusement to the inhabitants. As usual we were surrounded with Jews. After a delay of two days, we luckily met with a German, who sold us a wheel ; and though two inches lower than the other, we were contented to take it. Here we were most severely examined by the officers of the police, as to the nature of our journey, what reason we had to carry maps, &c. with us and what were our professions. Every foreigner who travels through Russia is considered as a merchant; and why we should pass through this part of the country, which offered no commercial interest, was more an object of astonishment. The idea of a foreigner travelling for amusement and information, was to them an inexplicable circumstance. We concealed our papers, satisfied their doubts, and were permitted to proceed. We engaged a Tartar to drive us, with one set of horses to Grodno, a distance of one hundred and forty-eight wersts.

From Novogrodec we entered an extensive forest of very old rotten fir trees. The road is merely an irregular track of deep ruts and wet sand, full of decayed trunks and stumps of trees. Twenty miles from Novogrodec, the forest terminated on the banks of the Niemen, which

we crossed on a floating raft. The river is here
about eighty yards wide, deep and rapid. From
the river we passed over a most extensive and
dangerous morass: it was impossible to travel
without the utmost caution, and not more than
two miles an hour. This stage was thirty miles
long, and is probably as intricate and dangerous
as any which could be passed. The horses became hourly entangled in marshy springs, and
every moment the carriage was likely to be
overturned, in consequence of our new hind
wheel being considerably lower than the other.
We lost a whole day on this dreadful stage, and
towards evening reached Belitza, a small bourg
of a few mean wooden houses, built round a
large open square, in the centre of which stands
a neat wooden church. The population is about
five hundred, partly Jews and Lithuanians.——
The Jews in this place are better looking than
formerly, but still *Jews*. The natives are extremely wretched, poor, and covered with rags.
The dress is a short frock coat, and cloth cap
without a brim—loose trowsers tied round the
ancle, and without shoes or stockings. The women wear a coarse wollen frock, tied round the
waist, and buttoned up the front—long sleeves
and deep frills.

The soil here is a fine loose loam. The plough
is extremely simple and seems to be generally

used in Lithuania. It is made entirely of one
branch of a fir tree ; the beam is formed of the
trunk, and the root forms the coulter; while the
lateral branches serve for the stilts or handles.
A considerable quantity of hemp is raised.

Having refreshed our horses at Belitza, our
Tartar insisted on proceeding another stage,
which he asserted was along an excellent hard
road. We accordingly proceeded a few wersts,
over a hard, dry, and well cultivated country;
but, towards evening, found ourselves on the borders of another morass. The weather of late
had been cold and rainy, and so soon as the 12th
of September, we perceived the approaching
signs of that early winter, to which these cheerless regions are, for so long a period, subject.
The evenings became frosty, and the nights extremely cold. We continued with caution to
proceed through this wild, dreary track, but
soon lost the regular road, and in passing over
a slight wooden bridge, it gave way, and entangled us in a most horrid morass, with a ditch
on each side. The night became dark, and the
clouds heavy and lowering. Our situation was
truly perilous ; but, at length we succeeded in
extricating the carriage, and by carrying a lighted torch before the horses, we immediately reached a Jew's hut, but who *singularly* refused us
admittance. We continued our progress, on a

tolerable track, and, in half an hour, regained the road we had lost, and reached a station-house, kept by a Pole. Here we found a small party of Polish officers, returning from Russia, and who had served in Napoleon's army. From them we received a variety of extraordinary anecdotes, relating to the campaign; the hardships they underwent, and the cruelties committed by both parties. To relate such tales, is only exposing the weakness of man, and can now be of no service—war will ever be followed by its train of evils, and individuals will speak of them, in proportion to the sufferings they have met with.— Among the prisoners was a Polish count, who had been a colonel in the French service;—he had marched from Seville, in Spain, to Paris, and onwards to join the *grand* army, which he met at Smolensko, on their flight,—there he was taken by the Russians, and sent to Orel, about two hundred miles south of Moscow.

At this miserable stations we were all lodged n the stable. The stables in this country, are the largest, and the most commodious part of the house. They are built parallel with the road, and are about one hundred feet in length, and forty feet in width. Each end is provided with large folding doors, and the carriages are always drove in at one door, and out at the other. In this place, travellers usually sleep in their car-

riage, while the postillions, servants, &c. with
their horses, are scattered on each side. From
the stable a narrow passage leads to a small dwelling house; but, from the filth and stench in them,
no stranger would dare to enter. In this stable
we prepared to pass the night. Our servants
spread some clean straw under the carriage, and
stretched themselves between the wheels. On
one side lay our drivers and their horses—before
us lay four Baskirs, and their large dogs; and, in
our front, were some Russians, and their horses;
besides, the Polish and French prisoners. Never
was a more motley group seen. We kept a lamp
burning on the top of the carriage. Our sleep,
as may be expected, was not of the most tranquil kind; we were soon disturbed, by a dreadful
bellowing, with the howling of dogs, and confusion of tongues. The cause we found to proceed
from our Tartar, who in a most piteous manner,
was complaining of the liberty which an old sow
and her young ones were taking with his sheep-
skin cloak, and with whom he was disputing possession this however, after some *violent* differences
of opinion was settled—peace was restored; the
Tartar continued his snore—the sow continued
her grunt—all was lost in sleep—the feeble
lamp-light flung its cheering ray around, and, not
until morning's dawn had summoned us from
our couch, did we bid adieu to the sow, and our
lively companions.

We proceeded on a narrow road, until we
reached Ioloudoke, a collection of mean huts.
Along this stage are two roads, the travelling,
and the post road; both are bad, particularly
the latter. At this stage the road to Wilna
branches off to the north. Here we dismissed
our Tartar, whom we found the worst driver that
ever managed the reins. Towards Tstouchino,
the road became more open and regular, and
the country better cultivated, with a hard clay
soil, and few trees. In passing along these tracts,
and for the last few stages, we could not avoid
remarking the calm and undisturbed state of the
country, without any of those marks of devastation and burning, which we had before so often
witnessed. The retreat of the French army having been cut off at Borisoff, the road hence, by
Minsk, to Grodno and the country round, was
untouched, and the only marks of spoilation,
which it now shews on one or two spots, resulted
from the early effects of the campaign.

The country through which we now travelled
was open and cultivated, but extremely sour and
sombre, without a tree to relieve the wearied
sameness. The weather was gloomy, lowering
and cold: the sun enveloped in misty vapours,
threw around an unwarming light; the bleak
winds waved over the immense fields of withered grass, and sighed along the endless plain; all

46

denoted the early approach of winter. Next
day the towers of Grodno came into view, and
compensated us.   It stands on a rising ground;
the surrounding prospect is most extensive, and
includes a view of the distant forests of Poland.
We descended into a deep broad valley, ascended
again and soon reached the barriers of the town.
Having now attained the frontiers of the Russian
empire, we deemed it most prudent to conceal
both our drawings and papers, as we had hitherto
met with several strict examinations, and were
compelled to write the account of each stage in
the carriage, when on the road; by these means
all suspicions were lulled.

Grodno is situated on the east side of the Niemen, five hundred and eighty-two wersts east of
Smolensko, or six hundred and eighty-seven
English miles from Moscow. It is irregularly
built, and exhibits a number of large churches,
and square towers.   In the form of the churches,
it somewhat resembles a town in Russia; they
have each two spires, and niches in the walls,
with figures. The religion is that of the Roman
church. The centre of the town is built with
brick, and the surburbs of wood; the streets are
badly paved, and very dirty. In various parts
of the town are the ruins of some magnificent
palaces and gateways, and other remains of fallen
splendour, which evince the ancient grandeur of
this spot. Here the Diets of Poland formerly

assembled, with the representatives from Lithuania,—and here Stanislaus, the last King of Poland resigned his crown, and dragged on a wretched life in a foreign land.

Next to wilna, Grodno is the largest town in Lithuania : the population is about eight thousand persons, but seems to consist of a mixture of various nations, who have settled here. Their employment consisted in manufacturing linen, cotton and silk; but, from late events, they have been reduced to idleness and poverty. We were detained three days, in the examination of our passports, and before a new order could be given us for horses to Warsaw; and here we were compelled to part with our faithful Prussian, who had acted as our interpreter; but, as we were to enter into Prussian Poland, where the German language was generally spoken, we felt the less lose : however we could not part from an individual, though in so humble a station of life and one who had gained so much of our esteem, without the deepest regret.

At the time we were at Grodno, large detachments of Cossacks, Baskirks, and other Russian troops, were quartered in the town, so that it presented a most varied picture. They were stationed partly as out-picquets to the grand army, which were marching about in every direction, to form a cordon of observation round the present frontier of Russia, to watch the ingress and egress of all strangers, and to be constantly hovering about in case of alarm.

Having now completed the extent of our investigations through a part of the Russian empire, and being on the eve of entering a new kingdom, we could not but contemplate the vastness and immensity of this unwieldy empire, to support whose overgrown size, the native of the most distant and untrodden regions, are called in. Hither flock the savage tribes, which prowl along the dens of the Caucasus, or the banks of the Oby—the wandering Samoide, and the houseless Tartar, here find a home and employment. The vastest bounds of the vastest empire in the world, pour along their contents, like a sweeping torrent—all tend to one point, all flock to one centre, and, under the wide waving banners of their mighty mother, all are enlisted, all are to serve.

Russia, as a whole, must be, more or less, weak from its expansion; it is too immense to be healthy. It wants the vigour of concentration, there is a kind of morbid bulk about it, which impairs its proper functions, and may one day put it out of breath. This is a remark, which must strike every traveller in this country; he will see it evinced in various features, and in many circumstances.

CHAP. XI.

WE felt, on crossing the boundary line of Russia, and entering into another nation, all that gratification to which the certainty of escape from bondage and despotism often exites. Before we could leave Grodno, we had the most frivolous and vexatious delays to contend with; the passports we had obtained at St. Petersburg could carry us no further, and we were obliged to obtain a governor's order to permit us to proceed to Warsaw. The delays and difficulties were endless. We had scarcely left the barrier gate when this order was inspected, our baggage ransacked, and the utmost trouble given to us. No less than three times were these endless and vexatious ceremonies practised in the spaee of three miles; and it was not untill after repeated trials of our patience, our temper, and our pockets, that we could disentangle ourselves from their snares, and bid the Russian frontiers adieu !

The Niemen, which we crossed on leaving Grodno, is deep and rapid, and about one hundred yards in width; its banks are steep, and broken with clay and gravel ruts: its scenery to the east, presents a pleasing landscape of forests and cultivated fields. The river is crossed by a floating bridge of planks. Numerous canoes scooped out of a single trunk of a tree, are seen on the river, similar to those of the American Indians; these are only large enough to contain one person who sits in the bottom of the boat and catches fish. Three miles from the Niemen we crossed a small stream, which is the boundary line between the Russian Empire and the duchy of Warsaw. a wooden bridge is thrown over this stream, one end of which is painted with black and white squares, denoting the Russian distinction; the other is red and white, that of Prussia. At the one end is stationed a Cossack sentry; at the other, a Polish police officer. We found no difficulty on entering the Polish side, as they seem, at present, not to know to which kingdom they belong, and perfectly indifferent about either; however of the two they are decidedly in favour of the Prussian yoke.

This first stage was over a rugged country, by a common track; the soil is covered with loose stones; the grass is strong and coarse. Large quantities of horse-raddish and wild celery (*apium graveolens*) grow most luxuriantly over the fields. On many of the fir trees were fixed hollow trunks of trees, as beehives. We changed horses at Kusniza, a small village, and proceeded through a wild rough country, to a mean village, on the borders of an immense morass. This swamp is crossed on hurdles, which form the road. To this morass an extent of dry, loose, drifted sand succeeded, and which was again bounded by a second morass, more extensive than the former, and more spongy, yet covered with dwarf bushes and reeds. This was about five miles in breadth, and stretched on both sides as far as the eye could reach. The adjoining country consisted of sand and light loam, with their crops of buck wheat. A rudely formed harrow is used, which is dragged by a rope, fastened round the neck of the horse. Here we changed horses at a solitary farm-house, pleasantly situated on a dry rising ground; but bounded in front by another of those singular and extensive marshes. This was the first stage in Poland which used the Prussian emblem; the postillions were dressed in Prussian livery, and the lively sound of the bugle echoing through the forests, was now substituted for the constant jingling of the Russian bell. The Russian wersts only extend to Grodno, from which the Prusssian miles commence, and the rate of posting rises to four-pence and a half for each

horse.   The Prussian mile here is equal to four
and a half English miles.

From Justrembne we rode through a large
forest of fir trees, forming a dark and solemn
avenue, and soon approached a fine lake, which
we crossed at a narrow point by a wooden bridge.
The scenery, though flat, is realy picturesque
and beautiful.   To Augustow, the next stage,
we proceeded by a very heavy road of loose
sand, and crossed the end of a small lake, by a
long wooden bridge.   Augustow is a small town,
of tolerable wooden houses, built round a large
wooden square, in the centre of which is a military guard-house.   The streets are long, narrow,
and full of mud ; the population is about twelve
hundred persons, who are all poles, fair, but not
robust : beards are not worn.   The dress is
generally a long cloth surtout, with a broad leather belt fastened round the waist.   We remarked
a fine breed of large dogs, and large flocks of
hogs, but of a most ugly form : few horned cattle
are reared, and no sheep.   The horses are small
and spiritless.   From this town, the road continues over loose sand, the country is open, level,
and well cultivated.   We passed through a small
forest, and three neat villages, adorned with little
gardens, and reached the town of Baggreda,
pleasantly situated on the side of a lake, which
it straggles along.   From this town we travelled

through a bleak sandy country, by a good road, but gradually entered on a better improved country. The habitations were now constructed of wicker-work, plaistered and thatched. We observed some large barns and farm yards, and an evident improvement towards comfort, beyond any thing in Lithuania. The houses were furnished with chairs and beds, &c. the inhabitants continue plain and simple, and without any peculiar character. There are very few Jews, and the German language is scarcely understood.

We now passed through a pleasant country, and woods of fir oak and elm; the former was nearly an hundred feet in height: the country was covered with flocks of cattle, of a small breed. Young rye was green above ground, the sowers were still busily employed, and every field presented an animated appearance. We now crossed the Narva, and entered the town of Lomza, situated on an eminence, and presenting a picturesque view. From Lomza a road leads to Konigsberg, and another to Bialystok. The Narva is a tolerably sized river, which has its source from three branches rising to the north in East Prussia, and from the east in Lithuania. These branches join at Ostrolensk, and afterwards fall into the Bug, one of the great and parrellel branches of the Vistula. By means of the Narva, great quantities of wood are annually

47

floated down to the Vistula, and hence conveyed to Dantzick. The Bug is more adapted to the conveyance of grain.

Napoleon passed this place about the first week of December, on his flight from Borisoff. He was accompanied by two officers and a Mameluke. He asked the landlord if he knew him, and appeared gloomy and reserved. The Russians, it is asserted, did not reach this place untill three weeks after he had passed it; nor did the people know of the complete overthrow of the French army.

The road from Lomza led us through a bed of fine, deep, loose sand, blown by the wind into various ridges, which continued to Ostrolenka. This little town stands on the banks of the Narva, which here widens into a kind of lake. Here we passed a camp of the Russian army, on its march to Warsaw; their blazing fires extended far around, and illuminated the dreary night. The road and sand continued parrellel with the river, untill it reached Rozona, which is very prettily situated on a rising ground, and inhabited by Jews. The shoes of the people are made with the hair on the skin, worn outwards. From this village, we hastened our rout towards Pultusk a mean, dirty town, with three large churches and a monastery: it is the residence of a bishop. The road continued good, and the extent of the forests in every direction was astonishing. Elm, oak, poplar, and fir, are the prevailing trees. The Narva meandered along the skirts of the forest, and, at several angles, exhibited picturesque scenery.

Leaving Wierzbica, we crossed the Bug, by a fine lofty wooden bridge, and entered again on a dreary sandy plain, which continued to Nieport. It is impossible to convey a just description of these sandy plains and morrasses, which alternately cover the face of the country, from Grodno to Warsaw, a distance of two hundred miles. They seem regularly to succeed each other, and present an appearance, as if the country had, at one time, been completely under water. The sand banks are always considerably elevated above the marshes; and their extent varies from five to fifteen miles in every direction. The rate of travelling over them is about two miles an hour.

We reached Nieport towards evening, and being within one stage of Warsaw, we deemed it prudent to delay passing through the intervening country, until next morning, in consequence of the numerous troops of Russian soldiers quartered in the vicinity. Here we met some German and dutch merchants, and had the pleasure of receiving the first intelligence of foreign news since we quitted St. Petersburg.

After a slight supper, we all betook ourselves to
our respective carriages, to pass the night. We
had not the shelter of a stable, and, from the
increased length and coldness of the nights, we
felt all the chilling effect of being obliged to
sleep in an open Russian carriage.

At the dawn of day we departed, and passed o-
ver an extensive and most beautiful plain, covered
with cultivated fields of Russian soldiers. From
a distance, we discovered the spires of the Polish
capital. We soon gained the suburbs, called the
Praga, crossed the Vistula, satisfied the police
officers, and entered the city.

The appoach to Warsaw, from the north, affords
the most pleasing view of the city. It stands on
a rising ground, on the south-west side of the
Vistula; which, on ascending, extends into a level plain, towards the south. The houses are
old, clumsy, and irregularly built. Many large
palaces in a state of neglect, and gothic churches
without spires, fill up; together with occasional
spaces, occupied by mean hovels and gardens.—
Passing through the town, the stranger is both
pleased and distressed, at the contrast of huge
piles of building mouldering into decay, and paltry hovels filled with Jews. The streets are narrow, badly paved, and without any regular footpath; on each side is a broad kennel to carry off
the rain. The houses are either of wood, as in
the suburbs, or of brick, stuccoed to imitate

stone. The principal houses are those of the nobles; but most of them are abandoned by their once opulent and noble possessors, and now converted into hotels and shops. These houses are built extremely plain, and without any ornaments; they are only conspicuous from their immense size. In the town there are forty churches, sixteen of which are monasteries, or nunneries. The cathedral stands in the centre of the city : it consists of a lofty body, without either spire or dome ; its interior is neatly decorated with private altars, and the seat of the late king. The other churches and convents are more heavy and clumsy. All the churches are built with the gable end to the street, and some of them terminated at each corner with a lower square tower. In the whole city, there are only five or six small spires, the highest not more than two hundred feet. The largest, and best built church in Warsaw, is that of the Lutherans. It is of a circular form, surmounted with a large dome. The late king, though a Catholic, gave from his private fortune, three hundred thousand florins towards building this church. From the gallery, at the top of the dome, we commanded a boundless prospect of the surrounding country. Nothing can be conceived more flat than the surface of the country ; the distant plains and forests seem to extend beyond the reach of the eye, and lose them-

selves in ether. The windings and sandy banks
of the Vistula are seen, far from the east, ma-
jestically rolling on its course towards the Baltic, while its floating bridge undulates with
every wave. On the north side of the river
are the mouldering ruins of the Praga, point-
ing to the unhappy pole the horrors of the
Russian massacre of 1794. On the opposite side
of the river is the other part of the suburbs, called the Kraka—where, in former times, during
the elective monarchy, the kings were chosen;
and which was often the scene of contention and
wars. In the reign of the late king the new constitution of Poland was formed, and the monarchy
became heriditary in his family. This has the
worst and meanest buildings attached to the city,
but it makes the most picturesque appearance.
These wooden huts are built in a most irregular
and straggling manner, each surrounded with
orchards full of fine fruit trees. Through this
part of the suburbs the road passes to the summer
palace of the late king, situated about a league
from the city. Viewing the scite of the town
from the top of this church, the houses appear
low and large. The scites are not extensive, but
the number of gardens spreads its boundary beyond what the population should allow. Excepting two tolerable streets, crossed at right angles
by other two, with the houses closely built toge-

ther, all the other parts of the town are divided into gardens, which vary in size, from a few roods, to four or five acres. They are all thickly planted with fruit trees, which gives the town the appearance of being placed in the midst of a luxuriant forest. In this respect, Warsaw appears even more singular and picturesque than Moscow. Such is a bird's eye view from the Lutheran church. In walking along the streets, an air of former grandeur every where arrests the attention, but now sadly divested of its former glory. In the principal street is the college, a large and not inelegant structure, at present shut up. The ancient palace of the Dukes of Saxony is now converted into a public school, where the students are well instructed in the various branches of literature, particularly the classics.

The palace is a large square building close to the river; the public rooms are few, but superbly furnished and painted: the whole was done under the immediate directions of the late king. In one small room were placed the portraits of his Majesty George III. of Great Britain, the kings of France, Germany, and Prussia, who were contemporary with Stanislaus, in the centre of this royal group is his own portrait. We next visited the summer palace of Stanislaus, situated on the banks of the river, about three miles from the city. The road passes through the suburbs of

Kraka, and enters a beautiful avenue, divided by nine rows of trees, which terminate in a large circular octagon, from which branch off eight other avenues, each at a short distance, crossed by others, and forming a kind of labyrinth. One of them passes a deep cut, made through a ridge of clay, on the top of which are erected elegant barracks for soldiers. Below this bank, in a sequestered vale, and on the edge of a small lake, near to the Vistula, is the elegant and beautiful summer palace of the late king. All which the exquisite refinement of education, and a chastened genius could invent, have been executed—no obtrusive gothic irregularity offends the eye, no voluptuous indelicacy hurts the feelings; neither magnitude nor vain shew disgust the taste—all is elegance, simplicity, and perfection. The house is small, and of an oblong form, between two narrow lakes, which wash its very foundation ; from which it is sometimes called *la Maison de Bain.* The rooms are beautifully painted and gilded— the pannels and doors are formed of elegant glass mirrors, and the floors inlaid with mosiac work.

About one hundred yards from the palace, in a retired grove, is situated the theatre, built partly from the model of Vespasian's amphitheatre. The stage is divided from the audience by a stream of water, and was intended to represent the ruins of the temple of the Sun at Palmyra ; the whole is beautifully covered with the dark foliage of the surrounding trees. The part allotted to the spectators consists of a circular series of steps, the last row of which supported a range of statues. The whole is uncovered, and the performance was usualy exhibited in the afternoon. To behold a theatric exhibition in so retired and calm a spot, and under the cooling shade of trees, must have afforded an exquisite treat to the lovers of the Drama. In an adjoining thicket was placed the concert-hall, where Pan and his Sylvan train might have responsed to soft sounds of music. Such was this beautiful spot, planned and executed by the good Stanislaus, who, with short-sighted hope, promised himself a quiet and sequestered abode, in which the evening of his life might have passed, and the pressure and turbulence of the government have been softened. This amiable prince beautified the environs of his capital from his private fortune; and, while he expended it in adorning the public grandeur of the capital, his ungrateful nobles wrangled, and allowed their glorious independence to be subdued, the sceptre of the realm to be broken, and the monarch to abdicate the throne, and end his days in a foreign land. Blush, ye jarring and oppressed Poles, to submit to a miserable existence under a foreign yoke, rather than shake off the odious bondage and trample on the inva-

48

ders of your country's liberty! What can ye
expect from your eastern friends? Can the
Russ teach ye the art of being free and independent? Can he improve the soil of your country,
or the cultivation of your minds? Or, can ye
forget his merciless cruelty in the siege of 1794?
On the bank, opposite to the barracks, the king
had planned the erection of a magnificent church,
in honour of the new constitution of Poland;
but it remains for another virtuous, and more
warlike Stanislaus, in honour of a glorious restoration of ancient Poland, freed from vassalage
and the subjugation of foreign powers.

Every traveller must be pleased with Warsaw.
The appearance of the people are sprightly and
gay—their complexions are fair, and, in their
figure, not unlike the English. The gentlemen
are particularly foppish in their dress—the ladies
are soft, comely, and of a small figure; they dress
very plain, except that a plume of feathers is
generally worn on the head. Black dresses
seem to be the most prevalent among them,
probably it is a mourning for the fate of Poland.
The streets are crowded with pedestrians, lively
and gay, but seemingly without any object in
view. There is not much appearance of wretchedness in the streets; the filthy sheep-skins of
the Russians are not seen, nor the indolence of
sleeping on the ground. An air of activity

prevails among the lowest orders, and their fine
fair countenances are not disfigured by an hideous
goatish beard. The shops are scattered every
where, and the streets crowded with stalls of fruit
and coarse sugar candy. The quantity, size, and
richness of flavour of the apples, pears, and
plumbs sold here, are astonishing. The pears,
are remarkably large, and possess an exquisite
flavour. Although such a vast quantity of fruit
is cultivated, yet they do not convert it either
into cider or perry. Poultry of all kinds is also
brought to the market in great abundance. The
public carriages are open phaetons, of a low form,
with one or two horses; the linings are generally
painted of a red colour, and which is easily kept
clean. These vehicles only carry two persons
but, unlike the Muscovites, the healthful exercise
of walking is preferred to the indolence of a
carriage. The horses are large and beautiful;
those of a piebald cast are very common, and
much admired. Large collars, of a red or green
colour, is the prevailing fashion of the harness,
which is covered with small brass rings, which
serve as tinkling bells. The hotels are numerous,
and generally kept in some of the old palaces.
At the entry of each hotel a porter is stationed,
dressed in a rich suit of livery, with a large
cocked hat and silver headed cane. He receives
the names of visitors, and conducts travellers to

their apartments, &c.　As in Russia, there are no beds, but sofas.　There are both stoves and fire-places, but no fire-grates.　Wood is the only fuel, which they have in great abundance.　Provisions of all kinds are plentiful; the bread is particularly fine, and very white.

The theatre is the only public place of amusement.　The house is large and elegantly fitted up, and the performers lively and interesting. The pit is an open space, without seats.　The drama generally consists of translations from the German with scarcely any native productions. The only writer of comedies whom we know is Bohomolec, who lived in the last century.　Poland can boast of no literary pretensions.　Its language is a dialect of the ancient Sclavonian; the alphabet consists of the common Roman characters, with the addition of nine duplicates, or accents, which are placed over certain letters, and which indicate a difference of sound.　Learning has not flourished; nor could the calm pursuits of literature have taken place, in a country so constantly the scene of wars and oppression. Yet individual genius has sprung up, and Martin Cromer, the historian of his country; and particularly Copernicus,* the astronomer, will live as

---

* In the former part of this work we had occasion to notice the celebrity of this philosopher. He was born at Thorn in 1472, and died in 1543, at Frauensberg.

long as science exists. The Polish language is spoken uncommonly fast, and with a hissing sound. The Russians and Poles partly understand each other. French is more generally spoken than German; all the *valets de place* are Frenchmen.

The town is not fortified; round the suburbs are earthen ramparts, a few feet in height, is thrown up, but without any means of defence. The religion of the people is that of the Roman church. The offensive shew of crosses and crucifixes every where obtrudes itself; these crosses are about thirty feet in height, and the figure as large as life : some of them are covered with rags and adorned with wreaths of flowers; others represent a skeleton. Nothing can be more shocking than this display of religious torture. The common people are extremely ignorant, and many of the priests are little better. One of the convents, which we visited, contained several fathers; they were habited in long loose white woollen cloaks, with a small black velvet cap on their heads. Few of them could speak any language but their own; and their time was taken up in grinding a small organ, in order to teach a canary bird to imitate its sounds.

The present population of Warsaw is estimated at fifty thousand individuals, of whom twenty thousand are Jews, and who seem to manage all

the trade of the city. In short, the whole retail
trade of Lithuania and Poland is carried on by
the Jews; their number, throughout the country,
is calculated at above two millions, which is probably the greatest collection of Jews in any part
of the world. It is a singular circumstance that
they are not allowed any place of public worship in Warsaw.

The Vistula is, here, a noble river; it is nearly one quarter of a mile in breadth, deep and
rapid. It takes its rise on the northern frontiers
of Hungary, about one hundred and fifty miles
to the south of Cracow, which it passes, and continues, as the boundary line, between the Duchy
of Warsaw and Hungary, as far as Sendomirz;
whence it takes a north-westerly course, and,
after a passage of one hundred and twenty miles,
passes Warsaw, and continues by Plock, Thorn,
Culm, Graudenz and Marienwerder, to Dantzick,
where it falls into the Baltic Sea; completing a
course of nearly seven hundred miles. From
Cracow it is navigable by long flat barges. From
Warsaw to Dantzick the voyage is most agreeable, and usually performed in from two to three
days.

CHAP. XII.

Berlin, October, 1814.

In quitting the capital of Poland, we could not but think of its present and its former state. We could not forget its once proud independence, when, with a population of fifteen millions of people, it supported its own sovereigns, and commanded the respect of other nations. We could not but lament to see so fine a country so devastated by its conquest; so tortured by its tyrannies; and so helpless to its interests. Distorted into every shape in which the agonies of tyranny could writhe them, its governments have assumed every form which the chimeras of despotism, or the madness of ambition, could invent. The fate of Poland must ever excite sympathy. With all the materials of freedom, independence, and glory, she has sunk to nothing;—her name is scarcely known among nations; and those very materials, which once constituted her pride, now constitute her misery. In the manufactory of her misfortunes they have been melted down,

and refined into the implements of the basest
born slavery. Long torn from her parent stock
of nobles; stripped of her rights, her virtues, and
her freedom; dismantled, dismembered, trodden,
and laid waste, she now, like the withered branch
of the sapless tree, which bends but to break,
bows down her head, shelters herself by her humility, and submits to invasion. Swept by its
streams, and blasted by its storms, lowly and
prostrate she now lies, drooping to her parent
earth; and never will she again take her rank
amid the nations of that earth; never will the
bright star of liberty again shed its light over
her plains, or sound its lay in the halls of her
barons, until the kindred spirit of a Stanislaus,
a Poniatowsky, or a Kosciusko shall again appear—shall again break her chains and awaken
into life the genius of her freedom. With these
she has fallen—with them her bright sun has set;
and long, over their tombs, may its last rays play,
till her sufferings be buried in the night of time.

Poland must now submit to a northern poten-
tate: she must increase the bounds of the boundless dominions of Russia. If the banks of the
Vistula are to be included within these bounds,
then the eastern provinces of Prussia may yet
feel the inconvenience of its insolated situation,
and her rich and commercial ports, from Dantzick to Memel, become a prey to the power of
Russia.

The road from Warsaw led us through a very
flat open country, with a fine sandy loam, well
cultivated but without any division of fields.
The ridges are very narrow, not more than four
feet wide, by which a vast deal of ground is lost,
by the frequency of the furrows. The stubble
appear strong, and the young crops of rye healthy and vigorous. The ploughs are, in general,
drawn by one pair of oxen, also the wains, but
the harrows are drawn by horses. The mode of
yoking and driving the last is somewhat singular,
and exactly corresponds with the mode of posting. A pair of horses is yoked to the harrows,
one of which the workman rides, and drives three
others, yoked abreast, in front. In this part of
the country water appears extremely scarce, and
the cattle seem to suffer from it. The horses are
small and active, and are readily procured at the
different stages. Blonie, the first stage at which
we changed horses, is a mean town of wooden
houses with a large square, and about six hundred
people; they are quiet and simple without any
particular character arising from their vicinity
to the capital, and whose lives afford that hnm-
ble, tranquil stream, which admits neither of
interest nor description. Proceeding hence, we
soon reached a prettily situated town, on a rising
bank, over a small river, forming a tributary
stream to the Vistula, and which we crossed by

a long wooden bridge. This town, like the last, presents, on a closer view, a paltry mean appearance. It possesses a plain brick church, and the ruins of an old *chateau.* This last stage is composed of the richest black loam which can be seen; it has all the appearance of black, greasy peat moss. The stubble here is very strong. Along this part of the country are several detatched farm houses, and the grain, throughout, is packed into large barns; not stacked as in other countries.

The road continued loose and sandy, and became agreeably shaded by shrubs, and fine trees of oak and fir, until it reaches Lowiez, a considerable town of four thousand inhabitants. The streets are clean, the houses large and well built; and it contains five churches. At the time we entered there was a fair, and the town appeared crowded. We could not procure loaging, and were obliged to proceed, about midnight, and had scarcely passed the environs of the town, when we were suddenly attacked by two footpads, one of whom leapt up behind the carriage, the other attacked the door; they appeared unarmed and perfectly intoxicated, and we had just time to prevent our German servant from firing on them. The postillions blew their horn, and went off at quicker speed. The robber still persisted in opening the side door, when we sud-

denly vociferated, *und voce,* such a dreadful yell
in his face, that he fearfully shrunk back, and
we escaped. An hour afterwards we lost the
road, but soon recovered it, and, apprehending
still further mischief, placed ourselves on the
boxes, both before and behind the carriage, and
kept a regular watch. Scarcely had we commenced our observations, when three men on
horseback came up, and reconnoitred us. They
rode round the carriage, disappeared, and returned again and again, evidently with intentions
not of an amicable nature. Having made their
reconnoissances, and finding there were five of
us, besides the postillions, well armed, and placed in a most imposing attitude, they at least
seemed irresolute and gallopped off across the
country. Robberies in this country we every
day learned, were very common, from the vast
numbers of French prisoners returning home,
and other disbanded soldiers, together with Jews,
who, having no profession live by plunder. Only
a few nights before, three German merchants
were attacked, in this neighbourhood, and murdered; their bodies were found the following
day.

From Lowiez the stage is rather bad, through
an open country, partly of loose sand and blackish
moss. We passed a neat *château,* the residence
of a Polish nobleman. The grounds are neatly

laid out and planted. The next stage was Pniew, a small miserable village of wooden huts, straggling along the road and containing not more than one hundred inhabitants. In this district agriculture is carried on with greater spirit than in any former part of Poland. The soil is a fine light loam and gradually increases in fertility as it recedes from the capital, and the crops appeared to have been very heavy. The plough is in universal use; it differs from that of Lithuania. The handles are long and upright, the beam short, but supported on an axle between two clumsy wheels: it is altogether a very clumsy machine, though accounted the most perfect in the country. Each plough is drawn by four oxen, which are managed by the ploughman alone. Near Kutno we observed twenty-four ploughs in one field, similarly yoked and managed. It is surprising to remark the docility of the oxen, and the easy manner in which they are guided. It is not an uncommon sight, in many parts of England, to observe ploughs as clumsily constructed, and heavier than the Polish plough, drawn by three, or five large horses, with a man to drive them, independently of the ploughman, and besides do not turn up deeper, nor more regular furrows, than the Polish plough; and it might even be questioned, if they perform as much labour, in a certain space of time.

In no country have we seen a richer soil, and more susceptible of agriculture, than in Poland. Every acre, from Warsaw, is capable of great improvement, and the country at large might become the granary of the north of Europe. The Prussian division evidently bears marks of general improvement ; the small farms are more protected, and its inhabitants saved from plunder. Farming, in Poland, is very different from that in Russia. Though the common people are equally slaves, and considered as disposable property, yet they are not obliged to give their labour, in every instance, to the proprietor, who seldom interests himself in the cultivation of his own estates ; but either to an agent, or one who leases a farm. In this case, the extent and value of a farm do not altogether depend on the nature of the soil, but on the number of villages or inhabitants residing on it ; as, from their assistance, the farmer expects to derive the chief source of his profits. A farm therefore of any importance, in Poland, must consist of between one and two thousand acres, while probably the greater part of it is covered with wood. When we find the farms of such an extent, how very extensive must the estates of the nobles be ! These differ in proportion to their local situation. In the more remote parts of the country, some individuals, particularly

the Czartoryski family, possess as much territory
as nearly equal in size to the fourth of Scotland.

We now see a part of those sources, whence
the immense granaries at Dantzick and Elbing
are supplied, and the advantages of the Vistula,
and its numerous branches, in the facility of transporting the productions of the country.

The frequent allusions to the state of agriculture of these countries, may be considered as an
useless waste of time; but whatever tends to
illustrate the practical resources of a country,
and the means by which its population may be
supported and improved, is more worthy the attention of the intelligent and rational mind, than
an exuberance of lighter, and perhaps more en-
tertaining, imaginary remarks.   When the earth
acquires an increased load of inhabitants, means
must be provided for their existence; and it is
only from the *soil*, and the labour of our hands,
that those means are to be attained, on which the
subsistence of man must altogether depend.

The surface of the country, now before us,
varied a little; its flatness gave way to gentle
undulations and straggling clumps of trees and
copses.   On the whole, the landscape became
rather agreeable.   The villages were surrounded
with small windmills, and neat orchards, with distant forests.   Nothing can exceed the beauty of
these forests, particularly the one round Som-

polno. Its breadth is about twelve miles, and its
length very great; the trees are either fir or oak,
and of great size; the ground is smooth, level,
and covered with the finest turf, and the postillion
chuses his own track. The ride through these
forests is delightful : neither noise nor motion is
felt from the carriage, and the dark shade of the
trees affords a pleasing sensation of tranquillity.
It is not however safe to pass them, particularly
at night, as we were often obliged to do. They
abound with robbers, wolves, and fallen trees.
We did not however meet with any interruption,
beyond the sight of some foxes, and the distant
howl of wolves. It was not the season of attack
from the latter, which, in the severe months of
winter, became a dangerous enemy to travellers.
The woods in Poland are infested with wolves,
and it is not an unusual circumstance for horses
and cattle to be carried off by them. An anecdote is related of a traveller passing through
these forests, and being attacked by a number of
wolves, his servant exclaimed, " protect my wife
and children," and instantly leaped into the midst
of them while his master escaped! In the middle of the forest, we reached a small open space,
in which were a few huts of some Jews, employed as carriers, and a receptacle for robbers. Leaving the forest we came in sight of a fine lake,
which gives the origin to the Notec river, which

forms the north branch of the Oder. On the opposite bank of the lake is situated the little town of Kleczew; we entered it under a fine arched gateway, whereon we observed fixed, for the first time, the Prussian eagle. The town is small and irregular; consisting of one long dirty street of wooden houses, but containing nothing of either interest or amusement to detain travellers: we therefore drove on. The country continued cultivated, and young crops of rye gave to the face of the soil a most cheering appearance. The people present a poor, miserable, dejected aspect, without any peculiar costume, except that of rags and matted hair. Stupidity and ignorance abound here. The houses are mean, low and dirty, generally raised on a wooden frame, filled up with straw and clay, and clumsily thatched with long bundles of straw. Most of the houses have gardens attached to them, containing beans, peas, cucumbers, gourds, &c. hops are occasionally seen, and appear to thrive well. A most singular mode of salutation is practised among the common people throughout Poland. Whenever any gift is presented to them, or acts of attention, they bend their bodies forward, and touch the lower part of the leg of the person to whom they are paying their obedience. When ever we had occasion to present any of them with small donations, we regularly received this salu tation. The Russ kisses the ground—the Pole is contented to touch his benefactor's leg!

We now reached the town of Posen, situated on the west bank of the Warta, the centre branch of the Oder. This river is only navigable by flat open boats. It is crossed by a small wooden bridge, and the road passes between the cathedral and the bishop's house. The town is large, and contains about fifteen thousand inhabitants. The houses are regularly built and stoccoed, but many streets exhibit a ruinous state. The churches are numerous and elegant. It is the see of a bishop, and one of the most ancient in Poland; it has also an university, public library, theatre, and public gardens. The streets being close and compact, the town does not occupy much space. The suburbs are clean, and agreeably laid out in avenues of poplars and straggling cottages. The inns are extremely dirty, and open to all intruders. The university is situated within a short distance of the town; it has greatly degenerated, but still contains twelve professors. The jail is full of highwaymen, many of whom we observed at the windows, and who appeared to have moved in a superior class of society. From every information we could learn, it was evident that travelling in this country is very dangerous. We continued to trace the flight of Napoleon in this town, from which

50

he proceeded to Glogau and Dresden. One of
the public walks is called after him, and in
general we found his name more respected here,
and in many parts of the country, than at Warsaw. We were detained several hours at Posen,
before we could get our passports, signed by the
police. One of the secretaries at length waited
on us, and said he knew we were Englishmen,
and expected to be well paid before he would
return the passports:—to this species of extortion
we were obliged to submit, and could not but
feel disgusted at so much mean venality in these
demi-official characters.

From Posen three public roads branch of, to
Breslau, Crossen, and Franckfort on the Oder.
The last we pursued, and passed through an open
flat country, partly cultivated, or in general
covered with fine dry sand, which retards the
speed of travelling to the rate of three miles an
hour. The sand is often drifted into ridges,
thirty to forty feet in height—in some places the
roots of the stunted oaks and fir trees were left
quite exposed. The German language is now
generally spoken, though mixed with the Polish.
We reached the town of Meseritz, situated on
the Obra, a small stream which falls into the
Warta. The town contains about six thousand
inhabitants, who carry on a small trade in the

manufactory of fine woollen cloth; the importation of which, into Russia, is strictly prohibited. This was the last stage in Poland; and
here we underwent the usual examination and
search. Every package was opened, and every
corner of the carriage examined. During this
vexatious ceremony, the police officer was constantly reminding us of his fees, but which were
gradually lowered from four, to one dollar, as
he found we had no contraband goods! From
Meseritz to Franckfort on the Oder, is three
stages. The road and country seem to contend
in the extremes of good and bad—picturesque
and barren—hill and dale—cultivation and extensive waste. It commences through a rich country, passes a small forest of oak, and enters on a
flat extensive moor: to this succeeds a rural
village, embosomed in orchards, with abundant
crops of fruit. During the first stage a gate is
placed across the road, which marks the division
of Prussian Poland from Prussia Proper—no
ceremony is used in passing this frontier. As
soon as we crossed this distinction, we began to
find ourselves in Prussia; the fumes of tobacco-
smoke assailed us in every direction, insolence
and extortion from the postillions, and German
indifference, marked the character of the country.

The peasantry of Prussia enjoy privileges,
different from those which have been already

described.—Those who occupy farms from the
crown, pay only a small rent, and they are also
assisted in the building of their houses. For this
indulgence their sons must be trained up for the
use of the army, and in case of emergencies they
are placed on active service; they must also
provide a certain quantity of provision for the
army, when passing through that part of the
country which they inhabit. In the time of
peace, these people are undisturbed, become
rich, and happy. In war, they are liable to lose
their children, and be burthened by the troops.

Franckfort is a beautiful inland town. It
stands on the west side of the Oder, and is called
Franckfort on the Oder, to distinguish it from
Franckfort on the Maine. It was formerly one
of the principal cities in Brandenburg. It has
some remarkably fine Gothic churches. It once
contained an university, but which has been
lately removed to Breslau, and the buildings
converted into a military magazine. A considerable manufactory of fine woollen cloths and
hats is carried on, and great annual fairs are held
here.

The Oder is about one hundred yards broad,
and is navigated by long open barges. This river
is far inferior to the Vistula, though its course is
nearly as extensive; it rises close to Ollmutz in
Moravia, near the source of the Vistula, passes

through the centre of Silesia, and falls into the Frische Haffe at Stettin.

From Franckfort on the Oder to Berlin, is three stages. The intermediate country is flat, barren, and covered with loose sand—however the road is one of the finest in the kingdom, and made at a great expense—on it, are several toll-gates, and each carriage pays one dollar. Munchberg is the only place of any importance on this road : it is a small town with one thousand two hundred inhabitants. The approach to Berlin is inconceivably beautiful—numerous avenues of poplars extend from all parts of the suburbs, and the crowd of passengers and carriages, announce the importance of a capital. At this elegant city we safely arrived, after a most persevering, and laborious journey, from St. Petersburg, including a distance of nearly one thousand nine hundred miles. And here we met with that repose which our fatigues demanded.

From Warsaw we had intended to proceed on the great south road to Cracow, and onwards to Vienna; but from the scarcity of horses, &c. and in consequence of the meeting of the Congress at Vienna, we were induced to alter our route, by Berlin; and thence we intend to proceed through Saxony, &c. The other route, by Cracow, would undoubtedly have proved more interesting than the present, but a traveller cannot, at all times, command his road, particularly through countries where he is obliged to travel according to the caprice of the police, as occurred to us at Grodno; from which we were sent round by the Prussian frontier, instead of the regular, and shorter road, by Bailystock, to Warsaw. This was probably done, that we should either avoid, or not behold, the Russian troops, stationed along that part of the country.

At the conclusion of these pages, it would be unnecessary to enter on any description of Berlin, a capital, so extensive and magnificent, and already so well known. Here the traveller, who has suffered fatigues and privations, through the dreary forests of Russia, and the marshes of Poland, will find the most luxurious banquet, and the most captivating society.

We have now, in the progress of this work, contrasted the appearance, manners, and character, of five capitals, with a vast extent of country between them; and a variety of human beings, more or less elevated or degraded, in the scale of human nature.

In such a retrospect, the contemplative mind and feeling heart, may find a rich source of lasting, and pleasing reflection; and inasmuch as it enlarges the sphere of our thinking faculties, and may lead us to survey that indescribable grandeur and beauty, which all the aspects of the physical and moral creation exhibit, so it must tend to place in a still more exalted point of view, that great power in nature, from whom all knowledge and good are derived.

APPENDIX.

—◦◦—

The following Table exhibits a list of the Stages connected with this work. The names of each Stage—the distances between them in wersts, Danish, and German miles—with their respective population, and the rate of posting,—are carefully annexed.

Stages.	Population.	Miles.	Stages.	Population.	Miles.
1 Copenhagen . .	100,000	4	29 Griefswalde . .	9,000	4
2 Roskilde . . .	2,000	4	30 Anclam	6,000	4 1-4
3 Ringstead . . .	1,200	4	31 Uckermunde . .	—	5 1-4.
4 Slagelse . . .	1,000	2	32 Falkenwalde . .	—	2
5 Corsöer	—	4	33 Stettin	22,000	5
6 Great Belt . . .	—	4	34 Gullnow	3,000	4
7 Odensee . .	5,500	6	35 Naugard . . .	2,500	4
8 Middlefarth . .	1,200	1-4	36 Griffensberg . .	2,000	2 1-4
9 Little Belt . .	—	3 1-2	37 Triptow	3,300	3 3-4
10 Kolding	1,000	4 1-2	38 Colberg . . .	7,000	
11 Hadersleben . .	1,400	5	39 Corlin	1,200	3 3-4
12 Appenrade . . .	—	4 1-2	40 Coslin	4,500	2 3-4
13 Flensburg . . .	14,000	4 1-2	41 Paukenin . . .	—	2 3-4
14 Schleswig . . .	6,000	3	42 Schlawe . . .	—	3 1-2
15 Eckenfhorde . .	—	3 1-2	43 Stolpe	—	3 1-2
16 Kiel	8,000	4 1-2	44 Lupow	100	2 1-2
17 Newmunster . .	—	3	45 Langbose . . .	50	2 1-2
18 Bromstadt . . .	—	2 1-2	46 Goddentow . . .	—	3 1-2
19 Ultzburg . . .	—	4	47 Newstadt . . .	—	2 1-2
20 Hamburg . . .	80,000	4	48 Gleicartz . . .	—	2 1-2
21 Schonberg . . .	—	4	49 Dantzick . . .	60,000	4 3-4
22 Lubeck	31,000	5	50 Derschau . . .	1,000	3
23 Greifsmuhlin . .	-—	3	51 Marienberg . . .	4,000	4
24 Wismar	6,000	3	52 Elbing	25,000	2
25 Nebuga	—	4	53 Truntz	150	2
26 Rostock . . .	13,000	4	54 Frauensberg . .	4,000	1 1-2
27 Damgarten . . .	1,000	5	55 Braunsberg . . .	6,000	2 3-4
28 Stralsund . . .	12,000	4	56 Hoppenbruch . .	150	3

Stages.	Population.	Miles.	Stages.	Population.	Wersts.
57 Brandenberg . .	—	3	99 Gridneva . . .	50	29
58 Konigsberg . . .	59,000	3 1-2	100 Jaztke	8,000	30
59 Caimer	350	3	101 Teplouka . . .	50	29
60 Lablau	4,000	4	102 Wiasma . . .	2,000	26
61 Mehleuchen . .	200	3	103 Semlevo . . .	40	23
62 Schilluppisscheken	30	3	104 Giachekovo . .	20	28
63 Tilsit	8.000	3 1-2	105 Dorogobouge . .	4,000	23
64 Szaineickehmen .	—	3	106 Mikailovka . ; .	20	24
65 Heidekrug . . .	—	4 1-4	107 Pneva	50	17
66 Prokuls	—	3	108 Bredikino . . .	—	23
67 Memel	7,000	—	109 Smolensko . . .	2,500	23
		Wersts.	110 Koritnia . . .	10	23
From Memel, by the			111 Krasnoi	800	18
Gulf of Finland to St.			112 Liadi	—	16
Petersburg, two hundred			113 Koziani	20	14
and six Leagues.			114 Doubrovna . . .	2,500	17
68 St. Petersburg . .	250,000	33	115 Orcha	2,000	28
69 Igiora	500	24 1-2	116 Kokanovo . . .	300	18
70 Tossná	300	32	117 Tolitzine . . .	600	15
71 Pomerania . . .	100	25	118 Maliavka . . .	—	15
72 Tischoudovo . ,	1,000	24	119 Kroupki	250	23 1-2
73 Spakia-Poliste . .	250	24	120 Lochenitzi . . .	150	17
74 Podberezie . . .	200	22	121 Borisoff	2,000	17 1-2
75 Novogorod . . .	8,000	35	122 Jodino	50	17 1-2
76 Bronnitzi . . .	2,000	27	123 Smolevitzi . . .	60	15
77 Zaiffovo	300	31	124 Touchnevka . .	20	21
78 Krestzi	2,000	16	125 Minsk	7,000	21 1-2
79 Rachino	1,000	22	126 Gritchina . . .	60	18 1-2
80 Jagelbitzi . . .	500	22	127 Koidanovo . . ,	800	14 1-2
81 Zimogorie . . .	4,000	20	128 Komele	20	21 1-2
82 Jedrovo	800	36	129 Novoe-Svergino .	500	18
83 Kotilovo . . .	600	36	130 Mir	1,000	21
84 Vishnei-Volotshok	12,000	33	131 Korelitzi . . .	500	21
85 Widropouskoe . .	—	38	132 Novogrodec . .	6,000	36 3-4
86 Torjock	4,000	33	133 Belitza	500	28
87 Mednoe	700	30	134 Joloudoke . . .	200	14
88 Tweer	—	26	135 Tstouchino . . .	200	14
89 Wosskresenskoe .	300	31	136 Kamenke . . .	100	21
90 Zadivovo . . .	300	26	137 Skidele	200	35
91 Klin	1,000	31	138 Grodno	8,000	—
92 Pecheki	200	22			
93 Tschernaia-Griasse	500	28	Grodno . . .	—	Miles.
94 Moscow	150,000	—	139 Kusniza	200	3
Moscow	—	27	140 Justrembne . .	' 30	4
95 Perkouchekovo .	80	26	141 Augustow . . .	1,200	3 1-2
96 Koubiuskoe . .	60	22	142 Raggreda . . .	1,000	3
97 Chelkova . . .	70	24	143 Grajew	500	2
98 Mojaiske . . .	1,000	27	144 Szcrucin . . .	—	3 1-2

Stages.	Population.	Miles.	Stages.	Population.	Miles.
145 Stawisk. . . .	300	3 1-2	162 Sompolno . . .	300	3 1-4
146 Lomza	1,000	2 1-2	163 Kleczew . . .	500	3 1-4
147 Miastkow . . .	15	2 1-2	164 Slupea	600	3 1-4
148 Ostrolenka . . .	1,200	4	165 Wrzeschen . . .	—	3 1-2
149 Rozana	350	4	166 Kostrzyn . . .	300	1 1-2
150 Pultusk	1,200	3	167 Lwarzedz . . .	1,000	1 1-4
151 Wierzbica . . .	500	2	168 Posen	15,000	4 1-4
152 Nieport	50	2 3-4	169 Bylin	400	2 1-2
153 Warsaw	50,000	4	170 Pinne	200	4
154 Blonie	600	3 3-4	171 Schillen	70	2 3-4
155 Sochaczew . . .	500	3 1-2	172 Meseritz . . .	6,000	4 1-2
156 Lowiez	4,000	3 3-4	173 Zielentzig . . .	3,000	2 1-2
157 Pniew	100	2 1-2	174 Drossen	—	4
158 Kutno	250	2 1-4	175 Franckfort . . .	—	5
159 Glasnow . . .	200	2 1-4	176 Munchberg . . .	1,200	4
160 Klodawa . . .	500	3	177 Vogelsdorf . . .	30	3
161 Babiak	150	1 3-4	178 Berlin	—	—

TOTAL, in English Miles 3,437

From Copenhagen to Hamburg, the average rate of posting is about 4d. an English mile, for each horse. From Hamburg to Memel about 4 1-2d. an English mile, for each horse. From St. Petersburg to Grodno, including fees to the postmaster, &c. is about 3d. a werst, for each horse. Throughout Prussia, and Saxony, from 9d. to 10d. an English mile, for each horse.

A Danish mile is equal to 4 1-2 English miles.

A German mile is equal to nearly 4 3-4 English miles.

7 Russian wersts is equal to 5 English miles.

THE END.